THE VAN DYKE FAMILY:

A GLIMPSE OF THE DUTCH SETTLEMENT OF NEW JERSEY

PAUL C. VAN DYKE

Heritage Books, Inc.

Cover illustration by
Mildred Dietz

Published 1997 by

HERITAGE BOOKS, INC.
1540E Pointer Ridge Place
Bowie, Maryland 20716
1-800-398-7709

ISBN 0-7884-0700-7

PEARL VAN DYKE HARVEY (1890-1965)

BE GLAD OF LIFE! Because it gives you

a chance to love and work, to play

and to look up at the stars.

Henry Van Dyke (1852-1933)

IN LOVING MEMORY

OF

PEARL VAN DYKE HARVEY (1890-1965)

CONTENTS

EIGHTH GENERATION

NINTH GENERATION

ILLUSTRATIONS

FIRST GENERATION

Preceeding Page

SECOND GENERATION

FOURTH GENERATION

FIFTH GENERATION

SIXTH GENERATION

SEVENTH GENERATION

EIGHTH GENERATION

NINTH GENERATION

PREFACE

It has been held in some quarters that history is a chronicle of facts piled on facts. A cynical view perhaps. To be sure, history is fact; a record of past events at a specific time and place.

This may explain why some writers romanticize history. Superimposed on historical material we find a mix of legend, myth and colorful anecdotes while omitting any reference to the source. In the same vein when material evidence is lost in antiquity leaving a gap, a melodramatic episode is often interwoven in the narrative suggesting, if not boldly proclaiming, that this is what actually happened. Reader interest, it appears, claims a high priority.

There is a better approach.

Obviously the truth should not be compromised. Nor is it necessary to be boring to be informative. History is a fascinating subject when seen by the people who made it - what they did, what they said, what they saw; how they confronted a multitude of life's problems. Therein lies the drama. Without people there would be no history on this small planet.

Why, then, not tell the story from the perspective of people living at the time? If the documents extant leave a hiatus, simply concede the fact. Sometimes the things we want to know cannot be found; the evidence is irretrievably lost. Still an interesting picture of the whole - a valid portrayal - can often be drawn if we scrutinize all the known facts.

In 1957 the author compiled a genealogy of his branch of the Van Dyke family with the aid of a family bible and the kind assistance of friends. Limited research in the archives at that time revealed that the Van Dycks (original spelling) came to America in the mid-seventeenth century and settled in the Dutch colony known as New Netherland; that they were industrious and prosperous farmers who subsequently migrated to Middlesex and Somerset counties in New Jersey when the area opened for settlement. Curiosity once aroused, questions came to mind. What was this history? What did they do? How did they live? And a host of other questions.

Recently uncovered among old correspondence was a letter dated October 8, 1956 from Richard Wilson Cook (1903-1981), compiler of a genealogy bearing the terse title Van Dycks. Said Mr. Cook, "I am sure members of your family and others will want to receive the history you have in mind preparing and I will be very happy to have you refer to and quote from my work on the Van Dycks." This, in turn, sparked a search for bits and pieces of the evidence, albeit when precious time allowed. Happily the past few years have afforded the opportunity to pursue the search more intensively, embarking on an exciting voyage of discovery.

Answers to some of the questions have been found tucked away in old documents that have seldom seen the light of day. The Van Dycks, and other Dutch families whom they knew, were part and parcel of this Dutch history. Hence all of them play a part. With evidence garnered from the archives, historical societies, libraries, and some unlikely places, the final step was to reduce the facts to simple narrative form and share the story with others.

Briefly, this is the story of the Dutch inhabitants of New Jersey as seen through their eyes. To lay the foundation, the first three generations trace the Dutch settlement history from the days of the intrepid seafaring Henry Hudson in the era of discovery. Thomas van Dyck of Amsterdam, Holland (First Generation), lived at the time of Hudson's historic voyages to the New World and the founding of the first Dutch colony on Manhattan Island which the Dutch called New Amsterdam, commonly known today as New York. Thomas' son, Jan Thomasse (Second Generation), came to America in 1652 with his family, including his infant son Jan Jansen (Third Generation), and a few years later settled in the small Dutch village of New Utrecht on Long Island, which ultimately set the stage for a massive migration into the New Jersey wilderness in the early eighteenth century. Nine generations in all recount the history closing with the death, in 1906, of John Schenck Van Dyke (Ninth Generation), who stood resolute as a young man and severed himself from the Dutch farm tradition; an interesting story in itself. The period spans nearly three centuries: from the first Dutch settlements concentrated on Manhattan Island, Long Island, and in the Hudson River Valley to a colony under English rule; from a rebellious colony to a bloody revolution in which they were ardent patriots; from an aristocracy to an unsteady republic taking form and substance under a constitution forged in Philadelphia; and, finally, from a fledgling nation to a great nation.

The Dutch easily assimilated into colonial society very soon becoming bilingual, thinking anew, and adapting to social, economic and political institutions brought to the New World by the English. They were <u>now</u> Americans. But, it should be added, in matters of religion and interfamilial relationships, they retained - some may say stubbornly held onto - much of their strong Dutch character and independence. Here the transition was slow, almost imperceptible; as subtle as the seasonal changes, measured however in generations.

In sum, these Dutch folk while constituting but a small segment of the population were a significant part of the American scene and exerted a palpable influence. And they have much to tell us.

While a genealogy has metamorphosed into a Dutch history, the genealogical aspect has not been ignored. Each generation contains a brief genealogical note identifying the family member, marriage and children. Related data is incorporated in footnotes and in an appendix to preserve the continuity of the text.

To facilitate inquiry there is provided:

Table of Abbreviations: Authorities and Sources
Index of Subjects
Index of Surnames

Every effort has been made to ensure accuracy while conceding that none of us is immune from error. Authorities relevant to major points are cited. Occasionally there cropped up along the way a fanciful tale lacking evidential support or documentation, its trustworthiness seldom having been called into question. Some response was indicated rather than quietly ignoring it. A common error is the repetition of an alleged fact or event, said to have taken place in the distant past, cunningly finding its way into print years later and gaining credence solely by repeated publication. As Richard Wilson Cook, a true scholar, said with reference to published material on the Van Dyck family, "Errors have crept in and been repeated so often that many people today believe such errors now to be facts." The preface to Cook's comprehensive work will be helpful to anyone contemplating serious research. It is incorporated as Appendix A.

It is the author's hope that this history will serve as a guide to those wishing to continue the quest on another exciting voyage of discovery.

Paul C. Van Dyke

Radnor, Pennsylvania

ACKNOWLEDGMENTS

Many persons have shared the writing of this Dutch history. Grateful acknowledgment is due and richly deserved; it is a debt I am pleased to pay.

The idea was born in 1957 when compiling a Van Dyck genealogy, in essence a supplement to the *Van Dycks* by Richard Wilson Cook (1903-1981), former president and longtime trustee of the Genealogical Society of New Jersey, published in 1954. Cook's superbly crafted analysis evoked not only a strong urge to delve deeper, but furnished the key in many cases to primary source material shedding light on the Dutch colonists in America. Without his scholarly work, the seed would not have taken root.

Additionally, looking back some thirty-six years, I wish to acknowledge once again valuable information and help from my cousin, Henry Everett Van Dyke, and my late paternal aunt, Pearl Van Dyke Harvey (1890-1965); also Donald Sinclair, former librarian at Rutgers University and Curator of Special Collections; Bruce French, Esquire, of Princeton; Kenneth W. Richards, State Library, Trenton; and Harold L. Hughes, Trenton Public Library.

Some years later I had the good fortune of meeting Mrs. Ursula Brecknell of Belle Mead, New Jersey. Her expertise in ferreting out old records and documents was, and is, amazing. Whenever in a quandary - usually in search of an elusive document - she came to my aid, always patient, understanding, and supportive. I am indebted to this fine lady for guidance along the way.

I tender special thanks to Elric J. Endersby, editor and publisher of The Princeton Recollector, containing a wealth of New Jersey history. With his kind permission I have drawn from this source the delightful memoirs of Margaret Van Dyke Malcolm (1824-1916), a distant cousin who was born in Mapleton, near Princeton, on a Dutch plantation in the days of slavery.

I am indebted to Frank Updike of Princeton who painstakingly researched the history of the Red Lion Inn and the Princeton Baptist Church at Penns Neck erected on the Straight Turnpike, once a busy stage route between New Brunswick and Trenton, but more familiar to the travelling public today as US Route 1. Fortunately, these ancient structures still stand, although many others have long since disappeared from the scene. And they have a fascinating story to tell. Upon discussing the founding of West Windsor Township (bordering Princeton on the south) and making inquiry, we were given access to the West Windsor Township minute books dating back to 1797 depicting local government as it wrestled with the problems and concerns of the people in that early time.

To Peggy Goodrich, author of Ike's Travels, the story of a great explorer of this century, Commander Isaac Schlossbach (1891-1984), I am most appreciative. To the explorer's younger brother, Dr. Theodore Schlossbach I extend sincere thanks for a limited edition copy of Peggy Goodrich's book autographed by Commander Schlossbach which is relevant to the Ninth Generation.

Other knowledgeable persons have made significant contributions. Among them: Mrs. Ruth Hayes Cortelyou Sincak, late of Kingston, N.J., former treasurer for many years of the Ten Mile Run Cemetery Association, and her brother, Norman G. Cortelyou, late of North Plainfield, N.J., both descendants of Jacques Cortelyou (1625-1679), a prominent Dutch surveyor and scholar who arrived in America in the same year as Jan Thomasse Van Dyck (ca1605-1673). Also Mrs. E. Renee Heiss of Vincentown, N.J., author of A Genealogical History of the Berrien Family (1982); Mrs. Dorothy Agnes Stratford, Corresponding Secretary of the Genealogical Society of New Jersey; David M. Riker, Trustee of the Holland Society of New York; William A. Johnson, Sr. and his son, John, Jr., who currently occupy the prerevolutionary dwelling of John Van Dike (1709-1777/78) together with their respective families, and till the soil as he once did, but no longer behind a team of horses or yoke of oxen. Also John and Barbara Stahl who in recent years restored historic Oppie's Mill at Bridgepoint, Somerset County; the late Mrs. Jeanette Gibson of Princeton for the origin of the stone marker at the entrance to the Ten Mile Run Cemetery; Fred Smith, Jr., of Interlaken, New Jersey, whose knowledge of Jersey Shore history is phenomenal; David William Voorhees, professor of American History at New York University, and an eminent authority on Jacob Leisler (1640-1691), currently editing some 2,000 Leisler documents; C. A. Weslager, noted authority on the history of the Delaware Valley; H. Gerald MacDonald, an authority on the history of railroading in New Jersey; Michael Kammen, Professor of American History and Culture at Cornell University and Pulitzer Prize-winning historian whose scholarly work, Colonial New York, is cited.

I am deeply appreciative, of the many courtesies extended by the staff members of libraries including Rutgers University Special Collection and Archives, Princeton University Library, Trenton State Library and Archives, the Princeton Public Library, the Historical Society of Princeton; also the Pennsylvania Historical Society, the Presbyterian Historical Society, the Philadelphia Free Library and the College of Physicians, all in Philadelphia; the Cape May County Court House Library, the Monmouth County Historical Association, Freehold, N.J., the Asbury Park Public Library, Asbury Park, N.J., the Villanova University Library and the Radnor Township Memorial Library, Wayne, Pennsylvania.

Countless hours have been spent by my sister, Florence Van Dyke Finne, typing the manuscript for which I express my heartfelt gratitude.

And there were contributors from the distant past whose personality and spirit live on.

To a talented journalist of yesteryear, Marguerite Durick, who visited the Ten Mile Run Cemetery in 1930 and promptly sat down and wrote a moving article published in the Sunday Times of New Brunswick, I am beholden. Interpreting the terse inscriptions on the eroded monuments, she keenly sensed the courage of those hearty Dutch pioneers resting in this quaint burial ground and captured it in her prose. Excerpts appear in the text.

An avid genealogist once said, "Sometimes I feel them looking over my shoulder". If only they could speak to us, what would they say? Fortunately, Margaret Van Dyke Malcolm of Mapleton (near Princeton) and Rachel Van Dyke of New Brunswick, born in the days of sailing ships and slavery, do speak to us through their writing. To these articulate cousins I owe a special debt of gratitude for they, too, are material contributors.

Margaret, you thoughtfully took the time in your mid-eighties, still keenly alert, discerning and with a clear incisive mind, to write your memoir recounting the days of your childhood, the daily activities on the Van Dyke plantation, your early schooling in the nearby village of Princeton in the back room of Captain Stockton's house, the stagecoaches arriving at noontime in Princeton, your father intently reading his bible on Sunday morning, the domestic servants engaged at spinning wheels in the kitchen, and, not the least, your black mammy of whom you fondly reminisced, "I never heard Father give her a harsh word, and what I am today, that Christian Negress made me ... Dear old Mammy, peace to your ashes." Portions excerpted from this treasure trove enhance our Dutch history.

And Rachel, when you were a teenager immersed in the study of Latin and the classics, you were motivated to pen your personal thoughts and recollections in a journal - usually, you said, at the midnight hour by the light of a candle in the quiet of your room - recording events of the day which you witnessed in New Brunswick in the early nineteenth century. What you have written is now history in the purest form. At this point in time I am sure you have no objection to my opening parts of it for others to read and enjoy.

Thank you, cousin Margaret and cousin Rachel.

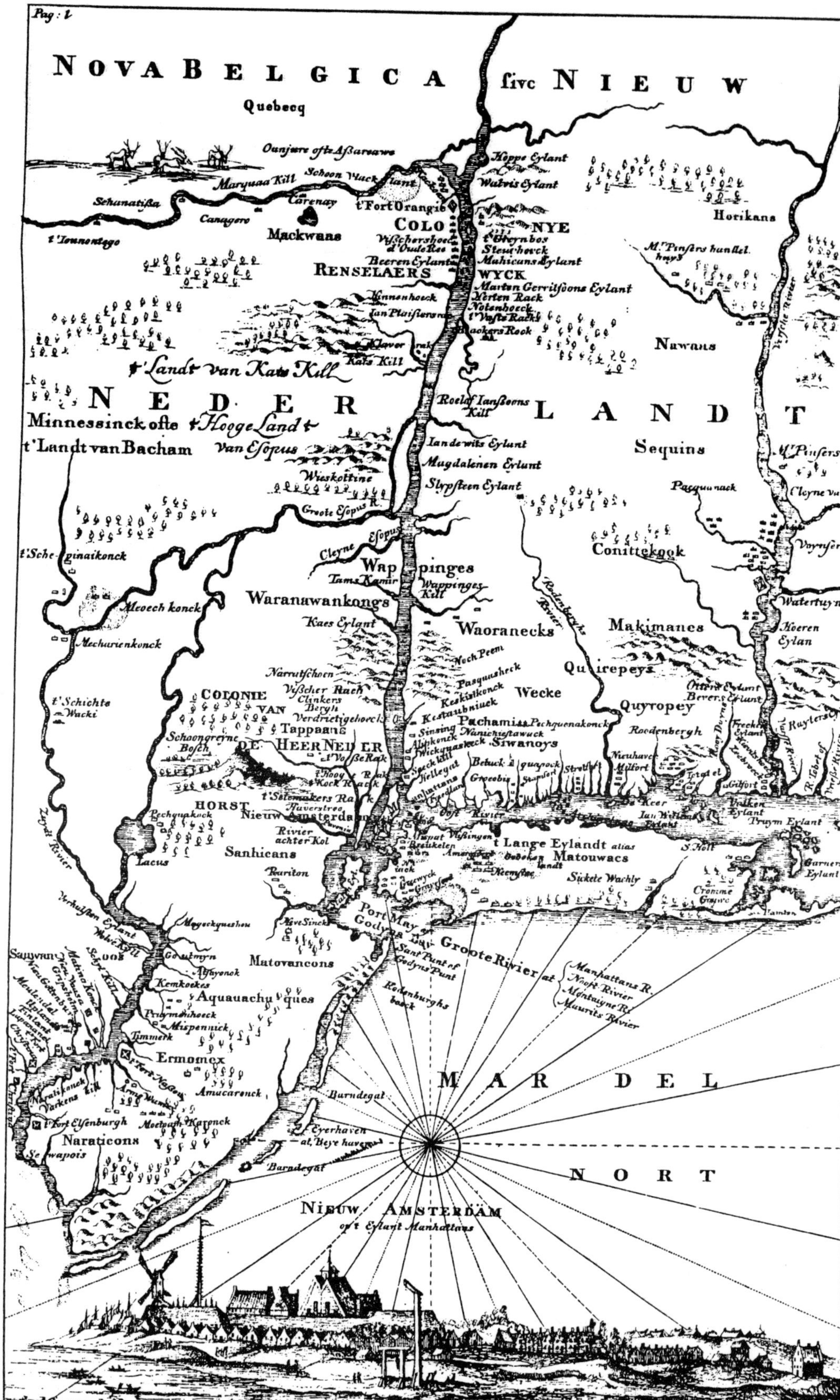

MAP of NEW NETHERLAND published in 1656 with a view below of New Amsterdam on the southern tip of Manhattan Island as seen by the Dutch cartographer. Some of the Dutch names, later Anglicized, are Kats' Kill, Staten Eyl, Breukelen, Rariton, Neve Sincks, Barndegat, Uplandt and Schyl Kill.

FIRST GENERATION

The Dutch Setting

THOMAS van DYCK
B Late Sixteenth Century
D
M

THOMAS van DYCK of Amsterdam, Holland,[1] was the progenitor of a long ancestral line that settled in parts of New York and Long Island originally known as New Netherland. In 1664 the English seized control of New Amsterdam in New Netherland and saw fit to change the name. At the same time they changed the whole course of American history.

There is no evidence that Thomas van Dyck, an elderly man in the mid-seventeenth century, came to America; nor is the name of his wife known (Cook 1).

Thomas was the father of three sons who with their respective wives and children in the company of other Dutch families settled in New Netherland when Peter Stuyvesant (1592-1672) was governor. They were:

Jan (ca1605-1673) (SECOND GENERATION)
Tierck (prob) (161_-)
Thomas (prob) (161_-)

The Golden Age

One may wonder why the Dutch came to America.

The North American continent in the seventeenth century was a vast, remote, uncharted wilderness, hardly an attractive place for civilized man. Furthermore the Indians had preempted the land. To civilized man they were also unattractive. Meanwhile, the Dutch were living comfortably in their homeland enjoying the benefits of a prosperous economy. The period has often been referred to as the Golden Age of Holland, an appropriate characterization because the times were in fact golden in every sense. Holland was a great sea power whose merchants, men of prestige and great influence, carried on a lucrative trade in many parts of the world including China, the East Indies and Africa. Material prosperity brought with it a cultural explosion as wealth poured into the country. The famous universities of Leyden (1575) and Utrecht (1636) were the finest in Europe. In the realm of the fine arts the magnificent paintings of Rembrandt van Rijn (1606-1669), probably the greatest Dutch artist of all time, Johannes Vermeer (1632-1675), Frans Hals (1579/85-1666), Jan Steen (1626-1679) and other Dutch masters won highest praise - even as they do today.

Why, therefore, would any Dutchman be interested in America?

The answer lies partly in the fact that this was an age of exploration added to another significant fact that it was an era of intense international rivalry. Sea power was an important element at stake. But when delving into colonial history, you discover that it was more subtle than that. And so it may be better to examine the facts before setting down broad conclusions.

The logical place to start is at the beginning. Perhaps a little simplistic but, nevertheless, the words of an astute law professor who was accustomed to chide his students when the discussion meandered from the point of law and sometimes, or so the class believed, when his thinking was not exactly in accord with theirs. "Gentlemen", he would plead in a cajoling manner, "begin at the beginning".

The New Netherland Colony

In the beginning New York was New Amsterdam. Wall Street was originally de wal, namely the wall along the northern boundary of the colony erected by the settlers as a protection from Indian raiders. New Amersfoort, the first Dutch settlement on Long Island, later became Flatlands. Breuckelen, now slightly anglicized, remains almost the same. Some people may forget, if in fact they knew, the Dutch were here first.

Not long before, in September 1609, Henry Hudson (-1611), an Englishman and master of De Halve Maen, or the Half Moon, of the Dutch East India Company composed of wealthy Dutch merchants, sailed through the Narrows into New York Bay passing Staten Island on the west and Long Island on the east. Earlier, in 1524, Giovanni da Verrazano (ca1480-ca1527), a Florentine of noble birth, well educated and a superb navigator for that day, exploring for the King of France, Francis I, anchored his wooden sailing vessel, La Dauphine, in the Narrows off the shore of Staten Island and began to explore the area in one small boat. In a letter to the French king he wrote, "We passed up this river [the Narrows], about half a league, when we found it formed a most beautiful lake three leagues in circuit [New York Bay], upon which they [the Indians] were rowing thirty or more of their small boats, from one shore to the other, filled with multitudes who came to see us." His explorations lasted less than a day, thus affording only a fleeting glimpse of the scenic harbor in its virgin state. "All of a sudden, as is wont to happen to navigators," his letter continues, "a violent contrary wind blew in from the sea, and forced us to return to our ship, greatly regretting to leave this region which seemed so commodious and delightful, and which we supposed must also contain great riches, as the hills showed many indications of minerals." Accordingly, it is most fitting that the magnificent suspension bridge that today spans the Narrows connecting Staten Island and Brooklyn, one of the mightiest suspensions of them all - its towers standing 690 feet high, the deck 4,260 feet long rising 228 feet above high water - was named in honor of the valiant gentleman explorer. It is no exaggeration to say that Verrazano's navigational skill four and a half centuries ago matched the expertise of the designers and builders of the Verrazano-Narrows Bridge completed in 1964.

But to Captain Henry Hudson, sailing under Dutch colors, must go the credit for exploring and making valid claim to New York Bay, Manhattan Island and the surrounding area. And, of course, the beautiful river that bears his name, called the North River by the Dutch. The flowing water constantly stirred by the ebb and flow of the ocean tides, the verdant forests, the rolling hills encompassing the river banks and the towering Palisades combined to produce a scene of grandeur for Hudson and his crew of Dutch and English sailors. Notwithstanding other exploratory claims, they were the first Europeans to fully explore this region of the New World[2].

Hudson's mission for the Dutch company was to find a shorter route to China and the East Indies. His friend Captain John Smith sent him a letter and a map suggesting that there might exist a northwest passage. Two previous voyages undertaken in a quest for a northeast passage around Asia proved unrewarding. But Hudson, a determined man, was not one to give up easily. On this his third exploratory effort, the Half Moon sailed up the inviting waterway as far north as present-day Albany. There, finding the channel greatly narrowed and the water not at all salty, he concluded that this was not the way.

It is not surprising, therefore, that Hudson's discoveries aroused very little, if any, enthusiasm in the directors of the Dutch East India Company. But a few years later thirteen wealthy merchants in Holland conceived the idea of a trading post and with no difficulty obtained a charter from the States General for exclusive trading privileges over that part of the east coast of the North American continent known as New Netherland. Colonization was furthest from their minds when they built Fort Orange, a trading post on an island in the Hudson not far from present-day Albany. Profiting from the fur trade was their principal objective. Having experienced moderate success, a new company, the Dutch West India Company, was formed in 1621 with an enormous amount of capital and, with the government's blessing, it was granted a monopoly over all Dutch trading on the North American continent. Soon they realized that if the new trading enterprise, far more ambitious that the first, were to succeed, settlers were essential, particularly soldiers and farmers to support the venture and protect the property against Indian raids as past experience proved. This presented a problem; indeed a formidable one. And attempts by the company to resolve it in various ways, but mainly by undemocratic methods, were ineffectual. Moreover, the company's officers casually ignored the fact that the average Dutchman was enjoying life in Holland. Why should he leave home?

Seeking to develop a major trading center on the North American continent and capitalize on a large investment, the company built Fort Amsterdam on the southern end of Manhattan Island and supplemented the garrison with farms or boweries ("bouwerijen" in Dutch) from which the "Bowery", a street in New York of unsavory reputation derives its name. Farms were needed to supply food for the soldiers and traders. The town surrounding the fort was appropriately called New Amsterdam, the first Dutch colony in America.

By July of 1626 a trading post near what later became Battery Park was established. A letter written in Amsterdam on November 5, 1626 by Peter Jansen Schaghen to the States General, addressed "High Mighty Sirs", said that the ship, the Arms of Amsterdam sailing from New Netherland on September 23, had arrived with a cargo of skins, specifically listing "7,246 beaver skins, 178 1/2 otter skins, 675 otter skins, 48 mink skins, 36 wild-cat skins, 33 minks, 34 [musk] rat skins. Many logs of oak and nut-wood". Schaghen's letter further said that "our people there are of good courage and live peacably. Their women, also, have borne chidren there, they have bought the island Manhattes from the wild men for the value of sixty guilders [and] is 11,000 morgens in extent[3]. They sowed their grain in the middle of May, and harvested it by the middle of August. They send thence samples of summer grain, such as wheat, rye, barley, oats, buckwheat, canary seed, small beans and flax" (General Government Archives, The Hague).

Thus the southern end of Manhattan Island and the southwest corner of Long Island were settled mainly to advance the profit-making objectives of a company largely controlled by Amsterdam merchants. That the Dutch colony was founded at all was more or less an afterthought, and, for the reasons cited, it failed to flourish. The patroonships along the Hudson, modeled after the feudal system and servitude in medieval Europe hoping to breathe new life into the colony, furnish another good example. This concept had little appeal for the average Dutch citizen and with the single exception of Rensselaerwyck near Albany died out in a few years.

Fifty-five years after Henry Hudson's discovery, New Netherland came to an end. Peter Stuyvesant, the last Dutch governor, found Fort Amsterdam overpowered by the British Navy with the fort's defenses totally inadequate and no enthusiasm on the part of the colonists to challenge four British men-of-war anchored in the harbor. When the final ultimatum was delivered, he ordered the white flag raised. On September 8, 1664 the British took control and changed the name to New York.

A postscript at this historic point is in order. The British military occupation in 1664 was repeated by the Dutch in the summer of 1673 when they surprised the British with a fleet of no less than twenty-three ships in the harbor leaving their enemy no choice but to surrender. But Dutch rule, it developed, lasted little more than a year. Quiet talks were being conducted in Europe between the belligerents that culminated in the Treaty of Westminster (February 1674) ceding New Netherland to Britain.

Meanwhile, in the aftermath of a dismal colonizing effort interpersed with sea battles, military conquests and treaties, the Dutch settlers found the struggle for existence in the New World rewarding. Those hearty pioneer families were here to stay. In due course, as our story unfolds, their children and grandchildren migrated westward across the great bay to New Jersey carving out new settlements in the wilderness and making New Jersey their permanent home.

The Van Dyke family was among them.

SECOND GENERATION

Genealogical Note

JAN THOMASSE VAN DYCK
B ca 1605
D 1673
M 163-

JAN THOMASSE (son of Thomas) VAN DYCK was born in Holland, about the year 1605 (Cook 1).

Marriage and Children

In his late twenties or early thirties Jan Thomasse married Tryntje Achias by whom he had seven children[1] who survived infancy. Cook corrects other accounts listing in error four additional children (Cook 2). Stout confirms Cook (SCHQ 4:263). All but the last child, Henderick, were born in Holland and were baptized in the Old and New Dutch Reformed Churches of Amsterdam. Records show:

Thomas Bp January 25,1639	D 1684-87	M 166__ Maritje Andriessen
Annetje Bp November 18, 1640		M 165__ Peter Jansen Staats
Agnietje Bp June 16, 1644 7:128)	D after 1711	M December 3, 1662 at Breuckelen Andriaen (Arie Willemse) Bennett(SCHQ (SCHQ 7:128)
Achias baptismal record not found	D ca 1707	M1 ca 1673 Jannetie Lamberts M2 December 1693 Magdeleena Henderse

Carel Bp September 22, 1648	D ca 1734	M June 27, 1680 Lisbet Aards Vander Hard
Jan Jansen (THIRD GENERATION) baptismal record not found	D ca 1736	M May 9, 1673 at New York Tryntje Thyssen (SCHQ 2:114) ;tb
Henderick Bp July 2,1653 in New Amsterdam (Cook 3,8)	D after 1710	M February 7, 1680 at Flatbush Janetje Hermanse

New Amsterdam

It was the beginning of a great adventure when Jan Thomasse Van Dyck and his wife, Tryntje Achias, with their six children and all their treasured possessions embarked on a Dutch sailing ship in the Amsterdam harbor bound for America. Crossing the vast Atlantic was hazardous. An ocean voyage could take twelve to fifteen weeks depending upon the wind, the ocean currents, unpredictable gales and violent storms.[2] Perils on the sea were not uncommon.

The year was 1652.

We know that their ship finally brought them safely to the harbor at New Amsterdam, the capital of the New Netherland colony on the southern tip of Manhattan Island. Upon setting foot on dry land, surely they said a prayer of thanksgiving for a safe passage. At the same place five years earlier Peter Stuyvesant stepped ashore to assume the governorship for the Dutch West India Company. The population then, it has been estimated, was 700. New Amsterdam grew very slowly. By 1660 there were approximately 1500 people (350 men, the remainder women and children) and exactly 342 houses according to a count by the brilliant young surveyor Jacques Cortelyou (Van Der Zee 341).

Upon entering the great harbor, Jan Thomasse must have been intrigued by Manhattan's skyline featuring a large windmill for grinding grain. Hugging the horizon were quaint houses and buildings with steep sloping roofs, either thatched or of wood, with stepped gables. The gabled end uniformly faced the street as in Holland. Drawing nearer the shore, he discerned piers, wharves and warehouses reflecting a typical port town in his native land. Practically all the structures were of wood, the common building material at the time. Every house, shop and public building contained a woodburning hearth with a chimney made of boards plastered with mortar or mud. Hence fire was a constant hazard. In 1657 Governor Stuyvesant signed an order that fire buckets and hooks be placed at the corners of all streets and at all public houses in New Amsterdam. The buckets were crafted of leather by local shoemakers (Van Der Zee 348, 349). Later the Dutch flavor was enhanced when brickmakers and masons came on the scene and houses were built wholly or partially of brick, at least for the wealthier citizens and the rich burghers who could afford it (Wertenbaker 47-50).

Unlike the motherland, New Amsterdam was a crude and primitive town. We picture Tryntje with her children on a cold winter day huddled in front of a rough stone fireplace where she cooked the family meal. The fire provided not only heat but interior lighting complementing whatever sunlight penetrated one or two small windows. The streets of the town were dusty or muddy lanes depending upon the weather; only a few were paved with stone. The Dutch, fond of water and canals, built the Heerengracht crossed by two large and three small bridges that ran along present-day Broadway. Boats docked at a pier near City Hall. People who dumped trash or filth into the canal were subject to pay a fine up to six guilders (Van Der Zee 342,348).

This was New York in the 1650s.

With only bare living necessities to sustain them and lacking reasonable sanitation, disease was prevalent in the Dutch colony. Death struck quickly. Peter Stuyvesant on a number of occasions exhorted the inhabitants to reflect upon their manifold sins and transgressions. For example, on April 1, 1663, he ordered a special day of "fasting and prayers", and directed that the people appear in church "to hear the Word of God," and beseech Him "to turn His righteous plagues and well-deserved punishments away" (Van Der Linde 64-67). When Jasper Danckaerts, the Dutch friar, infra, visited New Utrecht on Long Island on October 1, 1679, he personally witnessed the deadly scourge of disease and wrote in his journal: "We went, this morning, on a tour of observation of the country and of the neighbors, some of whom were better situated than others, but all of them had more or less children sick with the small pox, which, next to the fever and ague, is the most prevalent disease in these parts, and of which many have died. We went into one house where there were two children lying dead and unburied, and three others sick, and where one had died the week before ..." (Danckaerts 58).

Thus Jan Thomasse and Tryntje were very fortunate. Their seventh child, Henderick, born in New Amsterdam was baptized on July 2, 1653 (Cook 3), a year after they arrived in America. And all seven of their children, the record shows, survived, lived to adulthood and married (Cook 2-8).

In addition to fire and pestilence, there were vicious raids by the "savages", as the Dutch referred to the Indians. Merely another vexing problem which the Dutch governor was called upon to solve. Nor was it easy maintaining law and order and administering justice in a polyglot society. Although predominantly Dutch, there were other nationalities in New Amsterdam: English, French and Walloons, plus a smattering of Germans, Danes, Norwegians, Swedes, Portuguese, Spaniards and Jews. Peter Stuyvesant, often portrayed as tyrannical and aloof, had his hands full, yet conscientiously did his best in a perplexing role as governor and chief administrator.

If Jan Thomasse sought adventure and excitement in the New World, he found more than he bargained for in this turbulent Dutch town. The evidence indicates that New Amsterdam was a temporary abode while looking forward to a permanent place to settle in the New Netherland colony. Soon after New Utrecht on Long Island was surveyed by Jacques Cortelyou, whom we shall meet presently, Jan Thomasse and his family settled there.

New Utrecht, a far cry from cosmopolitan New Amsterdam, was virgin land and more appealing - peaceful, calm and serene. The silence was broken only by the songs of the birds.

The Founding of New Utrecht

Jacques Cortelyou (ca1625-1693), a Dutchman of French descent twenty years younger than Jan Thomasse Van Dyck, came to America with the Dutch settlers.

Jacques's progenitors were French Protestants, known as Walloons, who had suffered persecution in the Catholic provinces of present-day Belgium and France. Holland, more tolerant, offered a safe haven. Early in the seventeenth century Walloon refugees arrived in the ancient Dutch city of Utrecht where, according to church records, Jacques Cortillon and Elsken Hendricks (father and mother of Jacques) were married on April 14, 1612. Jacques, their second son was born about the year 1625. A rare book in the city archives contains thousands of autographs of students who came from all parts of western Europe to study at the renowned University of Utrecht between 1643 and 1685. Jacques' signature appears as "Jacobus Corteliou Ultraiectinus" in the year 1643[3] (SCHQ 1:103-106).

A young man of superior intellect, Jacques Cortelyou was chosen by Cornelis Van Werckoven, a distinguished member of the City Council of Utrecht and a colonizer for the Dutch West India Company, to accompany him to America in the capacity of tutor for his sons Pieter and Cornelis. A letter from the Directors of the West India Company to Governor Peter Stuyvesant refers to Van Werckoven as one "who goes there with a goodly number of souls, to take possession" (Cortelyou 7). The minutes of the City Council record: "His Honor had the intention, if it was pleasing to God, of himself making a journey there and back, begging that the absence of His Honor might be excused, and hoping that having returned, with the aid of God, he might continue in the service of this City with advice and deeds" (ibid 8). And so Jacques Cortelyou, then about twenty-seven years of old, bade his family and friends goodbye and boarded a Dutch ship for America in the entourage of the Honorable Cornelis Van Werckhoven.

The year was 1652.

The family of Jan Thomasse may have been in the company of those "goodly number of souls to take possession" on board the same Dutch ship. In any event, it is manifest from the records that Jan Thomasse Van Dyck and Jacques Cortelyou were well acquainted and may be counted among the first inhabitants of New Utrecht on Long Island.

Van Werckhoven's dreams of colonization were never realized. Finding himself in poor health, he returned to Holland in 1654 leaving Jacques Cortelyou as his agent to manage his business affairs. The following year he died. Meanwhile, Jacques grew in favor in the New Netherland colony. In the head office of the West India Company in Amsterdam his talent as a surveyor became well known. The directors wrote to Governor Stuyvesant on December 19, 1656: "As we have heard that there lives on the bouwery of the late Mr. Werckhoven a certain party, being well versed in engineering and surveying, who consequently

This Dutch scene is based upon a sketch by Jasper Danckaerts, a missionary from Holland representing a sect known as Labatists. It shows the entrance to New York bay at Sandy Hook as seen from the land of Jacques Cortelyou at Nyack on Long Island. The Journal of Jasper Danckaerts on Sunday, October 1, 1679, says: "Finding myself afterwards alone upon a small eminence, I made a sketch, as well as I could, of the land surrounding the great bay, that is, Coney Island, the entrance from the sea, Rentselaer's Hook, and so further to the right, toward Kil von Kol."

Courtesy The Brooklyn Historical Society

In keeping with tradition the Dutch dug a canal that ran along present-day Broadway. A public wharf at the terminus served ships laden with goods from all over the world. Edicts issued from city hall when Peter Stuyvesant was governor of the New Netherland colony and New Amsterdam, a bustling port city, was the capital.

Courtesy The Brooklyn Historical Society

might be of service to the said new Colony, as well as in laying out lots chosen for the dwelling-houses of the colonists as in other ways therefore your Honors will, upon request, persuade the said engineer thereto and let him go thither, to make a good beginning and location..."(Cortelyou 15).

By the year 1656 Jacques's career as a surveyor was fully launched in the Dutch colony in America. Since land formerly owned by Cornelis Van Werckhoven lay idle and undeveloped, Jacques himself seized the initiative and on behalf of the heirs of Van Werckhoven submitted a petition addressed "To the Noble and Right Honorable Director-General and Council of New Netherland" embodying the following request: "Whereas no lands here can be laid out and settled except with your Honor's approbation and consent, therefore the petitioner addresses himself to your Honors for consent to found a Town on Long Island on the Bay of the North River". The petition was granted on January 23, 1657 (Cortelyou 16,17).

Moreover, this remarkable Dutchman of French lineage, a brilliant scholar and a born leader, was among other things a mathematician and a formidable linguist speaking Latin and good French, as well as English to his English friends. This is confirmed by Jasper Danckaerts and Peter Sluyter, two interesting envoys from the Province of Friesland, Holland, who toured America in 1679-80 (then under English rule) seeking a suitable place for a colony of a religious sect known as the Labadists (Danckaerts xv-xxv). On four occasions they were guests of Jacques Cortelyou. Much more could be said about Jacques Cortelyou who was commissioned by Peter Stuyvesant as a "Sworn Surveyor" of "the lots within the city of New Amsterdam"; and subsequently made surveys in and about Bushwick, Communipaw, Bergen, Passaic, Staten Island, Esopus (Kingston), Schenectady, Harlem, Flatbush and other towns and villages in the colony (Cortelyou 26-31,36-41,46,48); and who married a Dutch girl, Neeltje Van Duyn about 1655/56, by whom he fathered seven children (Cortelyou 65-67).

Jacques laid out and surveyed the Van Werckhoven tract dividing it into twenty "lots" containing twenty-five morgen (fifty acres) each. The "lots" were then assigned to twenty Dutch inhabitants. Among them were Jacques Cortelyou and Jan Thomasse Van Dyck who may be regarded as founders of the little Dutch town of New Utrecht. Moreover, it was so named by Jacques in memory of the ancient Dutch City of Utrecht, his birthplace, and the home of his patron, Cornelis Van Werckhoven (Cortelyou 17).

Settlement Life

To endure in this rugged, pioneer country called for an equal measure of rugged, pioneer staying power.

Additionally, a knowledge of agriculture was essential. Dutch settlements on Long Island, as elsewhere, were basically self-sustaining. Only the most critical items were imported from Europe such as textiles, tools, farm implements, furniture, ink, and paper. Whenever ordered there necessarily followed a long waiting period for the goods to arrive on a Dutch sailing ship. Milk did not come in bottles nor eggs in cartons; nor butter and cheese in neatly wrapped packages. This, perforce, meant clearing the land, cultivating and improving the soil, growing wheat, barley, oats, corn, rye, potatoes, squash and other food staples, and most importantly feeding, nurturing and breeding farm animals, in particular cows, horses, sheep, pigs, goats, chickens.

This explains why Jacques Cortelyou's survey of New Utrecht contained "lots" of fifty acres. And Jacques himself, a learned man, lived on a working farm enlisting servants to perform the labor. Surveying assignments called him away for days and weeks at a time. An inventory of his estate included "A Negro man and Negro woman, 1 Horse, 3 Mares, 2 of one year, 1 Colt, 10 Cows, 5 of 3 years, 5 of 2 years, 4 of 1 year, 6 Calves, 6 Sheep; 1 Wagon with Yron (Iron) 2 Plows and 1 English plowshare. A Harrow with Yron teethes, 3 axes, 2 Grobbin hows [Grubbing Hoes], 3 Weeding hows, 1 Spade, 2 Dungh forkes, 3 Pitchforkes, 3 Wedges, 3 Lights, 2 Yron horse hopples, 6 wagon bitts, 1 Yron Crow [bar]; A grain stone. A Churan [churn], 8 Milk Tobs, 2 washing tobs, 4 milk Casks. A beefe Caske, another beef Caske, An old fishing nett, 8 old corn bags (Cortelyou 63,64).

In addition to agricultural pursuits critical to survival, municipal activities occupied much of Jan Thomasse's time. It is recorded in 1660 that he was "Overseer over all" and a "Sergeant". On June 12 of that year he accompanied Governor Peter Stuyvesant to Carnasie where a "piece of meadow was given to the town of New Utrecht" at which time he is referred to as "Assistant Secretary" of the town and "Custodian" of its records. In the same year Jan, joined with four others, complained in a letter to the Fiscal of damage done daily by hogs because of insufficient fences and pleaded for something to be done to "abate the evil". The New Netherlands Register records his appointment as "Magistrate" of New Utrecht in 1659, 1660, 1661 and 1673 and Documents Relating to Colonial History of New York on August 24, 1662 mention him as "one of three Commissioners of the village of New Utrecht". Subsequently he was "selected by the Council of War as one of four Schepens of the village" (SCHQ 4:262).

Indian Affairs

Relations with the Indians were precarious at best and at worst truly appalling. Some Dutch officials looked upon the Indians as barbarians who deserved to be treated in the same brutal and vindictive manner, an eye for an eye. This policy, they learned to their sorrow, served only to inflame the Indian's fanatic passion and thirst for revenge. In consequence, the Dutch paid heavily in the form of massacres, homes, barns, and grain stores burned to the ground, cattle and livestock killed or captured, villages laid waste. The family of Jan Thomasse was either directly involved in these tragic affairs or experienced the terror not far distant from the scene. Indians whose tree-limb and bark huts occupied land on the fringe of New Utrecht posed a threat. Life was never safe.

In September 1655, two years before Jan Thomasse settled in New Utrecht, the Indians in typical barbaric fashion assaulted Manhattan at night, an incident dubbed the "Peach War". Michael Kammen, professor of American History and Culture at Cornell University, cogently describes it:

> *Meanwhile, no sooner had Stuyvesant left New Amsterdam for that successful expedition that the Mahicans, Pachamis, Esopus, and Hackensack Indians made a surprise attack upon Manhattan - touched off by a trivial episode in Hendrick Van Dyck's peach*

orchard. On the night of September 15, these Indians, to revenge the murder of a squaw, made a shambles of many Dutch homes but did a minimum of personal injury. Instead of an eye for an eye, they smashed furniture, ripped up bedclothes, and ransacked homes. They then broke open beer and brandy barrels, drank themselves into a stupor, and a truce was arranged. Stuyvesant hurried back from the Delaware as quickly as he could and found the "Peach War" had spread to the far settlements. Massacres and kidnappings occurred, Dutch outposts on the Jersey side were burned and pillaged, fifty colonists were killed, twenty-eight farms were destroyed, five hundred head of cattle died or strayed, and thousands of bushels of corn were burned. The Indians seem to have lost some sixty men in the fighting[4].

In the first place the Indians thought that the land was theirs - the white man was a malicious intruder - based on the theory that they had been in exclusive possession for many moons, long before the Dutch arrived. The settlers on the other hand believed that they possessed something in the nature of a priori rights; they had come a long distance to this virgin land under Dutch jurisdiction, and therefore they had a right to settle in a Dutch territorial possession. But all things considered, they concluded that the best policy was to deal with the Indians and buy the land, especially since the Indians' demands were minimal, merely some tangible items worth a few guilders. However they often discovered that they did not hold a fee title. Consequently, to keep the peace, another purchase agreement was called for. And the Indians were ready to negotiate.

Six months before Cornelis Van Werckhoven departed the City of Utrecht, Holland, his agent in America purchased for him two tracts on Long Island, the New Utrecht area aforesaid and the Najack tract overlooking the Narrows for which he paid the Indians "6 shirts, 2 pairs shoes, 6 pairs stockings, 6 adzes, 6 knives, 2 scissors, and 6 combs" (Cortelyou 17). A few years later when Jacques built his home on the Najack tract, he bought the land again, not only once but twice! Even after that some Indians remained, purportedly "tenants", although they entertained no concept of the landlord-tenant relationship. The journal of Jasper Danckaerts, Jacques' guest on Saturday, September 30, 1679, based on conversations at that time, records: "The Indians live on the land of Jacques [Cortelyou], brother-in-law of Gerrit [Gerrit Van Duyn, brother of Neeltje, his wife]. He bought the land from them in the first instance, and then let them have a small corner, for which they pay him twenty bushels of maize yearly; that is, ten bags. Jacques had first bought the whole of Najack from these Indians, who were the lords thereof, and lived upon the land, which is a large place, and afterwards bought it again in parcels. He was unwilling to drive the Indians from the land, and has therefore left them a corner of it, keeping the best of it for himself. We arrived then upon the land of this Jacques, which is all good, and yields large crops of wheat and other grain" (Danckaerts 57).

A very tolerant man, Jacques understood Indian psychology - doubtless the product of a mature mind - and invoked patience and forebearance. The Indians' presence, nevertheless, constituted a worrisome problem creating mental stress. In 1679 Jacques was in his mid-fifties, but to Danckaerts he appeared to be a "man advanced in years" (Danckaerts 57). He was sixty-eight when he died in 1693 (Cortelyou 11,62).

Jan Thomasse was sixty-eight when he died twenty years earlier (Cook 1).

Justice and Morality

An interesting aspect of Dutch colonial life is revealed in an action for assault brought against Jan Thomasse Van Dyck. On September 15, 1661 a complaint charges him with "violently grasping a girl named Clara Gerrits by the throat, and assaulting one John van Cleef who would prevent him". He petitioned the court on September 22 for a pardon but was sentenced to pay a fine of 300 guilders. An action for damages by Jan van Cleef was referred to arbitration (NYCDM 229;Cook 1).

The facts surrounding these offenses are detailed in the Breuckelen Church Records which, fortunately, have been preserved[5], indicating beyond a doubt that excessive consumption of beer was the underlying cause bringing the parties to blows. The Dutch were great beer drinkers. The fracas erupted it is recorded, "while enjoying half a barrel of beer on the occasion of the departure of Sir Johannes Verveelen, burgher and brewer of Amsterdam in New Netherland" thus easily portraying a picture of an all-too-rowdy celebration precipitating an argument. But whatever the cause, inebriation furnished no excuse for Jan Thomasse's conduct at the gala party for the distinguished brewer so far as the Consistory of the Breuckelen Church was concerned. In a deeper sense the punishment ordered by the consistory was more severe than the fine of 300 guilders imposed by the court. Colonial society generally, and Dutch society particularly, were unified, not segmented. Justice and morality were quickly and firmly dealt with by both the court and the church. The Breuckelen Church Records offer an excellent example of the tremendous influence of the church on the lives of the Dutch people, illustrating the point more effectively than an erudite dissertation. We are indebted to Jos van der Linde, a Dutch scholar of Leiden, for the following English translation.

September 21, 1661

Jan Thomaszen, summoned by the consistory of Breuckelen together with his son on account of a certain unfortunate incident whereby he had drawn his knife and wounded Jan Cleeft in the village of New Utrecht, acknowledged that he, namely the afore-mentioned Jan Thomassen (while enjoying half a barrel of beer on the occasion of the departure of Sir Johannes Verveelen, burgher and brewer of Amsterdam in New Netherland), had gotten into an argument with a certain Claertie de Mof; that they even had come to blows; and that his shirt had been torn by the aforesaid [Claertie]. Thereupon, however, the aforesaid Kleeft had come and had pulled the afore-mentioned Jan Thomassen's hair, who [then] drew his knife and made four cuts in the afore-mentioned Cleeft's jerkin - indeed, wounding him eventually.

His son, Thomas Janssen, declared that because of filial affection he could not bear the fact that his father, Jan Thomassen, was grabbed by the hair and badly maltreated by the aforesaid Jan van Cleeft, so the afore-mentioned Thomas came to the help of his father and pulled Jan van Cleeft off by the shoulders. Thereupon, Van Cleeft grabbed the aforesaid Thomas, too, by the hair and Hendrick Matthijssen grabbed him by his feet; and [they] threw him to the floor. Thomas Janssen hereby contends, however, that he struck neither of the two again but merely grabbed Jan van Cleeft by the hair in order to be let go.

After discussing the matter among ourselves, it is [our] judgement, (as Jan Thomaszen strictly speaking is not a member of our Church of Jesus Christ in Breuckelen but so far has partaken of the Lord's supper there at his own request, while belonging to the congregation of Midwout and living in the village of New Utrecht) that because of his conduct, [he] will have to stay away from the Lord's table in the village of Breuckelen since his case is currently in the hands of the Hon. Lord Director-General and Councillors and since [he] has reconciled himself neither with the afore-mentioned Cleeft, who is seriously injured, nor with this congregation, which would be offended by it. His son, however, who was confirmed as a member of this place and showed more penitence and regret, would be admitted and at the same time warned to be on guard and careful in the future in order not to cause any offense to our congregation with such or other incidents. Both were notified and informed of this (van der Linde 24-27).

September 27, 1662

Jan Thomassen, living in Utrecht in New Netherland, requested to be re-admitted and to partake of the Lord's Supper beside our members, which had been denied him because of a certain knifing incident. [He] said he had settled with Jan van Cleeft to that end. Whereupon we resolved, and do resolve, while this afore-mentioned Jan Thomassen was standing outside, that it would be best to let this opportunity pass and to keep special watch on him, and then, at the time of repentance and regret, to re-admit him to our congregation; which was told him when he came in (van der Linde 48,49).

Can there be any doubt that Jan Thomasse learned true repentance, and in due course, after a "special watch", was readmitted to the Lord's table?

Demise

The New Netherlands Register documents the appointment of Jan Thomasse as "Magistrate" of New Utrecht for the last time on August 18, 1673. He died not long thereafter. The register, on November 16, 1673, records the appointment of Gysbertie Van Meteren as "Magistrate" replacing Jan Thomasse, deceased, thereby establishing Jan's death in 1673 in this three-month period (SCHQ 4:262,263). Surviving him were his children[6], thirty or more grandchildren and an unknown number of great-grandchildren (Cook 2-8). The conclusion may be safely drawn that by the year 1673 - a half century after the founding of New Amsterdam colony and a century before the Revolution - the Dutch were firmly rooted in America.

Other Dutch families living in New Amsterdam and in the small Dutch villages on Long Island - many of whom knew Jacques Cortelyou and Jan Thomasse Van Dyck - were destined in a few years to play important roles in New Jersey's history. A partial list includes Berrien, Beekman, Wyckoff, Voorhees, Vroom, Van Zandt, Van Ness, Van Kirk, Van Harlingen, Van Pelt, Van Derveer, Van Cleeft, Van Doren, Van Arsdalen, Updike, Ten Eyck, Terhune, Staats, Stryker, Schenck, Quick, Polhemus, Oppie, Lane, Hogeland, Hagaman, Gulick, De Hart. Some of them we shall meet in future generations.

Further in passing, the reader may wonder about numerous variations in the spelling of family names. For example: van Dyck, Van Dyck, Van Dike, Van Dyke. Be not disturbed! The explanation is that every scrivener had his own ideas about spelling and phonetics. There was no correct spelling. In the early days, for instance, Wyckoff was spelled at least twenty different ways (SCHQ 3:36).

Finally, the author acknowledges his indebtedness to Harry Macy, Jr., Associate Editor of The New York Genealogical and Biographical Record, for tracing the origin of the Jan Thomasse Van Dyck Family to Amsterdam, Holland. The facts uncovered are set forth in fascinating detail in "Amsterdam Reords of the Jan Thomasse Van Dyck Family" appearing in the October 1995 issue of the NYG&B Record,126(4):239-242.

THIRD GENERATION

Genealogical Note

JAN JANSEN VAN DYCK
B 1648/49
D ca 1736
M MAY 9, 1673

JAN JANSEN VAN DYCK, born in Holland 1648/49, was the son of Jan Thomasse Van Dyck (ca 1605-1673) and Tryntje Achias, his wife, who left their native land in 1652 to settle in the Dutch colony in America (Cook 7;SCHQ 2:114;SCHQ 4:262, 263).

Marriage and Children

On May 9, 1673 Jan Jansen married in New York (formerly New Amsterdam) Tryntje Thyssen (ca1648 - 1725) who was born in Leige, Belgium, and came to America with her father in 1663.[1]

Eight children were born of the marriage:

Catherine (Tryntje) B 167__	D after Dec.9, 1744	M__________ Daniel Hendricksen
Eva B 167__	D____	M_____________ Steven Koerten (Van Voorhees)
Mayke B 167__	D____	M April 22, 1694 Johannes Daniels Rinckhont (Johannes Richon)
Catalyntje Bp November 13, 1681	D____	M______ Garret Keteltas

Jan Bp November 19, 1682 (FOURTH GENERATION)	D Dec.18, 1764	M June 5, 1706 Annetje Verkirk
Mathys (Thys) Bp November 4, 1683	D Mar/April 1749	M__ Angenietje ____________
Jannetje B 168__	D after Aug.1758	M_____ Rutgert Van Brunt
Angenietje Bp April 29, 1686	D_____	M_____ Simon DeHart,Jr.

(Cook 7, 8; SCHQ 2:114; SCHQ 4:263,264)

Boyhood Days

Jan Jansen Van Dyck was the youngest child of the family when their Dutch sailing ship crossed the Atlantic Ocean, entered the Narrows and cast anchor in the bay at the foot of Manhattan Island. At three or four years of age, he could have harbored only a faint memory of the long, perilous voyage and perhaps a glimmer of Holland.

New Amsterdam was his boyhood home until Jacques Cortelyou completed the survey of New Utrecht on Long Island. In 1657, or not long thereafter, the Van Dyck family moved to the new Dutch settlement, a frontier country rich in flora and fauna and only recently inhabited by the Indians. In fact, some Indians decided to stay, Jasper Danckaerts informs us (Danckaerts 54-57). A picture emerges of a growing boy helping his parents with a variety of chores while they were busily engaged establishing a new home on virgin land; and thrilled by the profusion of wildlife, finding youthful pleasure hunting, trapping and fishing. Deer, turkey, wild goose, woodchuck and partridge were some of the game hunted in the forest and often a part of the family meal. Fish, lobster, oysters and crabs were plentiful in the bay (Danckaerts 53, 54; Van Der Donck 54-56).

On the southern shore of New Utrecht were the Narrows and Gravesend Bay. Looking east Jan Jansen could see Coney Island, Sandy Hook and the Highlands in New Jersey; and the broad sweep of the Atlantic in the distance. Across the Narrows to the west was Staten Island, a former Dutch settlement that had come to a tragic end when a wild band of Indians in 1655 pillaged the villages and farms, killing or capturing men, women and children, slaughtering their cattle and burning their houses and barns.

Domine Polhemus and the Reformed Dutch Church

New Utrecht consequently became Jan Jansen's permanent home. There, he and Tryntje raised two sons and six daughters. The family attended the Reformed Dutch Church in Midwout, now Flatbush (Cook 7), about an hour's walking distance from their home. Significantly, this was the first church edifice of the Dutch inhabitants on Long Island. A simple wood structure erected in the years 1659/60, measuring sixty feet by twenty-eight feet and fourteen feet high, it was the product of the minds and energy of the churchwardens and Domine Johannes Theodorus Polhemus, the first Dutch minister to the Long Island settlements. Voluntary contributions were given by the Dutch populace from New Amsterdam to Fort Orange (Albany) (GLIF 1:618).

Standing in the elevated pulpit in this primitive Dutch church, Domine Polhemus, the Good Shepherd, delivered the Christian message to his flock on Sunday. For the Dutch pioneers pitted against wilderness, Sunday was a special day of rest, a day to attend church for prayer and spiritual renewal. The domine's sermon marked the highlight of the day, a source of strength and moral courage. Later, after Domine Henricus Selijns returned to Holland in 1664, Domine Polhemus conducted services for the Dutch congregation in Breuckelen. How appropriate, then, that the faithful domine was laid to rest in a church where he preached the gospel! The Brueckelen Church Records document his death and burial: "In the year 1676, Thursday, the 8th of June, at about nine o'clock in the evening, our dear, loyal old shepherd and teacher Domine Joanus Polhemus piously passed away. He was buried here in the baptistry on the 11th last, right in front of the pulpit" (van der Linde xxi,xxii,156).

The dear, loyal old shepherd and teacher died in his seventy-eighth or seventy-ninth year. For fifty-two of those years he had been an ordained minister of the Reformed Dutch Church. Briefly, in 1624, he was called to a Dutch church at Gieten, a small community in Holland near Assen in the province of Drenthe, (GLIF 1:610). Thereafter, throughout a long and eventful career which took him from Holland to Brazil and then by accident at sea to America in 1654, he was an indefatigable missionary living under the harshest physical conditions. In a letter dated December 14, 1656 addressed to Governor Stuyvesant he was justly moved to complain, "I am compelled to respectfully complain to your honor that I must see the planks, given by your Honor out of compassion and presented to the community here to finish my house against this cold winter, being taken and lost this way or that ... so that my house remains open as it was, and I with my wife and children must live and sleep on the bare ground and in the cold" (GLIF 1: 615, 616).

The church's teaching expounded by the fervent preaching and pious example of Domine Polhemus was a dominant force in the lives of the Dutch inhabitants including, of course, Jan Jansen and his family. Lest there be a shadow of doubt, it is effaced by the conviction ardently expressed in his will: "first I bequeath my soul to God who gave it my Body to the Earth from whence it came to be decently Interred at the Discretion of my Executors hereafter named in Certain hopes of a Resurrection & the Union of my Body & Soul at the last day and of Eternal Life through the sole merrits of my Blessed Saviour Jesus Christ ...".(Appendix D)

Jacob Leisler and British Rule

Jan Jansen, in September 1687 at about age thirty-nine, took the oath of Allegiance to the British Crown when the oath was administered to all adult males on Long Island. Subsequently, on December 27, 1689, he was commissioned a lieutenant in New Utrecht by Lieutenant Governor Jacob Leisler, a controversial figure in American colonial history (Cook 7).

Born of Dutch parents and of distinguished Dutch heritage, Leisler (1640-1691) was temporarily serving as acting governor in the absence of Francis Nicholson who had fled to England because of political turmoil and unrest in the province. No one at the time could have anticipated that in another seventeen months Leisler would pay the extreme penalty of death, the result of trumped-up charges of treason for which he was peremptorily tried and found guilty. On a rainy Saturday morning of May 16, 1691, Leisler was publicly paraded in New York City to the executioner's block and beheaded before the largest crowd ever gathered there to that moment. It was an emotion-filled spectacle, unprecedented in the Dutch colonization era[2].

Leisler's trial and execution was a travesty of justice and a pivotal event in colonial New York. The Leisler affair is currently recognized by historians as a contest betwen two political factions contending for power and prestige linked to religion, economics, interfamilial feuds, and other factors. To Jan Jansen and Leisler's loyal followers, he was perceived as a martyr for the House of Orange and the Reformed Dutch Church, hence the inflammatory controversy left with them a trauma that was poignant and long lasting.

Nonetheless, as history convincingly proves, the Dutch are resilient. Life went on. Colonial government functioned by edict of the British Crown until the Declaration of Independence, eighty-five years later, was proclaimed by the colonists and with bells ringing in glorious celebration throughout the land, an event never foreseen or even dreamed of by Jan Jansen. In 1700 he was commissioned a Captain of a Foot Company of the Militia of the Town of New Utrecht (Cook 7). Appointments of this kind stemmed from the social and political conditions in the colony and therefore were secondary to his farm occupation. A tax assessment record dated September 29, 1676 discloses ownership of "one poll[3], 2 horses, 2 cows of 3 years, 1 cow of 2 years, 16 morgens [32 acres] of land; all with a total valuation of 84.10 pounds" (SCHQ 4:263). Upon Jacques Cortelyou's death the inventory of his personal possessions was taken by "Jan Van Cleef and John Van Dyck, inhabitants of New Utrecht," authenticated by estate papers dated January 20, 1693/94 and entered by Johannes Van Ekelen, Clerk of New Utrecht January 25, 1693/94 (Cortelyou 63). As records extant reveal, Jan Jansen Van Dyck was known in the colony as John Van Dyck.

The Land

To the Dutch settler land was more than a legal claim to a parcel of ground or a place for a dwelling to shelter the family. Land, in simple truth, was God's good earth with the potential for producing food. There were hungry children to feed. Clothing was needed to keep them warm. Wool and flax were spun and woven into cloth, a tedious hand operation from the moment of shearing the sheep and harvesting the raw fiber in the field. The days were filled with countless chores of a laborious nature.

With few exceptions the Dutch settlers were farmers all or part of the time. Although Jacques Cortelyou was a scholar and a surveyor by occupation, he, too, as we have seen, owned horses, cows and sheep, and raised grain on his plantation (Cortelyou 63,64). Similarly, Jan Jansen Van Dyck, residing nearby on a large tract, possessed an array of farm animals and cultivated the soil. The cardinal rule for survival was quite simple: farm the land or perish.

In this primitive agrarian society the horse and the cow were indispensable; the horse for transportation and the capability of pulling the wagon and the plow, the cow for body nourishment. The great importance of the cow is demonstrated in an interesting manner and in a most unlikely place. The Breuckelen Church Records, as one would expect, officially note baptisms, marriages and church membership. They also contain cow records. We find a page entitled Diaconies Koeijen or Cows of the Deaconry (van der Linde 204,205). Four cows were owned by the Deaconry which were available for "lease" for the benefit of the poor. This charitable concept called for some innovative thinking. The problem: how to achieve an equitable balance between the lessee-farmer charged with the responsibility of boarding and feeding the benevolent cow and the poor receiving the benefit given the fact that the cow's progeny and milk production were unpredictable. And she might die. The deacons of the church knew that. They were farmers, too.

A practical solution was found. To cite one example, the "Fourth Cow" (so designated) was placed in the hands of one Jan Jacobsen van Rheenen evidenced by a memorandum dated May 1, 1664 and signed by his mark. The document reads: "I, the undersigned Jan Jacobsen, living in Breuckelen, acknowledge to have received from the hands of the Hon. Consistory of the congregation of Breuckelen, for the benefit of the poor in the same place: a certain cow, [on the following conditions:] first, half-the-offspring; second, butter-lease of 10 lbs of butter during the present year and sixteen pounds in the following years - unless the aforesaid beast turns out to be a heifer, in which case [I will] give half as much this year which is customary - which [I] promise to pay in sewan instead of in butter for the benefit of the aforesaid poor; and finally, with the promise to cover half of the loss or to give the first off-spring if the beast comes to die. Done in Breuckelen May 1, 1664" (van der Linde 208,209). In this case the cow proved to be healthy and productive while under the care of Jan Jacobsen. During the years 1664-68 she produced two bull calves and three heifer calves. The record reads, "On April 23, 1668, the deaconry divided the offspring with Jan Jacobsen. The offspring of the year 1666, the year 1667, and the year 1668, became the share of the poor" (Ibid 208,209).

Sunset Years

Jan Jansen prospered as a farmer and land investor living to a ripe old age. In the normal course of events his children married and had children (Cook 7,8-20). Each son received a farm tract upon marriage. Mathys first settled in Breuckelen and later moved to Red Hook (Cook 19,20). His son Jan

(Fourth Generation) and his young family joined the Dutch migration into the Millstone Valley of New Jersey, the story which follows.

Tryntje Thyssen, his faithful wife, died in 1725, two years after they celebrated their golden wedding anniversary (Cook 7). Now, in his sunset years, Jan Jansen contemplated the distribution of his wealth among his loved ones. To this end he sold all his real estate consisting of a sixty acre tract on which stood his dwelling house, plus ten other parcels of land, to his son-in-law, Rutgers Van Brunt[4], for the sum of 1,676 pounds[5].

Having liquidated his land holdings, final division was made easy. His will divides the bulk of his estate in equal shares among two sons and three surviving daughters - Catherine, Jannetje, Angenietje - after leaving smaller monetary legacies to eight grandchildren and one great grandchild[6].

Demise

Jan Jansen, known as John to his family and friends, died in New Utrecht about the year 1736 at eighty-seven or eighty-eight (Cook 7,SCHQ 4:263). His burial plot, like that of many other pioneer settlers in this early time, has long since disappeared.

FOURTH GENERATION

Genealogical Note

JAN VAN DYCK
Bp November 19, 1682
D December 18, 1764
M June 5, 1706

JAN VAN DYCK of the Fourth Generation was the first born son of Jan Jansen Van Dyck (1648/49-1735/36) and Tryntje Thyssen, his wife, of New Utrecht, Long Island. He was baptized on November 19, 1682 (Cook 18;SCHQ 4:264).

A Brief Profile

Our story goes back nearly three centuries, a long time in American history. A summary statement will serve to place the facts in perspective.

In his late twenties or early thirties, Jan the Fourth accompanied by his wife Annetje Verkirk and their four children, all under seven years of age, ventured into the New Jersey wilderness, a land strewn with trees, thickets, streams and swamps inhabited for millenia by Indians. The roads were no more than primitive Indian trails, slightly widened, winding through rough, rugged terrain. Not long before, in the year 1711, he purchased a 300 acre tract situate at Ten Mile Run, Middlesex County, not far from the Millstone River, a principal tributary of the Raritan. There he built a home for his family, felled the trees, erected fences, cleared and cultivated the land.

Other Dutch families constituting a migratory movement did likewise. In a few years the Millstone Valley grew into a thriving agricultural community producing grain in large quantity. If Jan's grandfather, Jan Thomasse, had been told that this would come to pass or that his grandson would someday sit on a municipal council in the province of New Jersey, he would have laughed heartily. "Incredible!" he would have exclaimed; as fantastic as a prediction that the Wright brothers' flying machine that sustained a flight of fifty-nine seconds at thirty miles an hour, a feat accomplished at Kitty Hawk, North Carolina, in 1903, would cross the Atlantic on a non-stop flight from New York to Paris a quarter of a century later. Such is the course of history, unforeseen and, by the same token, exciting and dramatic.

Jan the Fourth, one of the early Dutch settlers of New Jersey, was part and parcel of its Dutch history. He adapted easily to English culture, language and custom. Although baptized Jan and still Dutch at heart, he preferred to be called John, the name by which he was widely known. Most deeds contain the English form.

Like his paternal grandfather who left his native Holland and brought his family to America in 1652 when Peter Stuyvesant was the governor of New Netherland, Jan exhibited the same adventurous spirit two generations later, a Dutchman willing to assume a risk and challenge the wilderness with his young family. It was a bold decision; a decision, however, he did not regret. He died in his eighties and is buried on his own land.

An adventurer, farmer, landholder and community leader, Jan has a stirring true-life story to tell.

Let us explore the Dutch settlement of New Jersey as seen through the eyes of Jan Van Dyck of the Fourth Generation.

Marriage and Children

On March 15, 1663 Jan Janszen Verkerk (ca1630-)[1] with his Dutch wife, Mayke Gysberts, and five children emigrated from Buren, province of Gelderland, Holland, to America and settled in New Utrecht, Long Island. Years later their son, Roelof Jansz Verkerk (ca1654-), met Catherine Simons, a young lady from Breuckelen whom he married in the Dutch Reformed Church on August 7, 1681 (GMNJ 41:50). Their second child Annetje was born January 13, 1684 (Cook 18) and baptized January 20, 1684 (van der Linde 123).

Annetje Verkerk became the wife of Jan Van Dyck on June 5, 1706[2]. She was twenty-two and he was twenty-three.

Ten children were born of the marriage:[3]

Tuentje (Juentye) *B April 18, 1707	D	M Johannes Emmons (Emans) *D March 24, 1752
Catrina *B April 10, 1708	D Prior to July 1792	M Gerrardus Beekman
Jan (John) *B November 5, 1709 (FIFTH GENERATION)	D 1777/78	M1 January 25, 1732 Margaretta Barcalo M2 July 24, 1750 Garritie (Charity) Bergen

Ruloff (Roelof) B May 18, 1711[4]	D June 4, 1788	M June 19, 1738 Catherine Emmons (Emans)
Mathys (Matthias) *B August 28, 1714 "at New Brunswick" (Bailey 397)	D 1784	M June 12, 1746 Neeltje Lane (SCHQ 4:264;Cook 18; GMNJ 66:64)
Abraham *B October 3, 1716	*D Probably March 12, 1742	
Simon *B October 12, 1718	D 1783-86	M Anne
Isaac *B June 28, 1721	D 1798-1803	M1 Ann Voorhees M2 Ann DeHart
Jacob *B November 12, 1723	D September 12, 1809 (SCHQ 4:141)	M1 June 1, 1751 Margrietje Terhuyne M2 Moyeke (SCHQ 4:141)
Anna *B June 16, 1725	D	M1 Albert Voorhees M2 Albert Terhune

Tuentje, Catrina, Jan (John) and Ruloff were born in New Utrecht, Long Island. It is reasonably certain that Mathys, Abraham, Simon, Isaac, Jacob and Anna, born in New Jersey, were baptized at the Six Mile Run Dutch Reformed Church founded November 15, 1710 and located in Franklin Township, Somerset County, near the Van Dyck homestead. Unfortunately the baptismal records covering the period of their births no longer exist.[5]

Settlement in the Millstone Valley

It was only natural that the early Dutch settlers should use the trails of the Indians who knew the topography and the most convenient paths on foot. One such path the Indians called the Assunpink Trail. According to Judge Ralph Voorhees, it extended "from the Falls of the Delaware at Trenton to the first fording place across the Raritan near the head of the Tide Water - now New Brunswick". In many old deeds it was called "The Path". Said

Judge Voorhees, "It ran over the highest and driest grounds" and "crossed the various streams in the driest and most favorable places, thereby avoiding the broad and wet meadows". Today it is known as State Highway Route 27 with some of the twists and turns straightened. Over this trail the Indians carried their furs and other articles to market (SCHQ 4:108;Menzies 39;Wacker 70,111,112). Thus in this early settlement period the socalled path served as a principal migratory route of the Dutch for transporting their household goods, farm equipment and live stock from the Raritan into the Millstone Valley.

The two Labatist missionaries from the Province of Friesland, Holland, Danckaerts and Sluyter, supra, used the Assunpink Trail in 1679 on their journey from New Brunswick to Trenton or the "falls of the South River" as it was known to them. On Friday, November 17, 1679 Jasper Danckaerts wrote in his journal:

> *The road from here to the falls of the South River, runs for the most part W.S.W., and then W. It is nothing but a foot-path for men and horses, between the trees and through the small shrubs, although we came to places where there were large planes, beset with a few trees, and grown over with long grass which was not the worst. When you have ridden a piece of the way, you can see the lands of the Navesink, far off on the left hand, into the ocean, affording a fine view. The land we rode over was neither the best, nor the worst ... When about half way you come to a high, but very rocky hill, which is very difficult for man or beast to walk upon. After crossing it, you come to a large valley, the descent to which from this hill, is very steep, by a very shrubby road; and you must dismount, in order to lead your horses down carefully, as well as descend carefully yourselves. We were in the middle of this valley, when a company met us on horseback, from the South River (Danckaerts 95).*

In the early eighteenth century news reached the Dutch farmers on Long Island of the rich alluvial soil and flowing streams in the Millstone Valley, land then being surveyed to be offered for sale. It was a powerful inducement, almost irresistible; they needed fertile ground for their expanding families. In dramatic fashion it triggered a migration of Dutch families with all their horses, cattle, sheep, and material possessions into the wilderness of East Jersey.[6] As a result, the Dutch in this prerevolutionary period made it one of the most important wheat growing areas in North America. While other reasons have been advanced, such as disenchantment with English rule and cultural differences, the availability of fertile ground plus navigable water ways were the main factors (Wacker 218).

In 1711, Jan the Fourth resided in New Utrecht, Kings County, Province of New York, the domicile of the Van Dyck family for two generations. A deed dated April 2, 1711 wherein Jan, the grantee, is designated "John van Dyck of new Utreck in Kings County in ye province aforesaid" documents the purchase of 300 acres on the Assunpink trail (Route 27) in the Millstone Valley, Middlesex County, Province of New Jersey, from John Moss, a wealthy land investor of Queens County, Province of New York (SCA). The consideration of 190 pounds may have been a bargain, even in that day; but in any event this transaction marked the initial step in the resettlement of the family. Soon thereafter, Jan with his wife Annetje and their young offspring - Tuentje, Catrina, Jan (John) (Fifth Generation) and Ruloff - set off for East Jersey. The journey over land and water was an exciting and unforgettable experience. In the company of other Dutch families, they very likely boarded a sloop anchored in the East River off the shore of Breuckelen. When the tide, current and wind were favorable, the sails were hoisted and the small, heavily-laden vessel sailed down New York Bay through the Narrows on a course around Staten Island and into Raritan Bay; thence up the Raritan, avoiding the shoals, to a convenient landing place at or near Inians Ferry at New Brunswick.

The voyage was an adventure brimming with emotion and tense expectancy, soon matched by a tedious trek overland into the Millstone Valley. The narrow primitive path, not long before an Indian trail, was a formidable challenge. Horses provided the principal motive power pulling heavily loaded wagons with their precious possessions including clothing, beds and bedding, blankets, furniture, spinning wheels, iron pots, earthen and pewter ware, kitchen utensils, plows, harrows and a wide variety of other farm implements. Along with the horses were livestock on the hoof necessitating constant watch to keep from straying. A wagon wheel might easily become mired in the sticky, sludgy mud slowing the pace or bringing the caravan to a halt. Nor was the mud and swampy terrain the only obstacle testing their patience and fortitude. A fallen tree, a large branch or rock could block the path. Streams and swollen rivulets were crossed at fords, if fordable at all, depending upon the rainfall. They were at the mercy of the elements.

Their children and grandchildren years later heard stirring tales about the great migration; perils lurking everywhere, perplexing problems calling for innovative solutions and doubtless some humorous incidents, for the Dutch are lighthearted and take life as it comes. Legendary accounts, if any were recorded, are lost. Even the year is unknown. The period may be dated between 1711 (John Moss deed) and 1714. Mathys, their fifth child, was born on August 28, 1714 in the "vicinity of New Brunswick", placing the Van Dyck family by 1714 in the New Jersey province. Jan was a member of the New Jersey militia in 1715 (Bailey 397;Lee 630;GMNJ 66:64).

In 1729 Jan substantially enlarged his plantation (as the Dutch commonly called their farms) with the purchase of 203 acres of adjoining land from Benjamin Harrison of Rocky Hill, tendering the sum of "one hundred one pounds and ten shillings". The deed, dated August 23, 1729, identifies Jan as "John Van Dike of the Ten Mile Run in the County of Somerset and Middlesex and Province aforesaid" (SCA). Part of Jan's land probably extended into Somerset County since the boundary line was questionable due to inaccurate surveys of that day.

Jan's will corroborates the 1711 and 1729 deeds of purchase and describes his plantation in simple terms, namely, "all my homestead Farm and Tract of Land whereon I now live containing about Six Hundred Acres which I purchased partly of John Moss and partly of Benjamin Harrisson, Together with about Eighty Acres of Woodland which I purchased of Samuel Drake." Upon his death his homestead farm was made a life estate for the support and maintenance of his wife by his will, a singularly revealing document hereinafter analyzed with reference to deeds extant.

Deeds of conveyance confirmed by Jan's will are not the only documentary evidence of his plantation located at Ten Mile Run. Early road maps setting forth the names of landowners, villages, mills, taverns, streams etc. shed more light on this early settlement history. On September 12, 1745, the popular Pennsylvania Gazette[7] contained an announcement by John Dalley of Kingston, New Jersey, that he "hath made an actual survey of the Road from Trenton to Amboy, with the River from Amboy to Brunswick Landing; and hath set up proper and durable Marks at every two Miles Distance, and at all Publick Roads turning out, that Gentlemen and Travellers may know the Distance from Place to Place, and whither the Roads lead" (NJRM;SCHQ 8:322). Examining the Map of the Road from Trenton to Amboy,[8] we find relevant historical facts. At a point where the road meets the east bank of the Millstone River we observe Rocky Hill Mills, originally conceived as the site for a dam and a mill by John Harrison, (1670-1709/10), known as the Great Landholder, built soon after 1702 and said to be the first gristmill on the river (Menzies 49). Alongside of John Harrison's mill we see another familiar personage, John Berrian, a well known lawyer-jurist prominent in the civic affairs of the New Jersey province who will appear shortly in our narrative. Then proceeding east on the Somerset County side of the road we find Judge Berrien's brother Peter, marked Peter Berian's. And continuing further east on the Middlesex County side we come to Jan the Fourth, designated John Van dyck's.

Other names appearing on John Dalley's road survey of 1745 informing gentlemen and travelers of the distance from place to place and whither the roads lead document much of the settlement history. Focusing our attention on Jan the Fourth, the site of his homestead in Middlesex County pinpointed on John Dalley's road survey we find is compatible with the John Moss deed of April 2, 1711 and Benjamin Harrison's deed of August 23, 1729. In terms of chain lengths it lay approximately 224 chains east of the Millstone or about 2.8 miles.[9] The settlement was known as Ten Mile Run.

These precious deeds and surveys evince a special appeal and charm, particularly when viewed against the background of colonial history. We conjure up an image of a man on a horse setting out in the early morning hours on one of his surveying assignments. The tools of his profession were plain and simple: a compass, a surveyor's chain made up of 100 links 66 feet long (called a Gunter's chain), and a surveyor's rod. Surveying was far from easy on rocky terrain covered with trees, thickets, impenetrable undergrowth, swamps and meandering streams. Of this, of course, he was fully aware and equal to the task, at least to the extent of eighteenth-century technology. A tree marked on four sides was considered adequate to represent a fixed point while degrees of the compass were measured in whole numbers, a more precise measurement in the form of degrees, minutes and seconds being either impracticable or impossible to define. Thus a description by metes and bounds conveying title to land would astound a modern-day conveyancer. Consider for example: "from thence running South thirty Seven Chains and a half to the Southernmost Line of Harrisons Great Tract where stands a Maple Tree in a Swamp Marked on four Sides." These words are not plucked from imagination to illustrate a point, but are contained in the 1729 deed from Benjamin Harrison of Rocky Hill[10] to "John Van Dike of the Ten Mile Run". The following description is typical of countless deeds of that day:

Manuscript copy of deed (selected portions) dated April 2, 1711 from John Moss of Queens County, Province of New York, to John Van Dyck (1682-1764) of New Utrecht, Long Island, conveying a tract of 300 acres on the Assunpink trail (Route 27) in Middlesex County, New Jersey.

Courtesy Special Collections and University Archives, Rutgers University Libraries

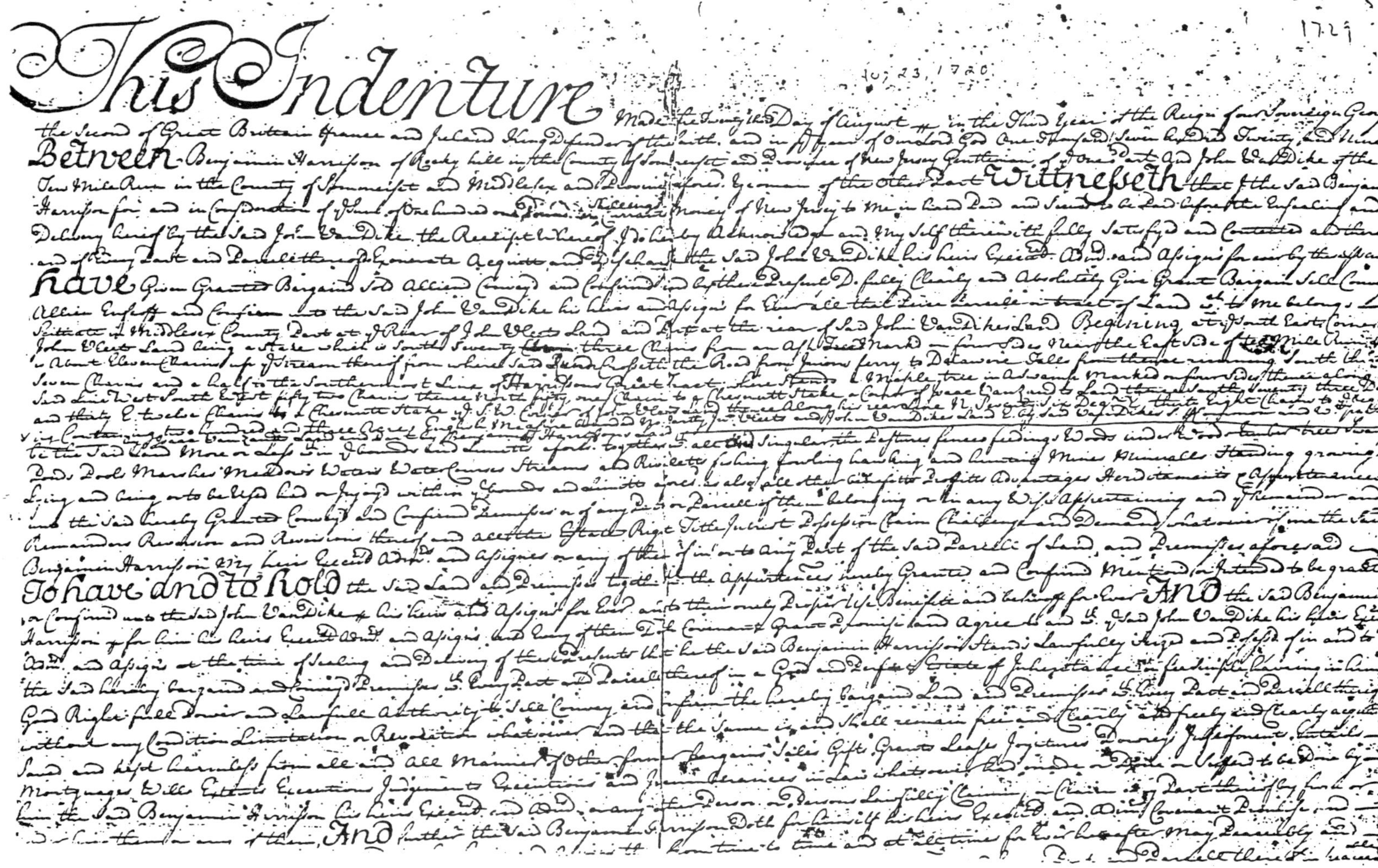
This Indenture Made the twenty third Day of August in the Third Year of the Reign of our Sovereign George the Second of Great Britain France and Ireland King Defender of the Faith and in the Year of Our Lord God One Thousand Seven hundred Twenty and Nine Between Benjamin Harrison of Rocky hill in the County of Somersett and Province of New Jersey Gentleman of the One part and John Van Dike of the Ten Mile Run in the County of Sommersett and Middlesex and Province aforesd. Yeoman of the other Part Witnesseth that I the said Benjamin Harrison for and in Consideration of ...

Manuscript copy of the deed (selected portions) dated August 23, 1729 from Benjamin Harrison of Rocky Hill, Somerset County, to John Van Dike (1682-1764) of Ten Mile Run in the County of Somerset and Middlesex conveying 203 acres.

Courtesy Special Collections and University Archives, Rutgers University Libraries

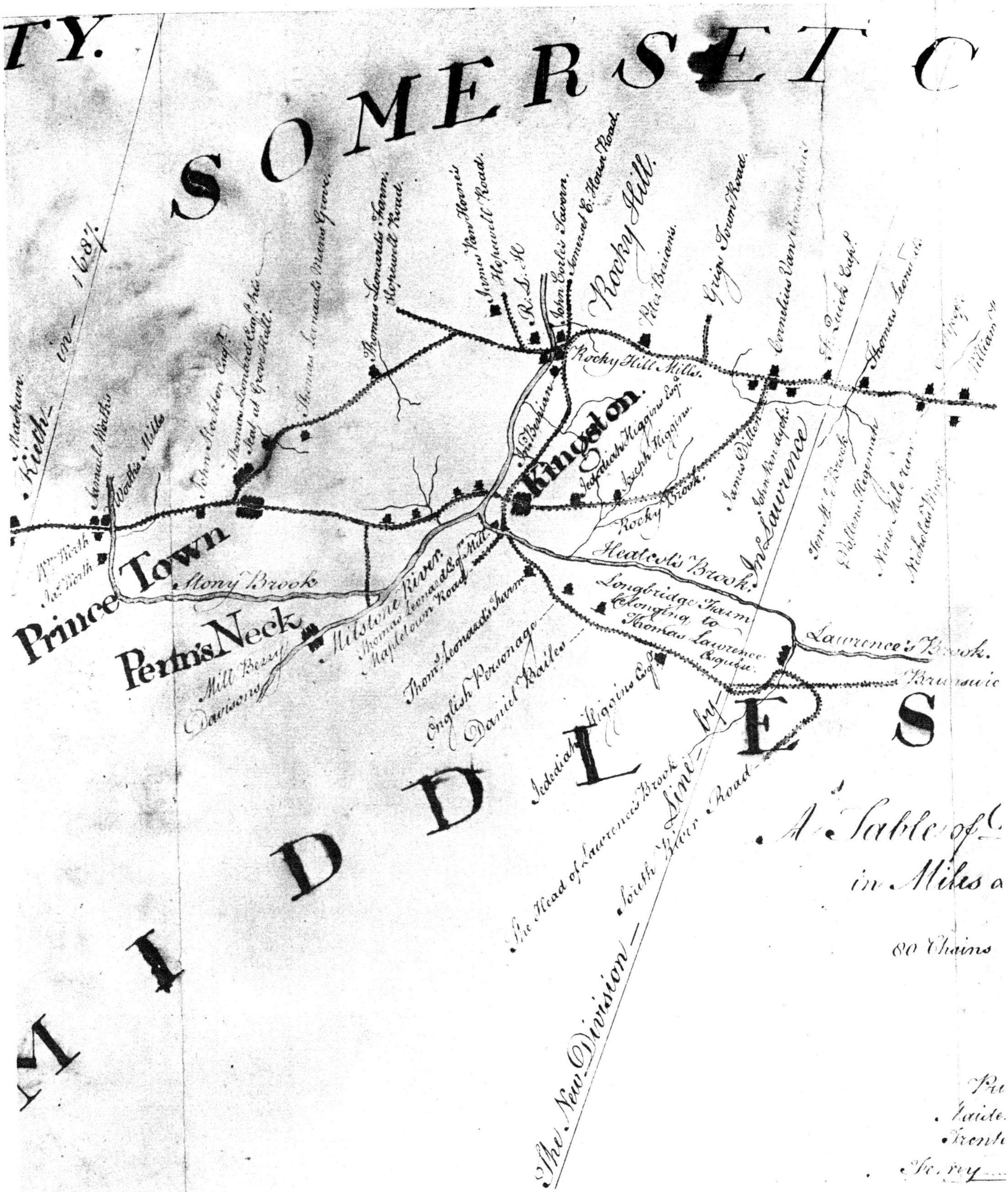

Early road map from Trenton to Amboy (selected portion) based on John Dalley's 1745 road survey. Among the inhabitants in that year were Judge Berrien, next to "Rocky Hill Mills", his brother "Peter Berrian's" nearby, and Jan the Fourth (1682-1764) designated "John Van dyck's".

New Jersey Road Maps of the 18th Century
Courtesy Princeton University Library

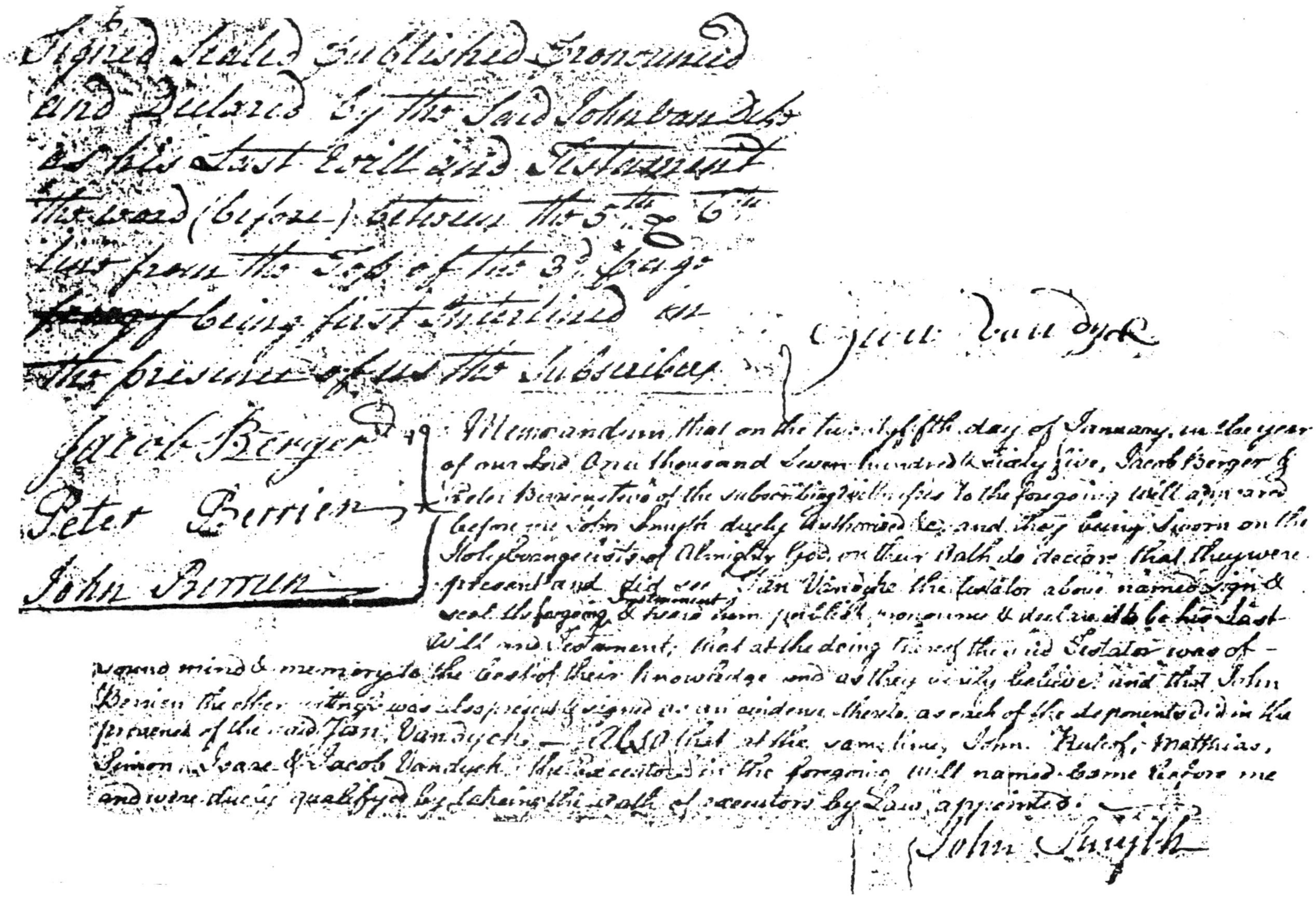

Signed Sealed Published Pronounced
and Declared by the Said John Van Dyck
as his Last Will and Testament
the word (before) between the 5th & 6th
line from the top of the 3d page
being first interlined in
the presence of us the Subscribers

Jan Van dyck

Jacob Berger
Peter Berrien
John Berrien

Memorandum that on the twenty fifth day of January in the year of our Lord One thousand Seven hundred & Sixty five, Jacob Berger & Peter Berrien two of the subscribing witnesses to the foregoing Will appeared before me John Smyth duely Authorised &c. and they being Sworn on the Holy Evangelists of Almighty God, on their Oath do declare that they were present and did see Jan Vandyke the testator above named sign & seal the foregoing Testament & heard him publish, pronounce & declare the same to be his Last Will and Testament; that at the doing thereof the said Testator was of sound mind & memory to the best of their knowledge and as they verily believe; and that John Berrien the other witness was also present & signed as an evidence thereto, as each of the deponents did in the presence of the said Jan Vandyck — Also that at the same time, John, Rulof, Matthias, Simon, Isaac & Jacob Vandyck the Executors in the foregoing Will named came before me and were duely qualifyed by taking the oath of executors by Law appointed.

John Smyth

Manuscript copy of the will (signature page) of Jan Van dyck made April 12, 1757 probated before John Smyth, Surrogate, on January 25, 1765.

Courtesy New Jersey State Archives, Department of State

WITNESSETH that the said Benjamin Harrison for and in consideration of the Sum of One Hundred One Pounds Ten Shillings Currant Money of New Jersey ... Do fully Clearly and Absolutely Give Grant Bargain Sell Convey Allien Enfeoff and Confirm unto the Said John Van Dike his heirs and Assigns for Ever all that Piece Parcel or tract of Land which to me belongs - Situate in Middlesex County Part at ye Rear of John Fleets Land and Part at the Rear of said John Van Dikes Land Beginning at ye South East Corner of John Fleets Land being a Stake which is South Seventy three Chains from an Ash Tree Marked on Four sides near the East Side of ten Mile Run and is About Eleven Chains up ye Stream thereof from where said Run Crosseth the Road from Inions ferry to Delawere Falls and from thence running South thirty Seven Chains and a half to the Southernmost Line of Harrison's Great Tract where Stands a Maple Tree in a Swamp Marked on four Sides thence along Said Line West South West fifty two Chains thence North fifty one chains to a Chestnut Stake a Corner of Isaac Van Zandts Land thence South Seventy three Degrees and thirty and twelve Chains to a Chestnut Stake of ye S.W. Corner of John Fleets Land thence Along his rear Line N. Seventy Six Degrees thirty Eight Chains to ye beginning Containing two hundred and three Acres English Measure ...

Estate Planning

At the time of his death Jan the Fourth was the owner of approximately 2,139 acres of land. His will devised the following tracts to six sons:[11]

- To his eldest son John a farm of approximately 230 acres in Somerset County "whereon he now lives which I purchased of Gershom Wiggins" and "my Silver Tankard which is marked with the first letters of my name in a Cipher."

- To Ruloff a farm of about 230 acres in Somerset County "whereon he now lives ... which I purchased partly of the widow [of] Thomsin Hollinshead and Francis Hollinshead and partly of Thomas Leonard Esq."

- To Mathias a farm of about 200 acres "whereon he now lives Situate at Maples Town in the County of Middlesex which I purchased of Thomas South" plus the sum of "fifty pounds" to be paid to him by son Isaac.

- To Simon a farm "whereon he now lives Situate near fresh pond in the County of Middlesex containing about Three hundred acres more or less which I purchased of Andrew Johnston, Esq."[12] plus the sum of "one hundred pounds" to be paid to him by son Isaac.

- *To Isaac a farm of about 264 acres "whereon he now lives, Situate at Maples Town in the County of Middlesex ... "which I purchased partly of Benjamin Pridmore and partly of Frederick Dolhason,"*[13] *conditioned upon son Isaac paying the said sums to Mathias and Simon within one year of his death.*

- *To Jacob, his youngest son, "all that Tract of Land Situate near RockyHill in the County of Somerset which I purchased of John Harrisson*[14] *containing about One Hundred and Fifty acres to the Same more or less"; also "one other Tract of Land near the same place containing about Fifty acres more or less which I purchased of Thomas Yates, Esq., and also One Other Tract of Land adjoining the aforesaid Last Mentioned Tract containing about Thirty-five acres more or Less which I purchased of Thomas Soden"* (Appendix G)

The final disposition of Jan's estate bespeaks exceptional thought and concern for the welfare and happiness of his family. His will incorporates a bequest of 800 pounds to be distributed by the executors in equal increments over a five year period "unto my three Daughters, Tuentje (wife of Johannes Emans) Catherine (wife of Garrardus Beekman) and Ann (wife of Albert Voorhees)". Lastly, to his wife Ann he left his homestead farm consisting of about 600 acres and 80 acres of woodland for and during her natural life, directing that upon Ann's death all remaining property be sold and the proceeds distributed in equal proportionate shares "to my aforesaid children named John, Ruloff, Mathias, Simon, Isaac, Jacob, and to their respective heirs and assigns forever."

This, simply stated, was estate planning Dutch style. Family oriented, hard-working and frugal, the Dutch carefully planned for their family's future. Their children held top priority. Financial planning was as important then as it is today in a more complex and sophisticated economy. It may be said without exaggeration that these Dutch folk did it superbly well. And without an insurance policy or a pension plan or a trust agreement or social security.

<u>John Berrien and Rockingham</u>

As a young man in his early twenties, John Berrien (1711-1772) left Newtown on Long Island where he was born and settled in the Millstone Valley (THSSC 73:46). The records establish that he was Jan Van Dyck's lawyer, confidant, and the scrivener of his will.

Once again referring to John Dalley's road survey of 1745, we note that John Berrien resided on the old Indian path (Route 27) near the <u>Rocky Hill Mills</u> in Somerset County while Jan lived on the Middlesex side of the path near Ten Mile Run. John Berrien was a third generation descendant of a Dutch immigrant. His father, Peter Berrien (1672-1737), born in Midwout (Flatbush), Long Island, was the son of Cornelis Jansen Berrien (ca1640-1688) presumably born at Alkmaar in North Holland, who came to America and married Jannetje Stryker, probably born at Rhuynen in the province of Drenthe, Holland (THSSC 73:42-46). As neighbors on the old Indian path possessing solid Dutch ties, a friendship developed which in the ensuing years extended to members of their respective families and led to intermarriage.[15]

Judge Berrien was seen in the community as a gentleman-farmer and mill owner. Well educated, energetic and exceedingly ambitious, he proved to be a man of many facets: a lawyer, surveyor, land commissioner, assemblyman and a judge (Menzies 127,128;Heiss 84-86). He arrived in the Millstone Valley shortly before 1735. On the Franklin Township Tax List of 1735 his name appears as the owner of 130 acres and one cow taxed at 7 shillings and 3 pence (Menzies 76). His younger brother Peter (1711-1781) followed around 1738 establishing a home for his family at Ten Mile Run on land inherited from his father (Heiss 6,88-91). By 1745 John Berrien's estate had substantially increased. Mills and stores were called "shops"; he was assessed for a "shop" consisting of 230 acres of land, 18 cattle and 44 sheep taxed at one pound and seven pence according to the 1745 Tax List (SCHQ 4:187). Soon he earned the reputation of a highly distinguished citizen; in part, a trustee of Princeton College (College of New Jersey), member of the New Jersey Assembly, a judge of the Somerset County Court (1739), subsequently a justice of the Supreme Court of the Province of New Jersey (1764), and an intimate friend of George Washington. One of Judge Berrien's sons was an aide to Washington at the Battle of Monmouth (SCHQ 1:85-87;SCHQ 4:187).

Judge Berrien's home situate about a mile east of the village of Rocky Hill in Franklin Township and about 500 feet from the Millstone River (SCHQ 1:85) was originally built by John Harrison, the Great Landholder, supra, between 1702 and 1710 as a summer cottage in the cool woods by the water where he could comfortably manage his mill and land holdings. Located about four miles from another settlement known as Prince Town (John Dalley's survey of 1745) and not more than a day's journey from his home in Perth Amboy, he found it pleasant and convenient. After the death of the Harrisons (father, son and son's widow), John Berrien acquired Harrison's small Connecticut-style dwelling with about 130 acres of land along the Millstone. His first wife, Mary Leonard, whom he married in 1744 and died in 1758, bore no children (Heiss 6). The following year he married Margaret Eaton of Eatontown (ca1723-1819), New Jersey, by whom he had six children, which easily explains why he extensively enlarged and remodelled his dwelling (Menzies 125-127;Heiss 6,84-88).

He christened it <u>Rockingham</u>.[16]

A quarter of a century later Rockingham would be famous in American history. Today it stands as a treasured historical landmark after having been moved twice to escape destruction from blasting at a nearby quarry. That it has survived threatened destruction and supine neglect is a "little short of a Standing Miracle", to borrow a metaphor from George Washington when praising the men of the Continental Armies who endured "almost every possible suffering and discouragement for the span of eight years", words from Washington's Farewell Address penned in the "Blue Room" at Rockingham in 1783 (SCHQ 1:87).

On April 12, 1757 a meeting took place, very likely at Rockingham, for the execution of Jan's will. Present were Jan, his lawyer, John Berrien, and his brother Peter Berrien; also Jacob Bergen, Jan's son-in-law. Jan was seventy-four and "thanks to God in good health", his will proclaims. After a reading of the will, John Berrien made a minor correction before Jan signed it,[17] whereupon the subscribing witnesses, Jacob Bergen, Peter Berrien and John Berrien affixed their signatures in that order (SA).

The draftsmanship reveals a meticulous lawyer concerned with every material detail. Aware of the surveying limitations generating the elements of a boundary dispute, John Berrien was careful to draft a provision for equitably sharing the cost and charges and any loss that might befall Jan's sons in the event that title to any parcel might be contested in court or declared invalid. To the surprise of everyone, at the age of sixty-one, an eminent public figure with everything to live for - a wife and six children under twelve years - he ended his life by drowning in the waters of the Millstone. His tragic and unexplained death, tradition says, took place in the presence of three friends who witnessed the execution of his will on the very same day, April 21, 1772, at Rockingham. He is buried in the Princeton Cemetery near the President's Plot (Heiss 86;Menzies 128). Jan died seven years earlier, thus having been spared the profound shock experienced by the jurist's family and his many friends.

No one residing in the Millstone Valley would have dreamed that in a few years Rockingham would be the home of George Washington. This took place in 1783 while Washington attended sessions of the Congress convened in Nassau Hall, Princeton. During a period of three months - August 24 to November 10 - George and Martha Washington received and entertained at Rockingham such famous guests as Robert Morris, the great financier from Philadelphia, General Nathanael Greene from Rhode Island, Thomas Paine, the pamphleteer, John Paul Jones, the naval hero; also Thomas Jefferson, Alexander Hamilton, and the first ambassador to the United States, the Burgomaster from Rotterdam, Peter John Van Berckel, after a perilous voyage of fifteen weeks.

It was a time of great rejoicing. On the morning of October 31, 1783 a horseman was seen galloping from the east along the Kings Highway (Nassau Street) toward Princeton. The message from Paris eagerly awaited by President Elias Boudinot and the Congress had finally arrived. John Adams, Benjamin Franklin and John Jay had completed long negotiations in Paris and a peace treaty between Great Britain and the United States had been signed. The signing of the Treaty of Paris took place two months earlier - on September 3.

Communication was slow in 1783.

Ten Mile Run Cemetery

Another historic landmark with a colorful history in Franklin Township, Somerset County, is the quaint burial ground on Old Georgetown Road. Jan the Fourth donated the land, a tiny part of his 150 acre tract purchased from John Harrison, Junior, in 1723, supra. It is known as the Ten Mile Run Cemetery.[18]

A granite stone near the front gate reads:

TEN MILE RUN CEMETERY
ORIGINAL LAND GIVEN BY
JNo. VAN DIKE
AS A BURIAL PLACE FOR HIS
FAMILY AND NEIGHBORS

While Jan's homestead on the old Indian path has long since been demolished - in the name of progress some people may say - family history is graphically preserved in this ancient cemetery. Standing for a moment among the old weathered stones with their terse inscriptions, one senses the distant past. History springs to life in a compelling way evoking scenes of those pioneer families who dared the hazards and endured the hardships of frontier life, among them the family of Jan the Fourth.

Entering by the front gate on Old Georgetown Road, we immediately observe familiar Dutch names on eroded, red shale monuments. Not far to our left, we see numerous stones marking the graves of the Cortelyou family.

Cortelyou!

The name sounds familiar.

Recalling that Jacques Cortelyou - that brilliant young scholar and surveyor of French descent born and educated in Holland - arrived in New Amsterdam in the same year as Jan Thomasse Van Dyck and settled in New Utrecht, it comes as no surprise that his sons and grandsons were among those pioneers constituting part of the Dutch exodus from Long Island into the province of East Jersey (SCHQ 1:103-106). In brief, the genealogical records establish that Jacques, the original settler, was the father of a son Jacques (ca1660-1731), who was the father of Hendrick (1711-1777) who married twice and had thirteen children; and the said Hendrick fathered a son Hendrick (1736-1800) who lived at Ten Mile Run and married a Dutch girl, Johannah Stootoff (Cortelyou 67,68,89-91) - which brings us to the Ten Mile Run Cemetery at this early time. There, lying peacefully are Hendrick Cortelyou of the fourth generation who, the marker informs us, was born on October 10, 1736 and died October 31, 1800 at age 64, and his wife Johannah Stootoff who died December 12, 1809 "aged 67 yrs,1 mo." Three of their children were taken from them: a son, Jacques aged 12 yrs.,8 dys.", a daughter, Ann, "aged 7 mos.8 dys.", and a daughter Sarah "aged 26 yrs.,3 mos.,7 dys." (SCHQ 4:136,137). Not unusual in those perilous times. The ancient eroded monuments evidence a total of fifty-three Cortelyous, twenty-seven Van Dycks, twenty-two De Harts (counting twelve stones bearing initials "D H") and ten Fourts, incontrovertible proof that these Dutch families ranked among the first inhabitants of the Ten Mile Run (SCHQ 4:64-66,136-142).

Further observing that Jan the Fourth and his wife Annetje Verkirk parented nine children who lived to adulthood and married and that Hendrick Cortelyou of Ten Mile Run was one of thirteen, all of whom lived in close propinquity, we may assume that in the natural course of events there were intermarriages. The assumption is correct.[19]

Still nestled in a quiet pastoral setting, this ancient cemetery has escaped the commercialism spawned by Route 27, once the path of the Indians. Whether some of them were buried in this spot at an even earlier time is unknown; they left no identifiable stones. In the early nineteenth century an epidemic of cholera or typhoid struck the community and a number of Irish immigrant workers on the Delaware and Raritan Canal succumbed to the disease and were buried in unmarked graves (ibid). A century and a half later they were honored by the Ten Mile Run Cemetery Association with a handsome Gothic-style monument erected near the resting place of the Van Dike family. Approaching the Van Dike plot, we read the inscription: "TO HONOR THOSE WHO GAVE THEIR LIVES IN BUILDING THE DELEWARE[20] AND RARITAN CANAL 1834"; and on the opposite side, "IN MEMORY OF ALL UNKNOWN BURIED HERE. ORIGINAL LAND GIVEN BY JNo VAN DIKE". The association was incorporated in 1925 under the laws of New Jersey by citizens concerned with the maintenance and preservation of this historic burial ground. The Cortelyou family has been active for three generations.

The granite stone near the front gate identifying the cemetery is appropriate. Its modern fresh appearance plainly indicated that it was of recent origin. Who placed it there? What is the history?

Seeking an answer, the author visited Mrs. Ruth Sincak,[21] then the treasurer of the Ten Mile Run Cemetery Association, who resided in Kingston. She courteously answered queries about the cemetery history and suggested that Mrs. Jeannette Gibson living in the area might be of help. Mrs. Gibson, it turned out, was very helpful. In a pleasant conversation in her home the following day, she provided a full and complete answer. This gracious eighty-six-year-old lady, conversant and alert, was the widow of William Walter Gibson (1891-1959) who is buried there.[22] While relating the facts, she modestly admitted that she was the inspiration for the granite marker! Several years before her husband's death, she said, he expressed a wish to be buried at Ten Mile Run with his Gibson ancestors.[23] This instantly stirred her mind on the subject of monuments. "Wouldn't it be a good idea," she suggested to William, "if a memorial stone were erected in front so that people passing by would know its history?"

William agreed. And so the granite stone seen today was crafted and anchored in place. Passersby now know the name and a modicum of the cemetery history.

In 1930 Marguerite Durick wrote an engaging article appearing in the Sunday Times in New Brunswick headlined, "THE TEN MILE RUN CEMETERY IS BOTH VERY OLD AND VERY QUAINT". Vignettes of pioneer life abound therein. Excerpts enhance our story:

> *One of the very oldest and very quaintest cemeteries in New Jersey lies a mile or so from the Rocky Hill highway, just between James Cortelyou's wheat field and the Phillips Schoolhouse. It is the Ten Mile Run Cemetery.*
>
> . . . .

Scratched on one little field stone are two letters D.H., D.H. very likely signifying DeHart. For in 1720 Cornelius DeHart bought 210 acres of land at Six Mile Run from the Indians, and then had to pay for the land again when white landowners descended upon him. This pioneer had a shot gun eight feet long and was famed as a deer hunter. It is probably Cornelius DeHart then who is buried underneath the rough red shale marker.[24]

The early French Hugenot and Dutch families used to lay their dead away on their private farms. Then neighbors agreed upon a common burying ground. The first interments in the Ten-Mile- Run Cemetery were thought to be in 1710, after the opening of the Millstone Valley. Until a few years ago there were heaps of unmarked red shale field stones over the oldest graves, but since they lacked aesthetic value and historical value too, for a stone's a stone [for] all of that, they were raked up and carted away.

Epitaphs were not very numerous in the Ten-Mile-Run cemetery. The early markers were plain and rugged like the early people of the community who struggled in the wilderness with stumps and stone-clotted fields and the dread of starvation.

. . . .

In a large plot toward the north of the cemetery all the dead of the Cortelyou family are buried. The common ancestor of them all was Hendrick Cortelyou, whose father was a tutor and surveyor and one of the first settlers in New Utrecht.[25] *The old Cortelyou Mansion was erected in 1690 on a farm extending from First to Fifth streets in the Eighth Ward, Brooklyn.*

Now, Hendrick Cortelyou was born in 1711, and he emigrated from the Isle of Manhattan to Somerset County, New Jersey. He married Antie Van Voorhees. His son and namesake fought in the Revolution.

You discover that the oldest date inscribed anywhere in the cemetery is 1762. Since there are no initials for further clues on the stone, you turn to an adjoining marker, erected to Henry Fourt, "A Patriot of the Revolution".[26] *He has compatriots in the little cemetery too. In the northwestern corner on a red-brown upright slab, you read that below this marker sleeps Samuel Grove, "A Hero of the Revolutionary War". All honor to them both!*

Captain Jacob Van Dik[27] *(this simplified spelling is just what you find on the marker) is another patriot of Ten-Mile-Run who wore the Continental Blue, and Hendrick Cortelyou, also. They belonged to the Somerset County Militia. Henry Fourt lived on until 1841 and died at eighty-five.*

Thank you, Marguerite Durick. All honor to them all!

The Founding of New Brunswick

When Jan the Fourth migrated to the Millstone Valley and braved the rigors of the New Jersey wilderness, he entertained no thought of political office. Rather his attention focused on clearing the land and providing food, shelter and basic necessities for his family. Little time remained for other things. Indeed he knew nothing about municipal corporations; he would not have recognized a corporate charter.

It seems strange, therefore, that his will identifies him not by his residence or domicile, but "of the corporation of New Brunswick in the County of Middlesex" The description is obviously a reference to a crossroads village on the banks of the Raritan River known as New Brunswick and its original charter when New Jersey was an English colony. George Washington (1732-1799), John Adams (1735-1826), Thomas Jefferson (1743-1826) and James Madison (1751-1836) were yet unborn. Rebellion was years into the future.

In substance the charter of New Brunswick is a twenty-one page legal document in the form of a petition by fourteen freeholders representing the inhabitants of "our Town [of] New Brunswick and Land thereunto adjoining", ceremoniously addressed to "George the Second by the grace of God of Great Britain Ffrance & Ireland King defender of the faith". The petitioners request a "Royal Grant by Letters Pattent under our Great Seal of our Province of New Jersey to Incorporate the freeholders Inhabitants of the said Town of New Brunswick and Land adjoining into a body Corporate & Politick". Significantly, this formal document couched in legal terminology extols the town's advantages as a port and commercial center, pointing out its strategic location "standing near the head of a fine Navigable River", which was of course the Raritan, and the "large and plentiful Country Lying on the back thereof", obviously a reference to the rich productive plantations many of which were owned by prosperous Dutch farmers. This rare and interesting document has been commonly called the Charter of 1730[28] (SCA).

The express intent of the founders was the creation of a city government based on the English pattern. The finespun draftsmanship sets forth the names of the men appointed to the various offices including the Mayor, Town Clerk, Recorder, six Aldermen and six Assistants, Treasurer, Sheriff, Marshall, Coroner, two Overseers of the Poor, and three Constables. John Van Dyck was named an Alderman-Assistant.

Observing that this large and plentiful country was a vast wilderness and sparsely settled, some questions arise: Why a city government? What was its purpose? And why was Jan, a Dutch farmer in the Millstone Valley, chosen to serve on the Common Council?

For credible answers it is necessary to step back into the early settlement history of Middlesex County.

One of the first settlers in the Raritan Valley was John Inian who arrived on the scene in the last half of the seventeenth century. John Pridmore was a squatter and an obscure figure who is said to have lived next to a swamp; hence the legendary name, Pridmore Swamp. But Pridmore neither bought nor sold land. Inian, however, was a large real estate investor as well as an enterprising

HISTORIC ROCKINGHAM, home of John Berrien (1711-1772), justice of the Supreme Court of the Province of New Jersey. George Washington wined and dined here, greeted famous guests, sat for portrait painters, wrote his Farewell Address to the Continental Armies and slept many times.

Photograph 1989

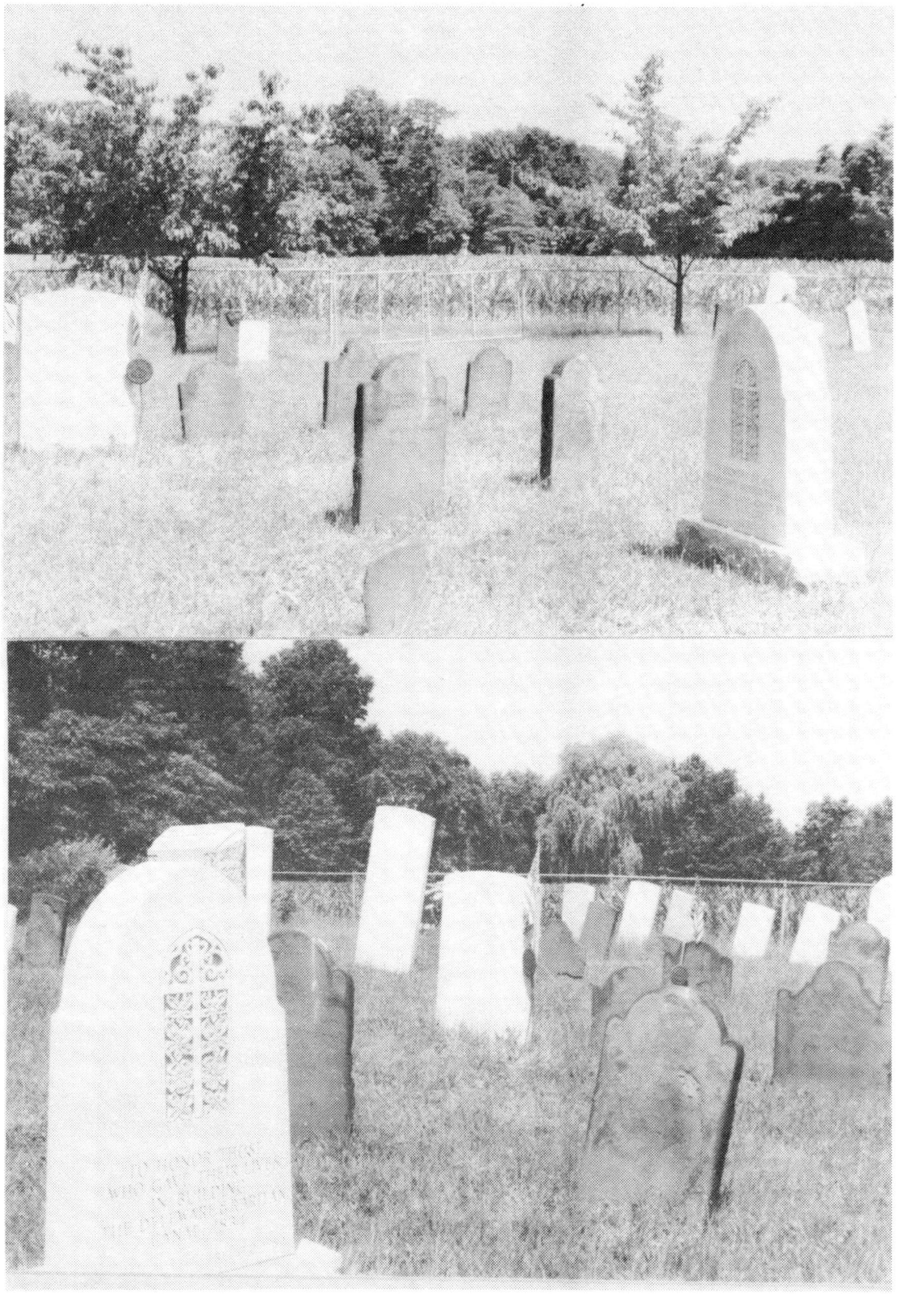

TEN MILE RUN CEMETERY, Franklin Township, Somerset County, dates back three centuries. Tombstones of Jan Van Dike and his wife Ann are seen to the left of the white gothic-style monument in the top photograph and to the right in the bottom photograph.

Photographs 1989

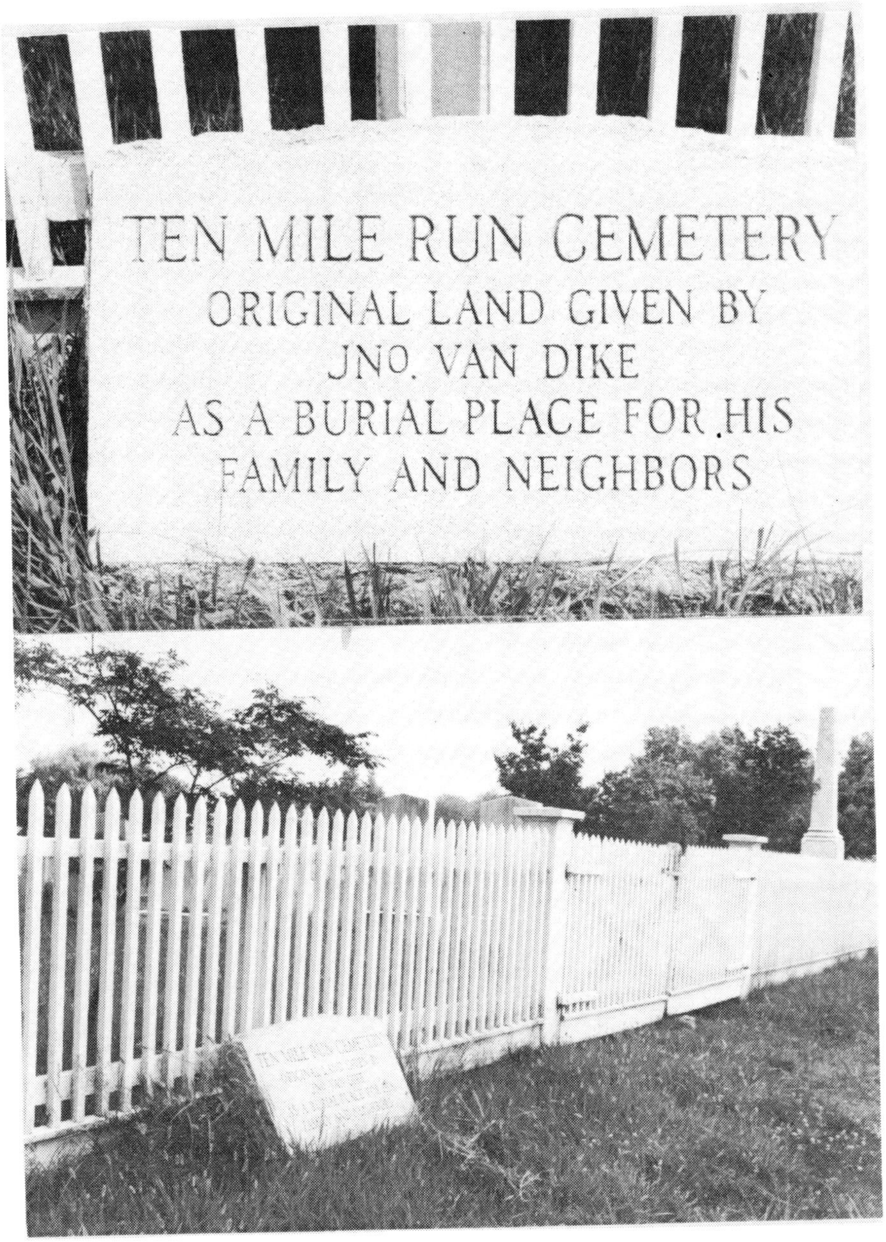

Identifying granite marker near the front gate of the Ten Mile Run Cemetery. Many Dutch settlers lie here including members of the Cortelyou, Van Dike, DeHart and Fourt families.

Photograph 1989

Wm Cox, Jacob Ockey, Dolly Hageman, Wm Chesemon, Josiah Davison & Law Williamson Aldermen.

ordain Constitute & appoint our well beloved Will[iam] Cox Jacob Ockey Dolly Hageman William Chesemon Josiah Davison & Laurence Williamson Esq[ui]rs Citizens of the said City to be present Aldermen of the same City to be & remain & continue to execute the said office until other fit Persons shall be elected and sworn into the said office of Aldermen as is herein after mentioned & directed. And we have assigned named Constituted ordained and appointed and by these presents do assign name Constitute ordain & appoint our

James Wilson Clerk

well beloved James Wilson to be Clerk of the s[ai]d City to execute and [illegible]form all things which unto the said office doth belong and appertain and to Continue in the same until another fit person be assigned nominated and sworn into the s[ai]d office. And we have assigned nominated Constituted ordained & appointed and do by these presents assign [illegible]inate Constitute ordain & appoint our

Evan Drummond Sheriff & water Bailiff —

well beloved [illegible]mond to be Sheriff & Water Bailiff of the [illegible] to execute and perform the said offices and to Con[illegible] the same until another fit person shall be assigned nominated & sworn into the said offices. And we have assigned nominated Constituted ordained & appointed and do by these presents assign nominate

John Thomson, Cort Voorhees, Minne Voorhees, Henry Longfield, Wm Williamson & John Van Dyke Common Council

Constitute ordain and appoint John Thomson Cort Voorhees Minne Voorhees Henry Longfield William Williamson & John Van Dyke to be the present Assistants of the same to execute & perform the offices of Assistants and to Continue in the same untill other fit persons shall be elected & sworn into the said offices. And we assigned name Constituted ordained & appointed and do by these presents assign name Constitute ordain and

Alex: Moore Treasurer

appoint Alexander Moore to be Chamberlain or

Manuscript copy (page six) of the CHARTER OF 1730 of the City of New Brunswick. Appointed by name in the document are six aldermen and six assistants, a clerk, sheriff and water bailiff, chamberlain or treasurer, coroner, marshall or sergeant at mace, mayor and others.

Courtesy Special Collections and University Archives, Rutgers University Libraries

individual, who established a popular ferry service which crossed the river from Highland Park to the foot of Albany Street in New Brunswick. The ferry operated continuously for more than a century, specifically from 1686 until the first bridge over the Raritan was built in 1791-93. Inian's Ferry is better known, in fact, than Inian himself (Wall 12-16).

Like John Harrison, Senior, who purchased thousands of acres from the Indians in the Millstone Valley, John Inian and his friends, in June 1681, bought a tract of 10,000 acres from the Indians along the south side of the Raritan opposite the Township of Piscataway. In the same year title was confirmed with the executors of Sir George Carteret (Wall 11).

John Inian was an astute negotiator, which is curiously manifested by an Indian deed setting forth the consideration tendered the Indians, namely: "200 fathoms of white wampum, 10 blankets, 20 overcoats, 10 guns and 12 kettles, 25 axes and 20 pairs of stockings, 20 shirts and 5 made coats, 4 pistols and 6 bars of lead, 1/2 barrel powder, 2 ankers of rum, 2 half-fatts beer, 1/2 anker of molasses, 20 tobacco boxes, 25 pounds shot, and 1/2 weight of bread" (ibid). The settlement with the Indians would have been fascinating to watch.

The land was surveyed and laid out into nineteen "lots", as land parcels were then called. Inian bought two lots containing about a mile of river front and two miles deep, or a total of 1280 acres. A few years later Philip French purchased Inian's two lots, laid out streets, and cut it into building lots or farms. Instead of conveying a fee simple title, he generally leased the lots, in some instances for 2000 years.

Briefly, then, Inian's two lots on the Raritan, subsequently developed by Philip French, was the genesis of the "Town of New Brunswick", so referred to by the founding fathers in the Charter of 1730. In that year the town contained no more than a few stores and houses and some outlying farms. To the west or "lying on the back thereof" were the Dutch plantations producing vast quantities of wheat, corn, oats, flax, wool, vegetables, fruit and dairy products. Rather quickly the little village on the Raritan developed as a commercial center for buying, selling and bartering. If the Millstone Valley was the bread basket, the "Town of New Brunswick" was the market place.

The farsighted incorporators understood that. Looking to the future, they sought to join the two areas into a single governmental unit thereby promoting the interests of both. Hence the Charter of 1730 defining the limits of the City of New Brunswick encompassed many square miles, bounded generally by the Raritan, the Perth Amboy-Burlington Road, the Millstone and the Brunswick-Trenton road. Such an enormous area containing only scattered settlements, plantations and small farms hardly looks like a city in today's world. Yet that is precisely what the founding fathers called it. And in the context of the Charter of 1730 and the English Common Law they were right!

Finally, Jan the Fourth, a freeholder in the Millstone Valley residing within the jurisdictional limits of the City of New Brunswick, a corporation as set forth in his will, qualified to serve on the Common Council.

Colonial Government

Colonial America, a strip along the North American continent lying between the Appalachian Mountains and the Atlantic ocean, was an aristocratic society dominated by the landed class and wealthy merchants in the urban centers. The privilege of voting, governing, holding public office and sitting on a jury belonged to a select few known as freeholders. Nor did aristocratic domination wither and die after the Revolution. That remarkable document, the Constitution forged in Philadelphia in the hot summer of 1787 by fifty-five brilliant men, marked only the beginning of democracy in America, a complex political process evolving slowly; and sometimes painfully.

A freehold in colonial times signified legal title to real estate that was inheritable or at least an estate for life. A freeholder in New Jersey was a man who owned 1,000 acres in a freehold estate or 500 pounds worth of real and personal property (Brecknell 26), a category representing only a small segment of the populace. Thus the aristocracy made up the governing body.

New Brunswick is a prime example. The Charter of 1730 mandated that aldermen and other office holders, either chosen or elected, shall be fit persons, that is to say a member of the landed class and a freeholder, thereby excluding the great body of people who were not of this class and qualified by property and status. For example, when James Hude was mayor in 1747, there were ninety-one freeholders (as shown by a list taken from the charter, ordinances and Philip French's Lease Book), while the 1745 census of Middlesex County counted 6,733 persons exclusive of 879 slaves. When William Ouke (upon Hude's death) assumed the office in 1763, there were ninety freeholders (Wall 26-30).

Consistent with this ingrained political philosophy, the Charter of 1730 vested executive and legislative authority in a Common Council composed of twelve aldermen and a mayor assisted by men aforementioned. Members of the council met four times a year. Carrying out the founding fathers' intent as set forth in the charter, they sat as a "body Corporate & Politick" for the purpose of decision-making. Lists of freeholders and the minutes of council meetings extant document that John Van Dyck was an alderman-assistant in the years 1730, 1734, 1735 and 1747, although undoubtedly he held the office in other years (NJHC 32-35;Wall 22,26-28).

The constant struggle incident to setting down roots generated social and economic problems far different from those dominating our contemporary world, a fact easily discerned from reading the ordinances, rules and regulations. A full agenda confronted the Common Council at their business meetings. Among the items for consideration were the maintenance of roads and bridges, the regulation of guns and firearms, the observance of the Sabbath or the Lord's Day (as they usually referred to Sunday), a curfew applicable to Negroes, Indians and Mulatto slaves, strangers to the city, taxes levied for the support of the poor, rules governing the market place and hucksters, fire prevention, and the appointment of chimney and hearth viewers.

Notably absent were any constitutional constraints that permeate the American political system today. To cite one example: the doctrine of separation of church and state would have been absolutely foreign to them. In this God-fearing society church and state joined hands in friendly fashion rather than stand cold and aloof. Religion was a powerful social and political force motivating colonial life. In many ways it was reminiscent of merry-old England where civil and ecclesiastical affairs were inseparably bound, calling to mind Henry VIII (1491-1547), a staunch Catholic upon whom Pope Leo X bestowed the honor of "Defender of the faith", a prerogative handed down to monarchs in the royal line of accession. Thus the deed of 1711 from John Moss to John Van Dyck executed two centuries later in the reign of Queen Ann (1665-1714) conveying 300 acres in Middlesex County contains the clause "our Sovereign Lady Anne by ye Grace of God of Great Brittain Ffrance & Ireland, Queen Defender of ye faith". And when those fourteen distinguished freeholders requested a royal charter from the King in 1730 for the City of New Brunswick, they deferentially payed homage to George II with the salutation "King defender of the faith".

Practically every citizen of New Brunswick, including the members of the Common Council, attended church once, if not twice, on Sunday, and refrained from any secular activity. Respectful and quiet observance of the "Lord's Day" was expected; moreover, demanded. Accordingly, the Ordinance Book records on November 12, 1733: "The Mayor Alderman & Assistants of ye New Brunswick Convened in the said City for ye good rule and government thereof Did make & ordain ye following Laws rules & ordenences viz ... The Law of ye Lord's Day is renewed & confermed. The Law relating to Children or Servantts not to play on ye Lord's Day renewed & confirmed" (NBHC 29). Similarly, the civil rights of a "stranger" - a term left undefined but unquestionably well understood - were casually ignored. The Common Council specifically decreed that "the Constables of this City and liberties thereof do from Time to Time make Strict Search and Enquiry after all Strangers that shall come and reside within this City or liberties and give a list of their names to the Mayor or Recorder or in their absence to the Senr. Alderman that Examination may be made and order taken to Save the City from Charges". When it later developed that socalled "strangers" continued to infiltrate the city to the displeasure of citizens who complained that the constables were lax in the performance of their duties, the Common Council took further steps and ordered, "The formar Law relating to Strangers is renewed and Confirmed with this amendment that ye Constables neglecting to bring in a list of Strangers DD according to ye aforesaid ordenence on ye first Monday in every month to forfit Six [Shillings]" (NBHC 27,29). We find no evidence of any objection on constitutional or other grounds. The atheists and agnostics, if any there were in this God-fearing community, were not heard from.

To be sure, this was a highly structured society that purposefully imposed heavy responsibilities on its citizens to take constructive measures rigorously enforced by onerous penalties. In their minds civic duties were as important as civil rights. Given the adverse physical conditions in the colony and the prevailing social climate, it is probable that government could not have functioned in any other way. The owner of a house or lot, for example, was ordered to pave the street in front of his property. At a council meeting on February 11, 1734 attended by Jan the Fourth an ordinance was passed reading in part:

> *Be itt ordained by ye Mayor Recorder & Alderman and assistants of ye City of New Brunswick ... the Street from the foot of the bridg near ffrancis Deldine's house through out on ye whole Breadth of ye Street to ye North End of Mr. Kimble's house be well and sufficiently paved with Stone by the inhabitants or*

Owners of Houses or Lotts on each Side of ye said Street each owner or inhabitant to pave over agt his or their respective house or houses Lott or Lotts to ye middle of said Street and from ye Corner of sd Kimble's house along ye Street to ye South Corner of David Chambers Lot be well and sufficiently paved with Stones or Brick six foot from ye houses and Lotts on [ye] side of ye Street ... And it is hereby [further] ordained &c that all and every housekeeper householder and owner of hoouses or Lots where such pavement is aforeordained be well and sufficiently done on or before ye 10th Day of August next ensuing the Date hereof under ye penalty of fourty [shillings]: with costs of suite for every owner of house or houses Lot or Lotts or Inhabitant where such pavemt is appointed to be done to be recovered by action of Debt before any one Magistrate of this City one third of which penalty to be pd to the informer ye other two-thirds to ye Treasurer to be applyed towards peaving the sd Streets as ye Commonality shall think fit and for ye better Regulating and paving the sd Streets (NBHC 33,34).

Lacking a fire department and with only private wells to supply the water - unless a pond, spring, or cistern happened to be convenient - the inhabitants themselves shouldered the responsibility of taking fire preventive measures. An ordinance was passed directing the appointment of:

... two Sufficient persons within this City to be Viewers of the Chimneys and hearths, who shall view the same once in every month and where they find any Defective to give notice that they may be swept or Mended in such Time as in their Discretion they shall think fitt and iff any person shall refuse their Direction herein they shall forfeit for Each offense three Shillings to the Said Viewers and that if any Chimney be on fire so as to blaze out att the top after the Publication hereof the Dweller in such a House shall forfeit for every Chimney so on fire the Sum of forty Shillings for the use of the City ... [And further] no Hay Straw Shingles or Shavings of Wood be laid within Sixteen foot Six Inches of any Chimney in this City under the penalty of ten Shillings for Each offense; [and] each Householder within this City from Mr. French's house to Lucas Voorhees's who hath one fire place in his house shall provide one good Leather buckett and all Others who hath two fire places or more in their houses Shall provide [two] good and Sufficient Leather bucketts for ye use of ye City for prevention of fire on or before ye first of June Next (NBHC 26,27,37).

Perhaps the city fathers thought that a leather bucket was little too costly an item to place this burden on all the householders. They were practical men.

Since slaves formed an integral part of the social fabric, the owner of a Negro, Indian or Mulatto Slave also bore an important civic obligation to his fellow citizens. And so an ordinance in the nature of a curfew was passed providing:

... that from henceforth no Negro Indian or Mulatto Slave above the age of fourteen years do presume to be or appear in any of the Streets of the City in the night time after ten of the Clock att night and that if any such Negro Indian or Mulatto Slave or Slaves as aforesaid shall be found in the Streetts after the hour aforesaid without a Certificate from Master or Mists or a lanthorn with a lighted Candle in itt so as the light thereof may plainly appear that then and in such Case itt shall and may be lawful for any of his Majesties Subjects within this City to apprehend such Slave or Slaves not having a Certificate or lanthorn with a lighted candle in itt and forthwith carry him her or them to the goal keeper of said City who is hereby authorized to put such Slave or Slaves into the Common goal and there him her or them to Detain till the Master Mistress or owner af such Slave or Slaves shall pay to the person who apprehended such Slave or Slaves eighteen pence and to the goal keeper eighteen pence money at 8s. per oz for each Slave so apprehended with the reasonable Charge for Victualing such Slave or Slaves if there detained above one Day (NBHC 25).

Significantly, the city fathers enacted one of the first zoning laws in America in setting aside an area for a public market. The best location, they concluded, was under the <u>court</u>. The site was undoubtedly well chosen as we interpret the rules embodied in an ordinance entitled "Regulations for the Markett", including the conduct of "Hucksters" who might be brought before the bar of the court to answer charges. This colonial zoning law reads:

Be itt ordained by the Mayor Recorder Aldermen and assistants in Common Councill Convened and by the authority of the Same itt's ordained - that the markett place under the Court room be and is hereby appointed to be the public markett place of this City and that all flesh poultry eggs butter cheese herbs roots fruits &c that shall be exposed to Sale on markett Days in any other place in this City than in the publick markett aforesaid shall be forfeited to the poor of this City whether found in the hands of the buyer or Seller and that itt shall and may be lawfull for the Clerk of the Markett Sheriff or any other magistrate of the said City the same to seize and thereof Dispose to the poor as aforesaid.

. . . .

And be itt further ordained by the authority aforesaid that no person or Huckster to sell again shall buy any flesh ffish fowl butter cheese eggs herbs roots &c or any other sort of provisions Saleable till itt hath been two hours in the Markett upon forfeiture of Six shillings and also what shall be sold or bought - And be itt further ordained by the Authority aforesaid that on Markett Days no person shall buy or Cheapen any provisions going to Markett upon the forfeiture of Six Shillings - And be itt ordained by the authority aforesaid That no unwholesome or Stale

Victuals be sold in the markett under the penalty of forty Shillings. (NBHC 26).

Highly structured indeed!

Finally, the record evidences a thriving business in the sale of grain transported by horse-and-wagon to the market from huge plantations in the interior. Once again the Common Council did not hesitate to exercise its governmental power to ensure fair dealing in grain transactions for it ordained that:

> *... Lawrence Williams Esqre be and is hereby appointed to be the Sworn Measurer and Sealer of all the measures for grain within this City and liberties thereof according to the Standard of that part of Great Brittain called England and itt shall and may be lawfull for him to Demand and take nine Pence money at 8s.p.oz for sealing every measure with the letters NB and also to Demand and Take two Shillings and Six like mony for measuring every Hundred Bushles of Grain and so in proportion for a greater or lesser quantity to be paid by ye party or parties requiring him to measure (NBHC 28).*

The farmers in the Millstone Valley were, of course, vitally interested in the sale and barter of grain in the public market place in New Brunswick and welcomed uniform standards to promote efficiency. What a pleasure it would have been to attend the Common Council meeting and listen to their discourse in this matter! We may reasonably assume that Jan the Fourth who served the interests of the farm population had something to say in the council's deliberations. Conceivably he may have proposed the measure.

In sum, these hard-and-fast rules, here partially abstracted from the ordinances promulgated by the city fathers of Ye Olde City of New Brunswick in the years 1730-37, testify to a conscientious effort to establish law and order in the colony and mirror the social order in Jan's lifetime.

Did they succeed? Did they govern wisely? Did New Brunswick grow and prosper?

History, as will be seen in the Fifth Generation, answers in the affirmative.

Retrospect

Viewing the total picture, Jan the Fourth emerges as an affable Dutchman who was fond of people everywhere regardless of social status or occupation. He understood human nature. It is not surprising, therefore, that he was held in high esteem by the inhabitants of prerevolutionary Middlesex County. Moreover, it explains the office he held in the governing body of the City of New Brunswick.

Speaking in Dutch to his Dutch friends and in English to his English friends, he uniquely bridged the cultural gap and filled a key role representing the Dutch farmers and others tilling the soil in the Millstone Valley. After all, it was the farm folk in the interior and the fruits of their labor that sparked the impetus making Market Day in New Brunswick a reality. In his sunset years Jan could look back with satisfaction mixed with a sense of pride upon his years of service on the Common Council. As previously seen, the draftsman of his will, the eminent lawyer-judge, John Berrien, saw fit to characterize him as "John van Dike of the corporation of New Brunswick in the County of Middlesex". An apt description.

In this aristocratic society the office of alderman was honorary and unsalaried. Twelve men sitting on the Common Council wielding near absolute legislative and executive power commanded great respect. Hence Jan by no means was a politician in the modern sense of the term, that is to say a citizen "running" for public office seeking popular support. The office sought him.

Now retired from the fields and barns sitting by the fire in a comfortable armchair, he could look forward to visits from his devoted offspring - Catrina, Jan (John), Ruloff, Mathys, Simon, Isaac, Jacob, and perhaps, Tuentje and Anna, joined by their respective spouses. And grandchildren, too, in large number. On their golden wedding anniversary, Jan and his beloved wife Ann could expect thirty or more grandchildren to warm their hearts and help celebrate the occasion.[29] Truly there was ample reason to rejoice and give thanks.

More especially, this was a time for calm and mature reflection. In quieter moments Jan's thoughts inevitably turned to rewarding achievements in a busy life. And to all the joys and, yes, sorrows as well, it appearing from the family record that his son Abraham died when a young man and never married, and his son-in-law John Emans (Emmons) and two of his children died within a few days of each other,[30] the scourge of infectious disease the most likely cause.

Also deeply etched in his memory, never forgotten, were those intrepid Dutch pioneers who, like himself, decided to pick up roots in the province of New York and settle their families on wild virgin land in the Millstone Valley of New Jersey.

Surely in solemn, retrospective moments Jan concluded that it was a good life. He and his Dutch friends willingly and with equanimity accepted all that life had to offer in those perilous times, its burdens and benefits, its reversals and rewards.

The Last Days

Jan the Fourth turned eighty-two in November 1764. The following month he died. His wife Ann predeceased him by about five months when she was in her eighty-first year.[31]

The year 1764 marked the turning point of British colonizing in America witnessed by a new proposal for taxing the colonists regulating commerce, including the Stamp Tax passed by Parliament in March of the following year, which instantly met violent opposition in the colonies. The iniquitous tax was the opening gambit foreshadowing the Revolution ten years later. But for Jan the curtain came down in December 1764. He could not have foreseen the bitter conflict soon to wreak havoc on his children and grandchildren - urgent meetings of the Committee of Correspondence in the glorious cause of American freedom, precious lives constantly placed in mortal danger, property pillaged, farms laid waste - the fate befalling the fifth and sixth generations.

Jan Van Dike and his wife Ann lie side by side in the Ten Mile Run Cemetery on a small parcel of his land. Reddish-brown tombstones, unadorned and partially eroded by the elements, mark their graves bearing the following inscriptions:

THE
Remains of
Jn° Van Dike Senr
upwards of 80 years
old when departed
this life

THE
Remains of
Ann wife __
John Van ____e Senr
when she died
upwards of
80 years old

Above: Tombstone of Jno Van Dike in the Ten Mile Run Cemetery. The white monument partially visible in the background marks the grave of his grandson Jacob of the Sixth Generation.
Below: Tombstone of his wife Ann who lies beside him

Photographs 1991

FIFTH GENERATION

Genealogical Note

JOHN VAN DIKE

B November 5, 1709
D 1777/78
M1 January 15, 1732
M2 July 24, 1750

JOHN VAN DIKE (as he signed his will) of the Fifth Generation was born in New Utrecht, Long Island, on November 5, 1709,[1] the first born son of Jan Van Dyck (1682-1764) and his wife, Annetje Verkirk (Cook 18). He was given his grandfather's name (Jan) in baptism in keeping with Dutch tradition.

To his family and friends he was known as John or John, Jr. His father liked the anglican form and in his will proudly referred to him as "my Eldest son John". As a token of affection he bequeathed to him his cherished possession: "my Silver Tankard which is marked with the first letters of my name in a Cipher".

Youth

John was very young - not over five years old - when his parents joined the Dutch migration into the Millstone Valley in East Jersey about 1711-14, supra. He doubtless had only a faint recollection, if any, of that exciting episode in the life of the family.

Prominent in his early memories were the horses, cows, sheep and other farm animals, and the plowing, planting, cultivating and harvesting acres of grain. Down a narrow road to the west he saw the flowing waters of the Millstone River and the Rocky Hill Mills frequently visited by the farmers with wheat, oats and corn to be ground which afforded a welcome opportunity for news gathering and friendly conversation.

The first grist mill on the Millstone was erected on the east side of the river at Rocky Hill, by the great landholder, John Harrison, Senior, who petitioned the proprietors in 1702 "for a patent for some part of Millstone River to make a damm for setting up a mill ... ordered he have it as desired". Upon Harrison's death in 1709/10 his eldest son, Captain John Harrison, Junior, inherited the mill and the unsold land whereupon it became known as Captain Harrison's Mill (Menzies 49). In rapid order other mills mushroomed along the Millstone. Soon the surrounding area was dotted with houses, barns, and outbuildings connected by small bridges and narrow roads, particularly roads to the mills. As more tracts were sold by the proprietors and new owners settled on the land, the Millstone Valley swelled into a busy agricultural community. Dutchmen with their large families were numerous among these early settlers (Brecknell 18-20;Wacker 164-169).

This was the scene at the time of John's youth. Doubtless he visited Captain Harrison's mill many times with wheat to be ground and accompanied his father on a wagon trip to New Brunswick with grain and produce for sale. There they purchased goods essential for home use such as silk, buttons, buckram, mohair, cambric, indigo, salt, tea and molasses (Brecknell 16).

Trenton and New Brunswick

To the Dutch farmers inhabiting the remote Millstone Valley often isolated by snow, sleet and heavy rain producing floods, Trenton and New Brunswick were seen as big cities. Originally small settlements by the water's edge, they grew rapidly over the next several decades acquiring wharves, piers and warehouses accommodating sailing ships laden with goods. Transformed into commercial hubs and exhibiting a metropolitan atmosphere, they were by contrast in colonial America big cities.

Setting out on a journey to New Brunswick was an adventure. We may picture John Van Dike as he grew to manhood atop a farm wagon driving a team of horses, the wagon well loaded with wheat for sale at the public market. Wagon and driver were uniformly jarred and jolted traversing the narrow, winding primitive road with holes, ruts, muddy depressions, sometimes huge pools of water produced by a heavy rain. Fording the streams was always hazardous. In the mental process of contemplating events that might or might not happen, thoughts were blurred. Anxious thoughts. Will the fair weather hold? Is the road open to New Brunswick? Can the streams be crossed? What price will my wheat bring?

If we could conjure up the magic of clairvoyance and hear him speak, he would paint a vivid picture of the big cities, particularly New Brunswick and Trenton with which he was so familiar, and regale us with anecdotes about settlement life as it in fact existed and those hearty Dutch farmers, their courageous wives and their children. Lacking, however, the power to turn the clock back, we must look elsewhere. Family documents such as letters, notes, bills of sale and account records, unfortunately, have not been found, and probably do not exist. How welcome an intimate diary or journal, if John, his wife or children, had ever kept one!

That is not to say that we are left wholly in the dark. There was one eyewitness who did keep a written record: Peter Kalm (1716-1779), a protege of Linnaeus (Carl von Linne 1707-1778), world renown Swedish botanist and a member of the Swedish Academy of Sciences, who toured America in 1748-51. His mission, basically scientific, was collecting seeds of plants and trees to enhance the horticulture and environment of his native Sweden. But possessing an inquiring mind as well as a passionate interest in everything, he talked freely to people in all walks of life. Thereupon he set down definitive accounts in his journal, published in 1753 in Stockholm, and known today in English translation as Peter Kalm's Travels in North America.

While visiting Trenton in October of 1748 - John Van Dike was then in his late thirties - the Swedish professor learned from his "landlord" (synonomous with proprietor or innkeeper) that when he first settled there twenty-two years earlier, there was "hardly more than one house"; but in that period it had increased to "nearly a hundred houses". In the words of Professor Kalm:

> *Trenton is a long narrow town, situated at some distance from the Delaware River, on a sandy plain; ... It has two small churches, one for the people belonging to the Church of England, the other for the Presbyterians. The houses are built partly of stone, though most of them are made of wood or planks, commonly two stories high, together with a cellar below the building, and a kitchen under ground close to the cellar.*

. . . .

> *The inhabitants of the place carried on a small trade with the goods which they got from Philadelphia, but their chief income consisted in attending to the numerous travellers between that city and New York, which are usually brought by the Trenton yachts[2] between Philadelphia and Trenton. But from Trenton to New Brunswick, the travellers go in wagons which set out every day for that place ... Between Philadelphia and Trenton all goods are transported by water, but between Trenton and New Brunswick they are carried by land, and both these means of transportation belong to the people of this town. On the boats which ply between this place and the capital of Pennsylvania [Philadelphia], people usually pay a shilling and sixpence of Pennsylvania currency per person, and everyone pays besides for his baggage. Every passenger must provide meat and drink for himself, or pay some settled fare: between Trenton and New Brunswick a person pays two shillings and sixpence and the baggage is payed for separately (Kalm 117, 118).*

Travelling through the beautiful Dutch countryside a few days later, the Swedish professor reached New Brunswick. Approaching the Raritan river valley from the west, he was deeply impressed. In his journal he depicted the community as a "pretty little town in the province of New Jersey in a valley on the west side of the river Raritan". He then continues:

> *The town extends north and south along the river. The German inhabitants have two churches, one of stone and the other of wood.[3] The English church is likewise of the latter, but the Presbyterians are building one of stone. The Town Hall makes a good appearance. Some of the other houses are built of brick,*

but most of them are made either wholly of wood or of brick and wood. The wooden buildings are not made of strong timber, but merely boards and planks, which are within joined by laths ... The houses are covered with shingles. Before each door is a veranda to which you ascend by steps from the street; it resembles a small balcony, and has benches on both sides on which the people sit in the evening to enjoy the fresh air and to watch the passers-by. The town has only one street lengthwise, and at its northern extremity there is a cross street: both of these are of considerable length (Kalm 121).

The conclusion is obvious that what was once a small settlement village lying along the banks of the Raritan had grown enormously in a relatively short time and enjoyed a substantial measure of prosperity. The reason, quite simply, lay in the history already recounted, recalling that only eighteen years earlier the incorporators conceived this little river town as an ideal location "standing near the head of a fine Navigable River" and "being the Most Convenient place for Shipping off the produce of a large and plentiful Country Lying on the back thereof" - in the words of the Charter of 1730. A farsighted and lofty concept! Presumedly, Professor Kalm had no knowledge of the Charter of 1730 or the founders' grand vision when he penned the following words in his journal:

New Brunswick belongs to New Jersey; however, the greatest part or rather all its trade is with New York, which is about forty English miles away. To that place they send grain, flour in great quantities, bread, several other necessaries, a great quantity of linseed, boards, timber, wooden vessels and all sorts of carpenter's work. Several small boats pass every day back and forth between these two towns. The inhabitants likewise get a considerable profit from the travellers, who every hour pass through on the highroad (Kalm 122).

How prophetic the founders were!

Education

Education held a high priority for the Dutch colonists, although subject to restraints of time, place and family affluence. For them it was almost as important as their religion - every family owned a bible - and the tenets of the Dutch Reformed Church. Education and religion, therefore, went hand-in-hand. After all, how could a boy or girl learn scripture and the catechism without the ability to read and write? John Van Dike, a member of the church and a revered churchwarden, exhibited a full comprehension of scripture and the catechism, as history shows.

As early as 1661 when Bergen was part of New Netherland, a log school was built and used as a schoolhouse and a church building until 1680 when the first meetinghouse was erected. In the early days of the Bergen settlement the consistory of the Dutch Reformed Church, the only church in the village, appointed the schoolmaster. The church rules provided that the consistory "shall be careful to provide good schoolmasters, who are able to instruct children in reading, writing, grammar, and the liberal sciences, but also teach them the catechism, and the first principles of religion" (Kull 389, Vol I). In 1688 the charter of the town granted by Carteret provided for a free school setting forth that the freeholders shall have the power "to choose their own minister" and shall contribute to his maintenance or "lay out such a proportion of land for the minister, and the keeping of a free school for the education of youth, as they think fit"; and further the said land once laid out "shall not be alienated, but to remain and continue forever from one incumbent to another, free from paying of any rent, or any other rate or taxes whatsoever" (ibid).

There is no record of a one-room school in the Millstone Valley prior to 1730, the year John turned twenty-one. It is highly probable that his father who was financially able engaged one or more private tutors for his children.

In December 1722 a schoolmaster by the name of Francis Harrison was living at Six Mile Run (Franklin Park), a short distance from the Van Dike homestead. Harrison was conversant in English and Dutch, and in 1730 wrote and published a small volume entitled The English and Low-Dutch School-Master characterizing himself as "Francis Harrison, Schoolmaster, in Somerset County, in New Jersey, America," and specifically identified his residence as Six Mile Run (Potts 450).

Observing the coincidence of time and place, it is possible that John Van Dike and his siblings learned their lessons under the tutorage of Francis Harrison, the able schoolmaster residing nearby. Noting further that John in later life held municipal offices including commissioner of highways and a justice who took acknowledgements of deeds and similar records, there is no doubt that he had mastered the rudiments of reading, writing and arithmetic.

Marriage and Children

On January 15, 1732 at twenty-two years of age, John married Margaretta Barcalo by whom he had four children:

Ann B 1733	D 1810	M 1753 Samuel Stout,Jr. (Cook 22)
Maregrita Bp November 27, 1741 at Harlingen (Cook 22)	D	M
John (well known as "John the Tory") Bp April 9, 1742 at Harlingen(GMNJ17:82)	D June 23, 1811 (VDFB/Princeton;	M April 17, 1761 Rebecca Van Dyck, daughter of Ruloff Van Dyck (SCHQ 6:189;Cook 22,23)

Cornelia[4] B December 8, 1743	D May 8, 1824	M ca1765 Henry Berrien

Margaretta Barcalo died July 5, 1749. On July 24, 1750 John married Garritie (Charity) Bergen by whom he had nine children (Cook 22,23):

Frederick Bp November 3, 1751 at Six Mile Run (SCHQ 8:126)	D June 23, 1811 (VDFB/Princeton)	M December 11, 1778 (date of N.J. License) Lydia Cole (SCHQ 6:189)
Abraham B April 11, 1753 Bp May 6, 1753 at Six Mile Run (SCHQ 8:128)	D March 9, 1804	M Ida Stryker
Jacob B December 24, 1754 (VDFB/Author;VDFB/Princeton) Bp January 26, 1755 at Six Mile Run (SCHQ 8:129) (SIXTH GENERATION)	D February 4, 1827 (Family Bibles)	M December 2, 1786 Sarah Schenck (Family Bibles)
Jane (Jannitie) Bp November 20, 1757 at Six Mile Run (SCHQ 8:132)	D	M Gerardus Skillman
Tuentje Bp July 15, 1759 at Six Mile Run (SCHQ 8:213)	D	M
Elsie Bp July 5, 1761 at Six Mile Run (SCHQ 8:215)	D	M Martin Voorhees
Ruloff Bp April 3, 1763 at Six Mile Run(SCHQ 8:216)	D	M Unmarried
Catrina Bp February 3, 1765 at Six Mile Run (SCHQ 8:218)	D	M Cornelius Vanderveer
Sara Bp October 25, 1767 at Six Mile Run (SCHQ 8:220)	D March 25, 1842 (SCHQ 4:261)	M October 4, 1791 John Van Cleef (SCHQ 4:261)

Above: Oppie's Mill recently restored located at Bridgepoint, Montgomery Township, Somerset County.
Below: The pond and triple arched stone bridge at Bridgepoint. Oppie's Mill is partially seen on the left.

Photographs 1989

Fireplace and walnut paneling in the home of John Van Dike
(1709-1777/78) restored by the Johnson family.

Photograph 1989

Above: Barn of John Van Dike (1709-1777/78) currently used by the Johnson family.
Below: Cellar of his prerevolutionary house exhibiting original stone foundation and hand-hewn floor beams.

Photographs 1989

Above: William A. Johnson, Jr. and his son John presently carry on the Dutch farm tradition on the former plantation of John Van Dike (1709-1777/78). In the background is a field of wheat.
Below: Dutch strap hinge on original barn door. "Peter Voorhees 1850" hand-carved on an old door found in the barn.

Photographs 1989

Settling in Somerset

Upon his marriage to Margaretta Barcalo in 1732, or very soon thereafter, John Van Dike settled on the 230 acre tract inherited from his father situate in the western precinct of Somerset County. The dwelling house and barns still stand at Bridgepoint, Montgomery Township, but what was then a large plantation farm has been fragmented by successive subdivision leaving today 81.46 acres. A few hundred feet down the road is Oppie's Mill, another historic building which has been restored in recent years by John and Barbara Stahl. With consummate skill and patience they have transformed a formidable structure into a comfortable residence while preserving its architectural integrity. The old mill dam creating a reflective pond is a picturesque sight enhanced by a triple arched stone bridge crossing a feeder stream. The setting in every detail is out of the past, a poignant reminder of the days when the Dutch held sway and the land was theirs.

A visitor enters the old Van Dyke farm through a narrow dirt lane, his presence immediately announced by a bevy of honking geese and a barking dog; perhaps the same greeting heard in years past. During most of this century the property has been owned and operated as a working farm by William A. Johnson, Jr., his son John, and previously by their father who took title and possession in 1928.[5]

Currently four generations occupy what was once the prerevolutionary dwelling of Jan the Fifth, an infant great granddaughter having recently joined the Johnson family. Although contemporary in outer appearance, its interior strikingly reveals its Dutch antiquity with beautiful wide-width floorboards, hand-hewn ceiling beams and Dutch doors. A huge brick fireplace with a high mantel is set against a wall of handsome walnut paneling.

The old Dutch barn a short distance to the rear of the house is supported by massive wood pillars and rugged beams about one foot square. You note the hand-forged nails and Dutch strap hinges on the weathered barn door. On the wall of the carriage house is neatly carved "C V PELT 1855" and "P Voorhees AD 1850 Bridgepoint". A door that had been stored for years in the barn exhibits a similar hand-carved inscription: "Peter Voorhees 1850". A deed search established that Peter Voorhees was the son of Frederic V.D. Voorhees and Cornelia, his wife, who owned the property in the nineteenth century when the farm contained 163.3 acres.[6] The initials "VD", it was found, stand for "Van Dyke".[7]

Reminiscent of the days of Jan the Fifth, young wheat is seen growing in the field on the opposite side of the lane leading to the house, but of course on a considerably diminished scale. The cattle population is also smaller. Two cows were in the barn. Grandfather Johnson, in his mid-eighties, who long ago delegated most of the farm duties to his son said with a chuckle, "They get me up in the morning." Grandfather does the milking.

A personal visit brings history to life. If those friendly Dutch folk who spent their lives here could return, they would instantly recognize their former habitation. Standing on the edge of the field near the house absorbed in its Dutch history and not a little moved by the pastoral beauty, you feel their presence, sense their thoughts, and hear sounds seldom heard today: the rooster's crow at daybreak awakening them to their daily occupations; the gurgling brook and the splashing water turning the waterwheel; the rhythmic clomp-clomp of horses' hooves and the subtle commands setting them underway and bringing them to a halt; the inevitable squeek and groan of the wagons and carriages passing by on the road.

Horses and horsedrawn vehicles call to mind market day when the Dutch inhabitants gathered in the village square to buy, sell and barter goods and wares. Meetings in the village square afforded a chance to chitchat about local happenings and personal matters; and, equally important, to learn the latest news filtering through from such urban centers as Trenton, New Brunswick, Elizabethtown, Newark, New York and Philadelphia. News spanned a period of days or weeks, not hours. There were no newspapers.[8]

Landholder

The purchase of land was an investment in the future of the family. Jan the Fifth, like his father, bought tracts of two hundred or more acres to provide land for his sons when they married and left the homestead. Following long honored tradition, the sons upon marriage settled on their allotted parcels. On the father's death title vested in them as provided by his will.

John Van Dike's will[9] provided:

- To his first born son John a 200 acre farm "whereon he now lives" in Somerset County "purchased of Jeames Murrey Esq", plus a three angle adjoining lot of about three acres "purchased of Sammuel Nevil Esq", and "the Wood Land of the Plantation whereon Cornelius Tenbrook now lives", subject to an important proviso discussed in the next section.

- To Frederick one-half part of a tract of land "purchased of Hew MacCan" situate in Elamantonk in Hunterdon County provided Frederick pay one hundred pounds to his estate.

- To Abraham the other one-half part of the above tract provided Abraham pay one hundred pounds to his estate.

- To Jacob about sixty-four acres in Somerset County "purchased of Garrit Williamson", also another ten acres near the same place "purchased of Samuel Nevil, the aforesaid three angle lot of three acres excepted; also another tract of about fifty acres in Middlesex County "purchased of Jacob Van Dike", probably his brother Jacob (Cook 18,19).

- To his wife Garritie a life estate in the homestead "whereon I now Live Containing about three hundred and Sixty Acres ... Partly Given and Bequeathed Unto Me by my Father John Van Dike by his Last Will and Testament and Partly I purchased of John Ver Kerk ... During her natural life or During the Time Which she shall Remain my Widow but if she Should

Happen to Marry Again it is my Will and I do Order She Shall Have Only So Many Household Furniture as She Brought With Her at the time of Her Marriage With me and one Negro Wench. (Appendix K)

The condition of remarriage was not intended as a forfeiture but rather a recognition of the solemn obligation of the husband to support his wife and children. Thus if Garritie should remarry, it became her husband's duty to support her.

Although tradition strongly favored sons with the bulk of the estate, John was exceedingly generous to his daughters: Ann, Maregrita, Jane, Tuentje, Elsie, Catrina and Sara. His will provided that upon Garritie's death or remarriage the homestead be sold and each daughter receive a one-eighth share of the proceeds and his minor son Ruloff the other one-eighth share plus one hundred pounds.

John the Tory

John Van Dike, baptized April 9, 1742[10] in Harlingen, Somerset County, the eldest son of Jan the Fifth and his first wife Margaretta Barcalo, is famous in Revolutionary history (Jones, E.A. 232-234). Not as a patriot however.

On April 17, 1761 he married Rebecca Van Dike, his first cousin, nineteen year old daughter of Ruloff Van Dike (brother of Jan the Fifth) and Catherine Emans (Emmons), his wife (Cook 22,23). Accounts portray him as a charismatic individual and a consummate storyteller. Long after his death, the legends appear to have lost none of the drama. Examining anecdotes and exciting tales, all purely hearsay, it is difficult to separate fact from myth.

Early in life he became enamored of the military. Given a career choice, he would have likely elected to be an army general or a navy captain. Tradition says that he "took an active part" in the French and Indian War (Jones, E.A. 232), but just how active a role has never been clearly defined. If he accompanied General Braddock's troops caught in ambush on July 9, 1755 upon advancing on Fort Duquesne (Pittsburgh) when Braddock was mortally wounded, and Washington (Braddock's young aide-de-camp) miraculously escaped death,[11] he was fortunate to survive. Ticonderoga - "sounding waters" so named by the Indians - commanding the ridge of a peninsula between Lake George Falls and Lake Champlain in upper New York witnessed another fierce battle in July of 1758, said to be the greatest battle fought on the American continent to that time, the British sustaining a loss of 1610 killed, wounded or missing. Young John Van Dike was there, too, so legend claims. Yea, right in the thick of the action bravely confronting the French and the Indians and hearing bullets whizzing by as he rushed fearlessly at the enemy![12]

As the Revolutionary fervor reached the boiling point in 1775-76, practically all the Dutch in the Millstone Valley opposed acts of Parliament considered grossly unreasonable and exploitative. One notable exception was John the Tory - a pseudonym well earned - who resisted all pleas of his parents, his brothers and other family members to join the patriot cause. Did he have an answer? What was the reason? According to accounts, he wanted to remain loyal to his oath to the King. His case has been dramatically presented, complete with dialogue, like the spirited oration of a lawyer for the defense when the facts in his case are weak. But let the reader be the judge: "'Col. John had a moral battle to face. Had he not sworn his allegiance to the crown of England in the Colonial war? Here was his country, kindred, friends, his home, his devoted wife and their little ones. Did he not owe them allegiance? These tore at his heart-strings, but that solemn oath which his inflexible conscience forbade him to violate triumphed. In vain all who loved him, zealous patriots all, pleaded. They were bound by no oath. For him he could see his duty in no other way. 'Well John,' said his father sadly, 'if you must go to the British deed back this place to me'. 'Yes, father,' said the son, 'on condition you will deed it to my wife and children, if I never come back.'" (Aitken 208).

Well!

Did not George Washington take a "solemn oath" to the crown? And countless other honorable men? Did not they have devoted wives and little ones?

If that precious "allegiance" which, it is claimed, he owed not only to the King but his friends, his wife and children could tear at his heart-strings, what did he think about his parents and his brothers? Or those fifty-six men with loving families who signed the Declaration of Independence putting on the line their lives, their fortunes and their sacred honor?

But enough! Whatever in fact he said in reply to the pleas of his family will never be known. Conversations were seldom recorded. Moreover, a deed of conveyance between father and son never existed. Title to land passed to all the sons in a Dutch family upon the fathers' death by will, as history demonstrates. The will of Jan the Fifth recites, "I do hereby disannul and make Void all former Wills and Testaments by me in any wise made ..." strongly inferring that his Last Will and Testament executed February 4, 1775 on the eve of the conflict superseded a former will containing a more liberal provision to his son John. Moreover, the devise to his tory son by his will probated before the surrogate on May 23, 1778 contains a significant proviso: "Provided he my Said Son John his heirs Executors or Administrators Shall well and truly pay unto my Executors here after named the Sum of five hundred Pounds Money at Eight Shillings per ounce Within Six Months after my Decease of which five hundred Pounds he has already Paid the Sum of two hundred and fifty three Pounds Nine Shillings and Seven Pense as by my Several Receipts therefore may appear" (Emphasis supplied; Appendix K). This is what in fact happened, which belies the mythical father-son conversation.

Finally, in keeping with Dutch tradition, the first born son of the family was usually named executor. In this case John the Tory was not so named, and for obvious reasons. Jan the Fifth appointed as executors his wife Garritie, his sons Frederick, Abraham and Jacob, his son-in-law Samuel Stout (husband of his eldest daughter Ann), and his brother-in-law, Henry Bergen.

When the war ended, John the Tory spent time in Nova Scotia with other loyalist refugees in exile, later returning to his home in Harlingen. In his remaining years he operated a tavern. An application for a tavern license filed in 1800 in the Court House, Trenton, avers that John Van Dike had "for one year past kept a tavern where he now resides ... near the Sourland Church" and had "sufficient house room, stables, and pasture to accomode [sic] travelers, three spare feather beds ... " (Brecknell 55).

The lone loyalist and plainly the blacksheep of the family with a gung-ho personality and a penchant for the military, John the Tory could scarcely escape notoriety and seemingly was destined to become a legendary figure. But for whatever reason, more has been written about him than all the courageous Van Dyke patriots who fought for independence and to whom we owe a debt of gratitude.

The Dutch Under British Rule

When Jan the Fifth settled on the 230 acre tract inherited from his father in the western precinct of Somerset County, the land was a vast wilderness with widely scattered farms and hamlets. Harlingen, Rocky Hill, Kingston, Millstone, Griggstown, Bridgepoint, Blawenberg and Neshanic were among the early settlements. Government was minimal. There were few people to govern.

Somerset grew steadily in the 1740s. By 1745 the population count was 3,239 including 343 slaves. Every sizable plantation had two or more slaves. Today there are over 200,000 people and no slaves. In the 1750s there were approximately seventy households established in the southern part of the county, later known as Montgomery, on tracts of two hundred or more acres. Their special needs were supplied by carpenters, butchers, tanners, weavers and other tradesmen usually hired by the day or week (Brecknell 12).

Local government was administered by a small, elected group of men called a committee who met once a year to oversee the building and maintenance of roads and bridges, render decisions concerning the poor and orphans, and collect a few taxes. County government, nearly as simple, functioned under a clerk and a Board of Freeholders.

Political power at the highest level stemmed from the King, the King's governor, and a Council composed of distinguished men all of whom were appointed. There was a General Assembly of elected freeholders, but, in reality, the King exercised the legislative function. The colonists were expected to bow to the King's wishes. This, in fact, is precisely what Benjamin Franklin (1706-1790) was told at a meeting shortly after arriving in London with his son William in July of 1757, nineteen years before the colonists proclaimed the Declaration of Independence. In Franklin's words:

> *John Hanbury, the great Virginia merchant, had requested to be informed when I should arrive, that he might carry me to Lord Granville's, who was then President of the Council and wished to see me as soon as possible. I agreed to go with him the next morning. Accordingly Mr. Hanbury called for me and took me in his carriage to that nobleman's, who receiv'd me with great civility; and after some questions respecting the present state of affairs in America and discourse thereupon, he said to me: 'You Americans have wrong ideas of the nature of your*

Constitution; you contend that the king's instructions to his governors are not laws, and think yourselves at liberty to regard or disregard them at your own discretion. But those instructions are not like the pocket instructions given to a minister going abroad, for regulating his conduct in some trifling point of ceremony. They are first drawn up by judges learned in the laws; they are then considered, debated, and perhaps amended in Council, after which they are signed by the king. They are then, so far as they relate to you, the law of the land, for the king is the LEGISLATOR OF THE COLONIES". I told his lordship this was new doctrine to me. I had always understood from our charters that our laws were to be made by our Assemblies, to be presented indeed to the king for his royal assent, but that being once given the king could not repeal or alter them. And as the Assemblies could not make permanent laws without his assent, so neither could he make a law for them without theirs. He assur'd me I was totally mistaken. I did not think so, however, and his lordship's conversation having a little alarm'd me as to what might be the sentiments of the court concerning us, I wrote it down as soon as I return'd to my lodgings.[13]

The die was cast.

Montgomery Township wherein John Van Dike resided had its beginning with William Franklin (1730-1813), governor of New Jersey, while his illustrious father for most of William's governship was in London pleading the cause of the Pennsylvania Assembly with the mother country and finding his mission increasingly difficult. Lord Granville's words must have made a deep impression on Benjamin Franklin who was compelled, finally, to make a personal decision, a decision critical to our nation's history. Soon after returning to Philadelphia in 1775, he tried to persuade his son to join the resistance. But in vain. A father-son confrontation reminiscent of John Van Dike and his tory son.

Patriotic fervor ran strong in Somerset County. The minutes of the freeholders assembled at the Court House in Millstone on July 28, 1775 record that Ruloff Van Dike, John's brother, was elected to a Committee of Correspondence for Somerset County authorized to instruct the Committee of Inspection in every township "to be vigilant and active in the discharge of their duty, in taking cognizance of every person of whatsoever rank or condition, who shall, either by word or deed, endeavor to destroy our unanimity in opposing the arbitrary and cruel measures of the British Ministry; and so deal with him or them as ... shall seem most conducive to prevent any injury to the glorious cause of American freedom" (SCHQ 5:246). So proclaimed seventeen men composing the Committee of Correspondence meeting at Millstone nearly one year before independence of all the colonies was formally declared. Could the zeal and dedication of these patriots have been more eloquently expressed?

Events leading to that "glorious cause of American freedom" rapidly unfolded. The Continental Congress having resolved "that William Franklin, Esquire, has discovered himself to be an enemy to the liberties of the country", he was placed under guard at his farm in Burlington (Snell 41). Being "adjudged a violent enemy to his country and a dangerous person", Governor

Franklin was arrested and sent under guard to Governor Trumbull of Connecticut who was requested by the Congress to treat him as a prisoner upon his refusal to sign a "parole" agreeing to remain quietly at Princeton, Bordentown or on his farm at Rancocus. Eighteen days later the Congress sitting in Philadelphia adopted the Declaration of Independence enthusiastically supported by his father who appended his signature to the engrossed copy. Indeed a remarkable contrast between a father, seventy years old, who stood for the rights of the common man and a son, forty-six, for something else.

In the period 1762-63 twenty-seven inhabitants of the southern part of the western precinct of Somerset, among them John Van Dike and his brother Ruloff, signed a petition addressed to "his Excellency William Franklin Esqr Governor and Commander in Chief in and over the Province of New Jersey and Territories thereon depending in America Chancellor and Vice Admiral of the same" requesting the grant of a "Pattent for a Township to be known by the name of the Township of Franklin" specifically describing the proposed boundaries. The petition appears to have been pigeonholed for some ten years (Snell 841). Did it by chance run into a political obstacle? Or was this royal bureaucracy? At length, about the year 1772, a patent for a township was granted, but the name was changed to Montgomery. Unless a rare bit of evidence should come to light, we shall never know the reason for the long delay or how Montgomery Township acquired its name.

On the tenth day of March 1772, the freeholders and inhabitants of Montgomery Township held their first township meeting, evidenced by the oldest public document now extant in the township, the volume in which is recorded the township elections (Snell 841). Chosen by a plurality of votes at the house of William Jones were a Town Clerk, two Freeholders, an Assessor, a Collector and Overseer of the Poor, two Surveyors of the Roads, and eleven Overseers of the Highways. Henry Van Dike, who wrote the minutes, was elected the clerk.[14] John Van Dike, Joseph Stockton, Christopher Hogeland,Jr. and Derick Longstret were appointed to a committee for "settling the presink business with the township of hillsborrow, and to raise the poore money of S^{d} western presink"[15]. And that completed the public business until a town meeting scheduled "Next Year at the house of wm Jones at Rocke Hill" (Snell 841). The men most active in the county engaged in local government were the commissioners of the highways, surrogates and justices who took acknowledgements of deeds, mortgages and similar recorded documents. John Van Dike was a commissioner of the highways in 1740 and a justice who took acknowledgements in 1773 (ibid 644,647).

Meanwhile, government at the county level incorporated a judicial branch, both civil and criminal, indispensable to the administration of justice and the maintenance of law and order in this fledgling society. The common law system of jurisprudence that the British brought to America found favor with the Dutch inhabitants of Somerset County. Of twenty-three freeholders serving on the Grand Jury at the Court House in Millstone on Tuesday, October 8, 1751, the majority were Dutch, among them John Van Dyke and his brother Rulof Van Dyke (as their names were spelled in the court's book of minutes for the day). Criminal Court bore the auspicious title Court of Oyer and Terminer and General Gaol Delivery, a name which has survived the years and used in some jurisdictions even as late as the twentieth century. The minutes extant record that the court opened with judges Samuel Nevill, Esquire, a Justice of the Supreme Court, and John Stockton, Benjamin Thomson and Tobias Van Norden,

Justices of the Peace for the County of Somerset. Thereupon twenty-three freeholders were called to the Grand Jury and found qualified. Among other Dutchmen on this Grand Jury panel with John Van Dike and his brother Rulof were Derrick Van Veghten, John Berryan, Christopher Van Arsdalen, Cornelius Tenbrook, John Hogeland, Isaac Skillman, Martin Voorhies, John Stryker, Gerardus Beekman, Peter Covenhoven, Hendrick Vroom, and John Tunison, manifestly attesting Dutch participation in the English judicial process. Only after the Grand Jury passed upon the sufficiency of the evidence to support a criminal charge could the defendant be held for trial (SCHQ 3:6,7).

A modern day jurist or lawyer steeped in the rules of legal procedure would find a trial in prerevolutionary New Jersey amazing. The times were vastly different from today; hence the English common law furnishing the basis for our current legal system was implemented to meet frontier conditions with its harsh demands. Justice was dispensed swiftly and decisively. Thus when the Grand Jury at the 1754 November Term of the Millstone Court returned a true bill of indictment, no time was lost; the prisoner was promptly brought before the bar of the court to plead guilty or not guilty. A trial then followed. However, if the crime were serious such as larceny, treason or murder, the court might allow a day to prepare the case and order the prisoner to appear for trial at nine o'clock the next morning. After calling and swearing a jury, witnesses for the prosecution and defendant were sworn. It is interesting to note that the defendant himself was not considered competent to testify, even if he had no witnesses. There was no record transcript to examine for trial error nor any post trial motions. The right of appeal did not exist (SCHQ 3:8,81-83).

Man and horse in this wilderness environment were inseparable. Loss of the precious animal could be devastating, not only to the owner but his wife and children. Horse stealing was therefore regarded as one of the most serious criminal offenses and was dealt with accordingly. The case of the Crown versus Thomas Salter et al that came before the 1754 November Term of the court is a good example. Four defendants were indicted for horse stealing and tried before a judge and jury. When verdicts of guilty against three of them were pronounced by the jury, they were brought before the bar of the court whereupon Justice Samuel Nevill ordered:

> *That the said Thomas Salter, John Brown (als.Murphy), and Benjamin Knight (als.Old England), be led to the place from whence they came and from thence shall be carried to the place of execution and there shall be severally and respectively hanged by the neck until they shall be severally and respectively dead (SCHQ 3:8).*

And the court wished to make sure that the prisoners did not escape - sometimes they did - and the sentence was carried out. Justice Nevill further ordered:

> *That one constable and three of the inhabitants of each township and precinct in this county of Somerset attend and watch the prisoners in this gaol of this county under sentence of death, in turn every night until their execution or other discharge, and that they take their turns as the Sheriff shall*

appoint, and that they keep on the watch from six o'clock at night until seven in the morning (ibid).

Upon a verdict of guilty rendered in a crime of lesser degree than horse stealing or murder, the public whipping post stood ready not only to administer punishment, but as a starkly visible deterrent to potential offenders. The case of The State versus John Henry Rice charging petit larceny in an indictment returned by the Grand Jury at the 1758 October Term of the Millstone Court is a case in point. After the defendant was adjudged guilty on his own confession, the court ordered:

> *that the said defendant be carried this day to the public whipping post at Millstone and there, between the hours of eleven in the morning and three in the afternoon, receive thirty nine lashes on his bare back and from thence to the gaol of this county, that on Monday the ninth of this instant, he be carried to New Brunswick and there, between the hours of eleven in the forenoon and four in the afternoon, he be tyed to a cart's tail and whipt through Albany Street with thirty nine lashes on his bare back, and from thence be carried to the gaol of this county, and that on Friday the 19th of this instant, he be carried to Bound Brook and there, between the hours of eleven in the forenoon and four in the afternoon, he be tyed to a cart's tail and receive thirty nine lashes on the bare back through the main street of Bridgewater, and he then stand committed until the fees are paid (ibid).*

The Church on the Millstone

About eight miles north of Princeton on US Route 206 in Montgomery Township, Somerset County, stands a large imposing white church. Two tall classic columns instantly catch the eye, one on each side of a portico forming the entrance. High above the roof in the style of the ancient Greek Parthenon is a belfry topped by a steeple. Thousands of people passing by every day are made aware of its name and origin; a sign on the lawn proclaims: "HARLINGEN REFORMED CHURCH established in 1727". Very few of the travelling public, however, know that it traces its history to the early Dutch settlers who gathered nearby in the wilderness for prayer and worship and, in 1727, founded a congregation under the jurisdiction of the Classis of Amsterdam.

The Greek revival edifice seen today - a far cry from the first Dutch house of worship - was the fourth building of this congregation built in 1851, and the third on this site. John Van Dike, in 1749, conveyed part of his land for the purpose to the church elders described in the deed as "one full Square half Acre". The original site was one mile north on the same highway where the Dutch built a small wooden structure with the materials at hand, and during the years of the Conferentie-Coetus controversy, infra, was allowed to fall into decay. No record of its size or appearance has been found. The Dutch referred to it as de kerk up de Milston or the Church on the Millstone. The old graveyard, still maintained by the trustees, marks its location (Hoagland 3,4;GMNJ 15:1).

All of which raises many intriguing questions. Who organized the Millstone congregation? Why did the congregation move to another location? What motivated John Van Dike to donate the land? How did it acquire its name?

The answers are found in the history of the Dutch Reformed Church in America, a history that is extraordinarily well documented.

Like his father before him, John drew strength and solace from the church. Nine of his children by his wife, Garritie Bergen, were baptized at Six Mile Run (Cook 22,23), not far from his boyhood home. The sixty-fourth item in his estate inventory lists a "1 large Dutch Bible and Some other Books"; the preamble to his will reads, "IN THE NAME OF GOD AMEN ... I John Van Dike ... being much indisposed in Body but through Gods Goodness of Sound and Disposing Mind and Memory" (SA). John lived at a time of spiritual revival sometimes referred to as the Great Awakening. However, long before this period of full-blooded evangelism, the church was a powerful cohesive force in the lives of the Dutch. Wherever they settled, the church went with them (Leiby 75;Wacker 166,167).

A deed of partition dated June 1710 conveying nearly 9000 acres to seventeen proprietors reserved 160 acres "for the benefit and behoof of the Minister and Consistory of a Church to be gathered there, upon the basis of the confession of faith adopted by the Synod of Dort[16] in 1618 and 1619" (Hoagland 3). This was another real incentive for the Dutch to buy land and settle there. In this early time there were no settled ministers in the Province of New Jersey. On February 11, 1715, two ministers in the Province of New York wrote to the Classis of Amsterdam, "The Dutch congregations very plainly are increasing every day. On the Raritan they are busy also in calling a minister" (SCHQ 3:174). The procedure to obtain a minister was by a formal letter or application addressed to the Classis of Amsterdam. The minutes of the Classis record that under date of June 5, 1718 such request was made, and, with the approval of all parties, the Reverend Theodorus Jacobus Frelinghuysen (1692-1748) of East Friesland, Holland, accepted the call. Upon his arrival early in January of 1720 he undertook the charge of four churches in the Raritan Valley: the Raritan (Somerville), Six Mile Run (Franklin Park), Three Mile Run (New Brunswick) and North Branch (Readington). Since these churches covered an immense area, large parts of Middlesex, Somerset, and Hunterdon counties in wild and uncultivated state, the congregations could be served only at widely spaced intervals.

Domine Frelinghuysen was a man of enormous energy; and, as the Dutch settlers soon learned, a vigorous, zealous and demanding evangelist. One writer portrays him as a "veritable John the Baptist - his voice the voice of one crying in the wilderness; his spirit a burning and shining light".[17] The heat generated, spiritual and otherwise, was intense. His evangelistic methods deeply offended all four congregations precipitating a bitter confrontation lasting for many years, and which the Classis of Amsterdam was called upon to settle - an onerous undertaking in the circumstances. Mail service between Europe and the American colonies was slow. The parties were adamant. Accusations against Domine Frelinghuysen ranged from a refusal of communion for one-half year to a communicant member who had settled her difficulties with her neighbor to the excommunication of four church leaders. To support them for expenses involved in litigation, travel and other duties, collections were taken among the church members documented by "Subscription Lists" some of which survive (SCGQ 1:36,37).

By 1723 the controversy, aptly characterized as the "Rebellion at Raritan in 1723"[18] was full blown; in effect, open warfare. Prolix letters were exchanged between the contending parties interspersed by appeals to the Classis of Amsterdam. To every charge Domine Frelinghuysen had a ready answer. One senses little in the way of tolerance or an effort by the domine to be conciliatory.

In these tumultuous times Domine Henricus Coens of Aqueknonk, in May 1727, organized the first church known as de kerk up de Milston or the Church on the Millstone, which held meetings in a small structure on the southeast corner of the graveyard aforementioned on the line now dividing the townships of Montgomery and Hillsborough. In a letter dated April 19, 1729 Domine Frelinghuysen informed dissident members of the Millstone congregation that "as far as he was concerned they were free to remain", passionately condemning Reverend Coens in preaching, baptizing and administering the Lord's Supper; and adding that he would never consent to his preaching in his church, but that he had no authority over the " barns in which he preached" (SCHQ 3:245). Scarcely consoling words to bring them into the fold! In the light of the turbulent history, it is not surprising that early records of the church are incomplete (Hoagland 3,4).

Patience and persuasion at long length having failed, the Classis of Amsterdam in a letter dated October 19, 1732 ordered Domine Frelinghuysen to make his peace with the "disaffected ones" within three months or they would be free to join the people of Millstone and choose a minister, and reinterated a prior order annulling absolutely the harsh ban of excommunication. Peace articles between the contestants were agreed upon and read from the pulpits of the Raritan churches in January 1734. But notwithstanding a declared settlement, there remained an undercurrent of dissatisfaction among some members into the 1750's (SCHQ 3:248,249).

And so was born and played out a schism in the Dutch Reformed Church in America continuing more than thirty years; on the surface a conservative group known as the Conferentie demanding ministers ordained in Holland and services in Dutch, and a more liberal faction called the Coetus wanting locally educated clergy, services in English, and greater autonomy. But as one reads the prolonged heated debate the root cause was more personal than theological.

After the death of Theodorus Frelinghuysen, his son Johannes (1729-1754), educated and ordained in Holland, was invited to preach at the Millstone church. While in Holland Johannes married, in Amsterdam, Dinah Van Bergh, daughter of a wealthy East Indian merchant, returning to America with his bride in the summer of 1750. A call was extended to him by three congregations, the Raritan, the Millstone and North Branch whose consistories jointly agreed "to provide first for an annual salary of one hundred and twenty-five pounds, current money, at eight shillings an ounce; the half of which, collected by the elders and deacons, shall be paid each half year; and a suitable dwelling with thirty acres of land"

(SCHQ 2:173). His ministry was highly successful, but unfortunately exceedingly short (Hoagland 8,9). When only twenty-five years old, he was suddenly taken ill and died, leaving his young wife Dinah and two small children. In addition to his pastoral duties, he still found time to instruct several young men in theology at his home in Somerville. The domine's dwelling house built in 1751 with a firm, stone foundation and walls constructed of brick (said to have been brought from Holland by the domine himself although undocumented) survives today as the oldest house in the borough limits of Somerville. It is called the "Old Dutch Parsonage"; also known as the "Hardenbergh House" (ibid). Both names are equally appropriate.

Dinah Van Bergh Frelinghuysen, the young, bereaved widow suddenly left desolate with two small children, intended to return to her native Holland. But fate intervening, her plans changed. Jacob Rutzen Hardenbergh (1736-1790), who belonged to the socalled "Dutch aristocracy of New York" and was one of the theology students, made a proposal of marriage. And Dinah, by reputation a woman of unusual piety and strength of character, finally accepted after much thought. Hardenbergh was ordained in 1758 becoming one of the first Dutch ministers to receive ordination in America. In the same year he received a call to fill the pastorate left vacant by the untimely death of Frelinghuysen, whereupon the Hardenberghs and the two little Frelinghuysens returned to the parsonage. During the Revolution, Hardenbergh courageously espoused the patriot cause. History asserts that he was "so ardent a patriot that the British set a price upon his head, and it is said that for months during the Revolutionary War he slept with a loaded musket at his bedside, and that on several occasions he was compelled to flee his home in order to escape capture by the enemy" (SCHQ 2:175).

For twenty-three years the Hardenberghs lived at the Old Dutch Parsonage, credited as the first seminary of the Dutch Reformed Church in America. Officially founded by a royal charter in 1766 through the persistent effort of Hardenbergh and with the cooperation of a few like-minded men, it was first known as Queen's College, and he was unanimously appointed its first president (ibid). Later, in 1825, it was renamed Rutgers College in honor of its benefactor, the New York philanthropist, Henry Rutgers; and finally, in this century, became Rutgers University in 1924. Thus two zealous Dutch ministers, Frelinghuysen and Hardenbergh, may be properly termed the founders of Rutgers and the Old Dutch Parsonage in Somerville its birthplace.

These men of action moved by strong moral principles were well known to John Van Dike, more especially, the inspiring young Domine Johannes Frelinghuysen who preached every third Sunday at the Church on the Millstone in its newly erected building. They must have enjoyed a very cordial relationship. No evidence has been found of John's involvement in the Conferentie-Coetus controversy. Observing the vehement charges and countercharges in a polarized and embittered atmosphere, John may have found himself not in total accordance with the divergent views of either faction. Whatever the facts, it is clear that when tempers cooled and the "Rebellion" had run its course, he was pleased to donate a half acre of ground for a new edifice suggesting that his sympathies lay with the members of the Millstone congregation.

The Harlingen Reformed Church

In the early years the Millstone church bore three different names. Originally, as we have seen, it was the Church on the Millstone. In the middle of the eighteenth century it was called the Church of Sourland. In 1801 the Dutch congregation officially renamed it Harlingen (GMNJ 15:1).

For thirty-three years until his death in 1795, the Reverend Johannes Martinus Van Harlingen (1724-1795), ordained by the Classis of Amsterdam, faithfully served the Dutch people preaching in their native tongue. In his memory the minister, elders and deacons, pursuant to an Act of the New Jersey Legislature signed a certificate at a congregational meeting on October 1, 1801 changing the name, in their words, "to renounce our former name of Sourland & to assume the name Harling [sic] corporation church or Congregation, by which only we wish to be regarded & known hereafter" (GMNJ 16:69). By 1794 English was supplanting Dutch as the prevailing language. In that year the Reverend William R. Smith, a brother of President Smith of Princeton College, was called from the Presbyterian Church at Wilmington, Delaware, to preach in English every third Sabbath, the other two at Neshanic (Hoagland 9:GMNJ 15:2).

The early church records - in Dutch - are contained in two books in possession of the church. With the benefit of an accurate translation published in 1940 we are given a detailed exposition of the first church building erected on the present site. There were ninety-four subscribers who contributed stated sums. We find that "Jan van Dyck" (as John's name appears on the Subscription List) contributed eight pounds and two shillings, and his brother "Roelof van Dyck" eight pounds, entitling them to a designated number of seats or places which they legally owned and could pass along to their children (GMNJ 17:2-4). The Building Fund Articles infer that prior to a congregational meeting in January 1750, John had promised to donate the land, which doubtless served as a catalyst for the building project. A reading of the articles elicits meticulous planning, firm resolve and dedication. Witness the following abstract:

> *According to the Lord hath willed it that the hearts of this congregation are inspired to build a church in His Honour, and have indicated as overseers and builders these honorable men who are here below inscribed, Messrs Peter Nivis, Johannis Stryker, Gerrit Dorlandt, Abraham van Arsdaalen, Roeloff van Dyck, chosen to complete this good work, and authorized by these articles to complete it by steps as both indicated in the articles. According as that work is completed with the blessing of the Lord in the year of the Lord 1752.*

. . . .

> *In the year 1749/50*[19] *the 15 January, the council and some of the upper Milstone congregation have foregathered and have agreed to build a church together about Henry Cannada on land of Jan van Dyck, where the most suitable place [is] ... The church shall be for a lawful Low-Dutch reformed [dominie] who shall be lawfully called and sent. The plan of the church shall be what the builders consider good and what anyone subscribes for this building shall be a voluntary gift to the edifice and for every*

pound that he subscribes he shall be obliged to work with horse and wagon whenever the builders deem it necessary, or if he should not appear on the day being notified his fine shall be four shillings, and he who does not come with horses and wagons shall be fined eight shillings.

For this building there shall be chosen five builders at the next meeting in order to get on with the work and to get in the money that has been promised. When the building shall have been completed, then shall the builders number the places and write them down in a book and builders shall even up the money disbursed with the [number of] places and divide the same equally among all places so that all the places come to the subscribers [and] each one shall have places for the money spent. If the finances are insufficient then every place shall be taxed higher equally until everything shall be paid excepting the free place for the Domine and the church council and a place for the Domine's wife, and those the builders get for their troubles. If anyone be unwilling to pay what the builders have taxed him, his place shall be sold at auction, and his already disbursed money shall remain to the church. In case money should remain over, this shall be made over as profit for the church in order to repair the same whenever necessary (GMNJ 17:1-3).

The following month, on February 19, a deed[20] was executed by John Van Dyke conveying "One full Square half Acre of land" to the church elders. The language of the deed expresses the religious convictions of the parties evidenced by the following excerpt:

WITNESSETH that the said John Van Dyke for the love and affection which he hath and beareth for the promoting of the Gospell amongst said Congregation and for divers other good causes and conditions thereunto moving, he the said John Van Dyke Hath granted, Bargained, Aliened, Released and Confirmed ... unto the said Simon Van Arsdalen & Lambert Dorland, Elders as aforesaid and their successors as Elders as shall be appointed from time to time hereafter for Elders for Ever over said congregation, One full Square half Acre of Land. BEGINNING at the westerly corner of Hendrick Canada's land, on the east side of the King's Road, for the building and setting a meeting House on said half Acre of land for the use and benefit of the said Low Dutch Congregation Established Conformable to the Rules of the Senate of Dortregt Held in the year of our Lord God 1618/19 and for a Protestant Orthodox Minister to preach to said Congregation and none other.

The overseers and the builders completed their "good work" in 1752 as they had planned. The Building Articles further provided that "there shall be three churchwardens chosen from the congregation, and the builders shall render their accounts to the churchwardens of everything they have received". Following this directive, the majority of the Congregation on December 5, 1752 chose Jan Van Dyck, Henry Canada (later "Kennedy"), Cornelius Van Aarsdalen as their churchwardens; and on January 29, 1754 the churchwardens admitted the receipt from the church builders of "the sum of eleven pounds seven shillings and two pence in full for all receipts by us from the church" (GMNJ 17:63). The building cost about 350 pounds and was in continuous use until 1803 (Hoagland 4,11).

The church records listing pewholders show that "Jan V:Dyck" held pews number 9, 10, 11 and 16 and his wife and children number 9, place 2, and number 10, place 8; and his brother "Roelof V:Dyck" pews number 6, 9 and 11 and for his wife and children number 8, place 3, number 10, place 2, and number 10, place 7 (GMNJ 17:32-37). The men occupied the pews along the sides while the women and children sat on chairs in the body of the church. The building has been described as "in the ancient style of Dutch architecture, with high gables and steep roof - an aisle at one side, from which a door opened: along the sides were short pews for the men, while the body of the church was divided into small squares, occupied by chairs for the women and children" (Hoagland 4). It probably conformed to a square (some of the earlier churches were octagonal) with two pillars in the center supporting a steep sloping roof symmetrical on four sides. Above the roof was a belfry ending in a steeple surmounted by a trim weather vane. The interior was plain and of the utmost simplicity, reflecting the reformation in sixteenth century Europe and Calvanist dogma that frowned on beautiful art - paintings, murals, mosaics, frescoes, statuary. The outstanding feature was a high pulpit at the far end with a sounding board overhead so that the domine's voice could be clearly heard. Since preaching the Word was the heart of worship, the pulpit was the focal point (Wertenbaker 77-81).

As the belfry was located at the apex of a four-sided roof, the bell rope hung loosely to the middle of the floor amid the women and children. Here the faithful sexton stood on the Sabbath at the appointed time tolling the bell with long, rhythmic strokes summoning the people to worship; then probably wrapping the rope around one of the pillars. For many years this bell rang out over the fields, villages and hamlets in the Millstone Valley on the Sabbath, Independence Day, and on other special occasions.

Days of Slavery

Webster defines a plantation as a "settlement of people in a particular region" or a "settlement in a new country". In the 1730's the western precinct of Somerset County was sparsely populated by newly settled farmers. The great majority were Dutch with their growing families, having settled on virgin land - new country. Thus, by definition, John's 360 acre tract (230 acres inherited from his father plus 130 acres subsequently purchased) was a plantation.

Encompassing over one-half square mile, a tract of this size was needed to support a family of thirteen children. Like all Gaul, a Dutch plantation was divided into three parts: woodland for fencing and fuel for cooking and heating; land for growing crops; and pasture for grazing cattle and sheep. Obviously a substantial labor force was required which was supplied by the family, hired hands (if available), servants and slaves. The estate inventory of John Van Dike made May 23, 1778[21] lists his slaves by name and value in English pounds:

1 Negro man named Tom	80 pounds
1 Negro man named Jack	80 pounds
1 Negro man named London	90 pounds
1 Negro man named Tom	50 pounds
1 Negro wench named Bet Aling	20 pounds
1 Negro wench named Cate	80 pounds
2 small wenches named Cate & Inde	40 pounds

How could John, a pillar of the church, countenance slavery?

In the Dutch colonies slavery evolved slowly and insidiously mainly as a means of providing agricultural labor because Dutch farm servants in Holland could not be persuaded to leave their homeland except by inducement with large sums of money and promises (Wacker 190). Simply stated, slaves were cheaper. The Dutch West India Company introduced negro slavery very early, as did the original proprietors, Berkeley and Carteret. Interested in planting settlements in the New Jersey province, generous land grants were offered to potential white colonizers to induce them to settle with their indentured servants and slaves. Accordingly, Berkeley and Carteret - or their counselors and advisors on their behalf - so provided in New Jersey's first constitution bearing the fulsome title, "The Concessions and Agreement of the Lords Proprietors of the Province of New Caesarea or New Jersey, to and with all and every of the New Adventurors, and all such as shall Settle or Plant There." Substantially abbreviated and usually referred to as the Concessions and Agreement, this unusual instrument provided among other things:

> *Secondly. Item. To every master or mistress, that shall go before the first day of January, which shall be in the year of our Lord 1665, one hundred and twenty acres of land; and for every able man-servant, that he or she shall carry or send armed and provided as aforesaid ... the like quantity of one hundred and twenty acres of land; and for every weaker servant or slave, male or female, exceeding the age of fourteen years, arriving there, sixty acres of land; and to every Christian servant, to their own use and behoof, sixty acres of land.*

Explicit enough. This and similar provisions did much to promote slavery and servitude.

As early as 1660 there were slaves on Manhattan Island. Domine Henricus Selijns (1636-1701), twenty-four year old Leiden graduate and Dutch Reformed minister living in Breuckelen, reporting the first days of his ministry in New Netherland in a letter dated October 4, 1660 to the Classis of Amsterdam addressed "Reverend, Wise and Godly Teachers" said:

> *In the morning, I preach in Breuckelen, but after the conclusion of the sermon on the catechism, in New Amsterdam at the Bowery, which is the place for recreation and pleasure in Manhattan where people from the town came for evening prayers*

as well. Besides the villagers, there are 40 negroes whose country of origin is the Negro-Coast (Van der Linde 226-229).

Four years later a second letter, dated June 9, 1664, requesting leave to return to Holland when his four year contract with the Dutch West India Company terminated, alludes to the negro as one of the problems troubling him. We discern that the young Dutch minister was disenchanted with his pastoral assignment in that he had been serving two congregations in New Netherland, Breuckelen on one side of the East River and Governor Stuyvesant's bowery on the other. True, his duties were rather onerous, as he emphasizes, but the institution of slavery was a thorn in his side probably more than his words convey:

> *Trusting that it would not be displeasing to Your Reverences, and very profitable to the Church of Christ, we found it easy - when it was [in fact] very difficult - to serve, besides the aforementioned congregation, the congregation of the General's Bowery as well. These places are separated from one another by the river flowing between them.*
>
> *The situation whereby in the morning we preach in the village of Breuckelen and in the evening at the aforesaid Bowery, is still continuing as we described it to you before; with the exception of the Lord's Supper, because as it is not customary among Your Reverences to administer the afore-mentioned Lord's Supper in the evening, we deemed it best and most edifying, after consultations and careful deliberations with our very dear colleagues of the congregation in New Amsterdam, to preach there in the morning before that time and [then] to administer the Lord's Supper, in accordance with the Christian custom in our fatherland.*
>
> *As for the Holy Baptism, we were sometimes asked by the negroes to baptize their children, but we refused, partly because of their lack of knowledge and faith, and partly because of the material and wrong aim on the part of the afore-mentioned negroes who sought nothing else by it than the freeing of their children from material slavery, without pursuing piety and Christian virtues. Nevertheless, [we] have taken great trouble to the best of our ability, which was proper, through private and public catechizing, which bore little fruit among the old people, who do not understand, but gave more hope with regard to the young, who have improved reasonably well. And not admitting them to the Holy Baptism for aforesaid reasons, is also the custom among our aforesaid colleagues (van der Linde 228-231).*

In colonial New Jersey, as in most of the other colonies, the slave population steadily grew and exerted a profound influence on society in the next century. In Middlesex County, for example, the number increased from 303 in 1726 to 1564 in 1800 and in Somerset County in the same period from 379 to 1863, approximately five times. Under normal conditions we would expect that slavery would be condemned, at least by the majority of people, and gradually die out. But the times were not normal. To settle and survive in the wilderness required physical labor. Simply stated, the law of supply and demand coupled with human want prevailed pushing aside moral principles. As a result, the institution gained a foothold on American soil.

Not even the example and precept of honorable men beloved by their countrymen, including presidents of the new nation, could deter it. Well known is the fact that Washington, a farmer-planter, owned slaves, as did Jefferson and Madison, who throughout their lives consistently deplored the institution of slavery as morally reprehensible while struggling to find some practical method for gradual emancipation.[22] At the constitutional convention in Independence Hall, Philadelphia, in the summer of 1787 slavery was a hotly debated issue, finally compromised notwithstanding a solemn declaration in the same building eleven years earlier that "all men are created equal".

In New Jersey there were few runaway slaves advertised in the newspapers (Brecknell 12). Slaves, for the most part, lived in close personal relationship with the family and were humanely treated. An excellent example is found in the memoirs of Margaret Nevius Van Dyke (1824-1916), a great granddaughter of Mathys (1714-1784), brother of Jan the Fifth.[23] Margaret as a young child lived on the old family plantation known as the "Stone Cottage" built by Mathys in 1756 on the banks of the Millstone at Mapleton. The property remained in the Van Dyke family until the last quarter of the nineteenth century and still stands (Bailey 397, 398, 417). Well educated and possessed of a brilliant mind and intellect, Margaret recalled in her eighties her childhood years surrounded by a loving family complemented by servants and slaves. In Margaret's eyes they were not slaves, but human beings - loved and respected members of the family. In a leather-bound journal, a gift from her niece, Lillie Van Dyke, in 1905, she penned in a neat, legible hand a moving account entitled, "As I Remember the Scenes of My Childhood". Of slavery Margaret wrote:

> *In Winter we always had buckwheat cakes for breakfast, and always had mush for breakfast, either in a pap, or mush and milk. Ed thought it made him grow. He was very anxious to be a man, and would eat bowl after bowl of the stuff, then measure by a sideboard to see if he had grown - a legend of the Negroes. We were born in slavery times and much of their doings and sayings was mixed with our educations.*
>
> *There were plenty of servants in my younger days to do everything, days of slavery. There was Nell, and Peggy, who was born the same day that Father was, Father in the spare room and Peggy, or Mammy as we children used to call her, in [the] kitchen garret.*
>
> *We all idolized Peggy, my Black Mammy. I never heard Father give her a harsh word, and what I am today, that Christian Negress made me, taught me all my housekeeping tricks. I owe [love and patience] to her for she took wonderful care of her 'Galloping Greyhound', as she lovingly called me. She taught me to work, not as labor but as a reward for some trifle, and now I regard labor as the price of Life, its happiness, its everything. To rest is to rust. She figured largely in my bringing up, all the*

whippings that I remember distinctly, and I now think that I never had a stroke too much. I wonder if there is never a chink in the world above where she can listen and see how well I have needed her instructions and advice. Dear old Mammy, peace to your ashes (Princeton Recollector, January 1979).

Life on the Plantation

When John's estate was inventoried by Henry Van Dike[24] and Thomas Skillman appointed by the Somerset County Surrogate's Court in May 1778, there were forty acres of "Green Wheat" in the fields valued at fifty pounds and a large quantity of wheat stored in the barn appraised at ninety pounds; also flax seed, hay, buckwheat in bulk, and Indian corn in the crib. Among the farm animals were two brown horses, one black mare, one gray horse, two colts, one small mare, twenty-seven sheep, nine hogs, seventeen milk cows appraised at eighty-five pounds and five calves at thirteen pounds. Farm equipment included two plows, one drill plow, one harrow, one wood stand, one new wagon, one old wagon, two sets of wagon gears, one wheat mill, one grind stone, spades, shovels, scythes, sundry lots of lumber in the chamber, and seven bee hives (SA).

His home equipped in characteristic Dutch style included a Silver Tankard (bequeathed to him by his father), two earthen mugs, iron pots and a brass kettle, a long looking glass, two tables, a black walnut desk, one eight-day clock, two pair of tongues, two pair of hand irons, ten old chairs, seven new chairs, one arm chair, a small cubbard, small table, writing desk, tea table, Dutch cubbard, bedsteads and bedding.

There were also four spinning wheels and one socalled "woolen wheel"[25] that had obviously seen plenty of service over many years. Spinning was a daily ritual according to Margaret Van Dyke who cleverly learned the art from the household servants. Said Margaret:

> *I was of Dutch and French descent, and by that strong law of atavism many national traits cropped out - creative beauty, and stern economical habits, a good mixture I "trow". [When still a small child] I could milk, make butter, spin flax into thread as fine as we could sew with, and fine woolen yarn for stockings. Nearly all this knowledge I stole from Mammy. When the female servants' work was finished, each day in the Winter, they went to their spinning wheels kept in the kitchen, covered over with a linen cover or sheet. I would watch [and] when the women went to the barn, off would come the cover and I would tangle a whole Hank of Flax for them. I kept on with that mischief until I could spin as good a fine thread for sewing, or weaving, as they, but much flax went to waste in my getting there. So it was with the woolen wheel in the garret, and I could spin yarn for stockings when fifteen years of age. (Princeton Recollector, January 1979).*

Twenty-seven sheep and two bushels of flax seed listed in the inventory of John Van Dike plainly testify to the fact that his clothes were homemade of wool and linen. John probably never saw a piece of muslin (cotton cloth) or cotton thread. Prior to the Revolution cotton was virtually unknown in New Jersey. In parts of the South, it was grown but on a very small scale. Picking out the cotton seed by hand was a laborious task. After the Revolution an imaginative Yankee schoolmaster, Eli Whitney (1765-1825), brought King Cotton into being with the invention of the cotton gin patented in 1794. The cotton gin could clean in one day as much as a handpicker in a year.

Preparing wool for spinning involved an ancient time-honored process known as carding. This was a slow tedious operation using a hand instrument with sharp metal teeth called a wool-card. The wool fibers were pulled through the teeth, then carefully hand combed and cleaned until formed into fleecy rolls ready to be spun into yarn for knitting socks and warm clothing or into tighter thread for weaving on the loom. Flax culture, similarly reaching back to ancient civilization, was even more tedious and time consuming. Grown in the open fields, the flax plants when ready for harvesting in the early summer were pulled up by the roots and left to dry in the sun. Then followed a long series of procedures briefly described as follows: drawing the stalks through a wooden or heavy wire comb to extract the seed-bolls; then vigorously pounding with a heavy mallet in a flax-brake in order to separate the fibers; next came the hackling, essentially a combination of dexterous hand maneuvers combing the fibers until layed out in smooth continuous threads; and, finally, spinning into skeins of linen thread. Many hours were consumed in this process.

Skilled artisans and tradesmen made their rounds over a wide area performing not only essential services but freely discoursing on the world outside - people, places and things. In a time of lamentably slow and fractured communication, they were natural news gatherers. Eagerly awaited about once a year was the itinerant shoemaker to repair worn shoes or make new ones. This centuries-old craft passed on from one generation to another and learned at an early age embraced the subtle art of designing and meticulously cutting out and sewing together the leather pieces, namely the sole, heel and uppers, creating before their very eyes a custom-fitted pair of shoes. We may reasonably assume that his services were in great demand at the homestead of John Van Dike with his many little ones and where he may have boarded a week or more. It is easy to imagine that the fabrication of a shoe from the animal's skin in the cobbler's skilled hands drew an enthusiastic audience.

Life on the plantation was never dull. With plenty of things to do and much to learn - as Margaret's lively account portrays - the days were filled with exciting activities, happy moments and warm memories. John's daughters mastered the art of spinning on those spinning wheels listed in the estate inventory in addition to milking, butter and cheese making, pickling, preserving, candle dipping, carding, heckling, weaving, bleaching, embroidering, quilting, and sewing among other homemaking skills taught by their mother or by the household servants.

But of all the feminine activities mastered in the home, the genteel art of spinning practiced by daughters, mothers, and grandmothers on the Dutch farms was the principal occupation. Firmly embedded in our culture, the word spinster survives to this day.[26]

John's Death, a Mystery

After a diligent search no evidence has been found proving when, where or how John Van Dike, born November 5, 1709 in New Utrecht, Long Island, met his death.

Nevertheless, there have been published over the years ancestral lists, stories and accounts to the effect that he was killed at the Battle of Monmouth on June 28, 1778. Unfortunately people believe the printed word to be the fact. What is the source? A story published in this century - long after that historic battle in the eighteenth century - is attributable to a great, great granddaughter of Jan the Fifth, Margaret M. Chambers, wife of Edwards Hall. Based on family lore and rooted in hearsay, the story came from the lips of a spinner of tales, John the Tory. Said Margaret Chambers Hall, "Grandmother Margaret Van Dyke Houghton told me some of the stories that her father Col.John Van Dyke[27] used to tell her" (Aitken 208).

Margaret Van Dike, born January 17, 1763 who subsequently married Abner Houghton (Houton/Horten), was the oldest of eight children of John the Tory and his wife, Rebecca Van Dike (SCHQ 6:189), and hence the granddaughter of Jan the Fifth. At the time of the Battle of Monmouth she was fifteen years old. Quoting the words of Margaret Chambers Hall: "Grandmother told me she was busy at her spinet that awful twenty-eighth of June 1778. The heat was intense. She heard the dreadful boom, boom of the cannon from the Battle of Monmouth. A Whig paper of the time described it as 'the severest cannonade, it is thought, ever happened in America'. Grandmother said it seemed to her as if the very earth trembled". All of which seems creditable and might well be accepted as Grandmother Margaret's recollection of events that day while sitting at home in Harlingen. Then follows this sentence: "Her grandfather that Godly patriot 'John Van Dyke, Jr., of New Jersey' gave his life that day for his country on that bloody battlefield" (Aitken 210).

And it ends just like that! No explanation offered. No documentation.

Who witnessed John Van Dike's death? Who possessed firsthand knowledge? What are the facts?

There are some relevant facts. On May 23, 1778, a month before the Battle of Monmouth, four members of John Van Dike's family appeared before the Surrogate Judge of Somerset County to probate his will: his two sons, Frederick (1751-1811) and Jacob (1754-1827), his son-in-law Samuel Stout (1713-1803), and his brother-in-law Henry Bergen who were appointed executors by his will.[28] On this day, the record shows, they were duly qualified and sworn under oath to administer the Estate of John Van Dike, Deceased, compelling proof without more that the father of the family was no longer living.

Is it conceivable that members of John Van Dike's family who dearly loved him would have thought of probating his will unless convinced under the facts known to them that he was deceased?

Another fact merits consideration. These were dark days in the struggle. Violence reigned. Somerset County lay in the path of the opposing military forces. British soldiers, often undisciplined, pillaged homes and farms (SCHQ

1:279-286;SCHQ 4 :29,30). Montgomery Township where John Van Dike resided was in the thick of it (Brecknell 24;SCHQ 5:161-171). Brutal tory raids, frequent skirmishes, wanton destruction and senseless killing were common. "Royalists plundered friends and foes ... warred upon decrepit old age, warred upon defenseless youth ... they butchered the wounded, asking for quarter, mangled the dead", said Governor William Livingston speaking before the New Jersey Assembly in 1777 (Wall 214).

John Van Dike was then an aged and feeble man in his sixty-ninth year scarcely able to engage in military combat.[29] In this barbaric climate his life was even more endangered. There were myriad ways in which his death could have occurred and his body buried in an isolated spot. A believer in the Declaration of Independence and an outspoken patriot, his convictions may have spread afar and earned him enemies. It is conceivable that he was killed by stealth or simply by accident in one of the forays in Somerset County.

But it was not on the Monmouth County Battlefield.

His devoted wife, his loving children, his brothers and sisters as well as many friends were shocked, devastated; their grief inconsolable. For weeks running into months, they agonized and prayed for his return, meanwhile combing the countryside in search of a clue. If his body had been recovered, he would have been given a Christian burial and his remains interred in the Van Dike plot in the Ten Mile Run cemetery on the land of his father. [30]

The death of John Van Dike remains a mystery.

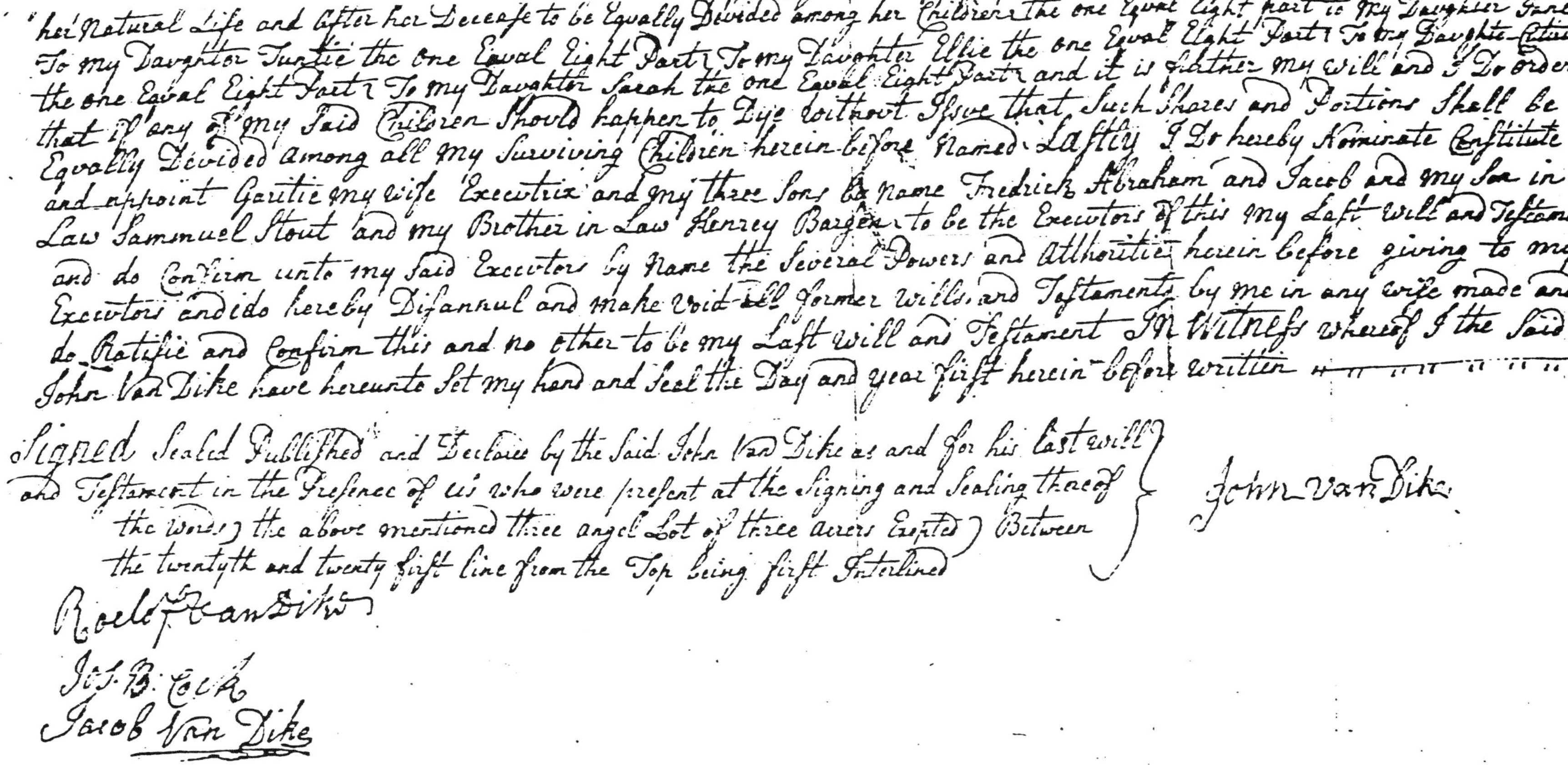
"her Natural Life and After her Decease to be Equally Devided among her Children the one Equal Eight part to my Daughter Jane
To my Daughter Juntie the one Equal Eight Part To my Daughter Eltie the one Equal Eight Part To my Daughter Catrine
the one Equal Eight Part To my Daughter Sarah the one Equal Eight Part and it is Farther my will and I Do order
that if any of my said Children Should happen to Dye without Issue that Such Shares and Portions Shall be
Equally Devided among all my Surviving Children herein before Named Lastly I Do hereby Nominate Constitute
and appoint Gautie my wife Executrix and my three Sons by name Fredrick Abraham and Jacob and my Son in
Law Sammuel Stout and my Brother in Law Henrey Bargen to be the Executors of this my Last Will and Testament
and do Confirm unto my said Executors by Name the Several Powers and Athorities herein before giving to my
Executors and do hereby Disannul and make void all former Wills and Testaments by me in any wise made and
do Ratifie and Confirm this and no other to be my Last Will and Testament In Witness whereof I the said
John Van Dike have hereunto Set my hand and Seal the Day and year first herein before written

Signed Sealed Published and Declared by the said John Van Dike as and for his last will
and Testament in the Presence of us who were present at the Signing and Sealing thereof
the words the above mentioned three angel Lot of three acres Excepted Between
the twentyth and twenty first line from the Top being first Interlined

John Van Dike

Roelof Van Dike
Jos. B. Cock
Jacob Van Dike

Manuscript copy of the will (signature page) of John Van Dike (1709-1777/78) dated February 4, 1775 and probated May 23, 1778.

Courtesy New Jersey State Archives, Department of State

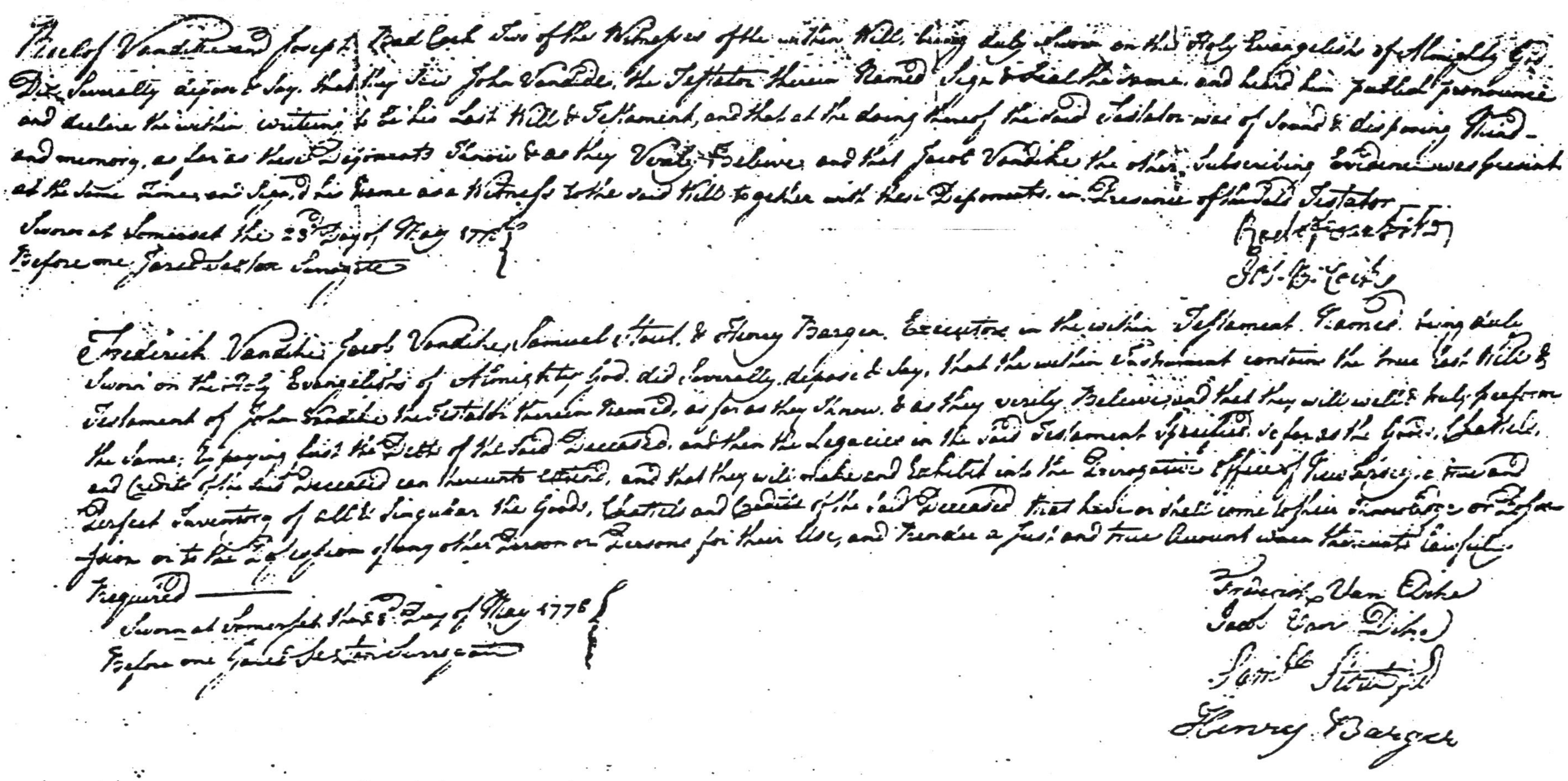

Rich. of Vandike and Joseph Read Cook Two of the Witnesses of the within Will being duly Sworn on the Holy Evangelists of Almighty God Did Severally depose & Say that they saw John Vandike the Testator therein Named Sign & Seal the same and heard him publish pronounce and declare the within writing to be his Last Will & Testament, and that at the doing thereof the said Testator was of Sound & disposing Mind and memory as far as these Deponents Know & as they Verily Believe and that Jacob Vandike the other Subscribing Evidence was present at the same time and Signed his Name as a Witness to the said Will together with these Deponents in Presence of the said Testator

Sworn at Somerset the 23d Day of May 1778
Before me Jared Saxton Surrogate

[illegible]
[illegible]

Frederick Vandike Jacob Vandike, Samuel Stout & Henry Barger Executors in the within Testament Named being duly Sworn on the Holy Evangelists of Almighty God did Severally depose & Say, that the within Instrument contains the true Last Will & Testament of John Vandike the Testator therein Named, as far as they Know & as they verily Believe, and that they will well & truly perform the same by paying first the Debts of the said Deceased and then the Legacies in the said Testament Specified so far as the Goods, Chattels and Credits of the said Deceased can thereunto Extend, and that they will make and Exhibit into the Surrogate's Office of New Jersey a true and perfect Inventory of all & Singular the Goods, Chattels and Credits of the said Deceased that have or shall come to their Knowledge or Possession or to the Possession of any other Person or Persons for their Use, and render a Just and true Account when thereunto lawfully Required

Sworn at Somerset the 23d Day of May 1778
Before me Jared Saxton Surrogate

Frederick Van Dike
Jacob Van Dike
Saml Stout
Henry Barger

Manuscript Copy of probate record in the Estate of John Van Dike before the Surrogate Judge of Somerset County on May 23, 1778.

Courtesy New Jersey State Archives, Department of State

SIXTH GENERATION

Genealogical Note

JACOB VAN DIKE
B December 24, 1754
D February 4, 1827
M December 2, 1786

JACOB VAN DIKE of the Sixth Generation was born December 24, 1754 (VDFB/author,VDFB/Princeton) in Harlingen, Montgomery Township, Somerset County, the third child of John Van Dike (1709-1777/78) and Garritie Bergen (1722-1787), his second wife (Cook 22). He was baptized at Six Mile Run on January 26, 1755 (SCHQ 8:129).

In his youth he was sometimes called "Little Jacob" (SCHQ 6:190) distinguishing him from his Uncle, Jacob Van Dike (1723-1809), thirty-one years older, who lived nearby in Middlesex County.[1] After attaining the rank of captain in the New Jersey militia, he was well known in the community as Captain Jacob Van Dike, a title so familiar that it was preserved on his tombstone in the Ten Mile Run Cemetery.

Marriage and Children

On December 2, 1786 Jacob married Sarah Schenck, seventeen year old daughter of John R. Schenck, a wealthy Dutch landholder and owner of two plantations in Penns Neck, West Windsor Township. The first settlers in the Schenck family were Roelof Martense Schenck, born about 1630, who came to New Amsterdam from Amersfoort, Utrecht, Holland, with his brother Jan Martense and sister Annetje in 1650, two years before Jan Thomasse Van Dyck and his family arrived (SCHQ 5:89).

Unlike his father and grandfather who married early in life and sired large families, Jacob was nearly thirty-two when he married Sarah Schenck and by whom he had three children:

Sarah	B February 27, 1789	D June 6, 1811
John Schenck (SEVENTH GENERATION)	B September 25, 1801	D December 3, 1852
Jacob (VDFB/Author; VDFB/Princeton)	B July 15, 1806	D

In sharp contrast with his forebears, Jacob's adolescent years were fraught with tension, a period of great social unrest ultimately climaxed by a bloody conflict, a war with England.

The Revolution

When the British Parliament passed the iniquitous Stamp Act in March of 1765, Jacob was ten years old. Stirrings of discontent instantly ran through the colonies. In no sense, however, should the Dutch colonists be considered insurrectionists. As we have seen, they adapted to English law and custom, participating in civic affairs and a government patterned on English institutions. All they wanted was to lead their lives peacefully and be treated fairly.

The following year Parliament repealed the Stamp Act, in large measure reacting to strong opposition in the colonies. But shortly thereafter it passed other repressive measures including a tax on glass, paper, paint, tea and other imports to raise money to pay the salaries of colonial officials making them independent of the Assembly. With each new measure the tension mounted. And the war came.

Jacob was twenty when the first shot was fired at Lexington, Massachusetts, on April 19, 1775. In July of that year Ruloff Van Dyck, his uncle (Cook 18,23), was elected a member of the Committee of Correspondence by the freeholders of Somerset County (SCHQ 5:245,246). These were dramatic events, deeply felt, which rapidly matured him. Sensing the great injustice, Jacob embraced the patriot cause, a cause for which he fought and was honored for loyalty and bravery. Said the New Jersey Patriot published in Princeton on February 15, 1827:

> *Suddenly, at his residence near Griggstown in this county on the morning of the 4th inst. [February 1827] CAPTY. JACOB VAN DYKE, aged 72 years. At the commencement of the Revolution, he took a decided part in favour of the colonies, being young, active, and enterprising. He in conjunction with several revoultionary worthies of his neighbourhood, rendered useful and important services to the country, by carrying on a successful partizan warfare, when the state was overrun by British troops. Although he was never attached to the regular army, he continued in service throughout the war, - was present at the battles of Princeton, Monmouth, and Germantown, and distinguished himself by the bravery of his deportment and the prompt discharge of*

BIRTHS.	BIRTHS.
Jacob Vandike was born december 24th 1754.	William Van Dyke was born April 8th 1822
Sarah Schenck daughter of John & Eve Schenck was born Jany 24th 1769.	Elizabeth Ann Van Dyke was born Jan. 26th 1827
Mary Schenck daughter of John & Eve Schenck was born Jany 9th 1776.	Alice Van Dyke was born Dec. 17th 1848
John Schenck Vandike was born Sept 25th 1801	Mary E. Van Dyke was born March 16th 1850
Jacob Vandike was born Jany 15th 1806	Frank Van Dyke was born Dec. 11th 1851
Sarah Vandike wife of Isaac Opie was born July 27th 1787.	Charles Van Dyke was born Dec 27th 1853
	John S. Van Dyke was born May 23rd 1857

Birth records (reduced) in the family bible of Mary Schenck Scott (1776-), sister-in-law of Jacob Van Dike (1754-1827). Purchased in New Brunswick in 1804, this book soon reverted to Jacob's family and became a family heirloom.

Author's possession

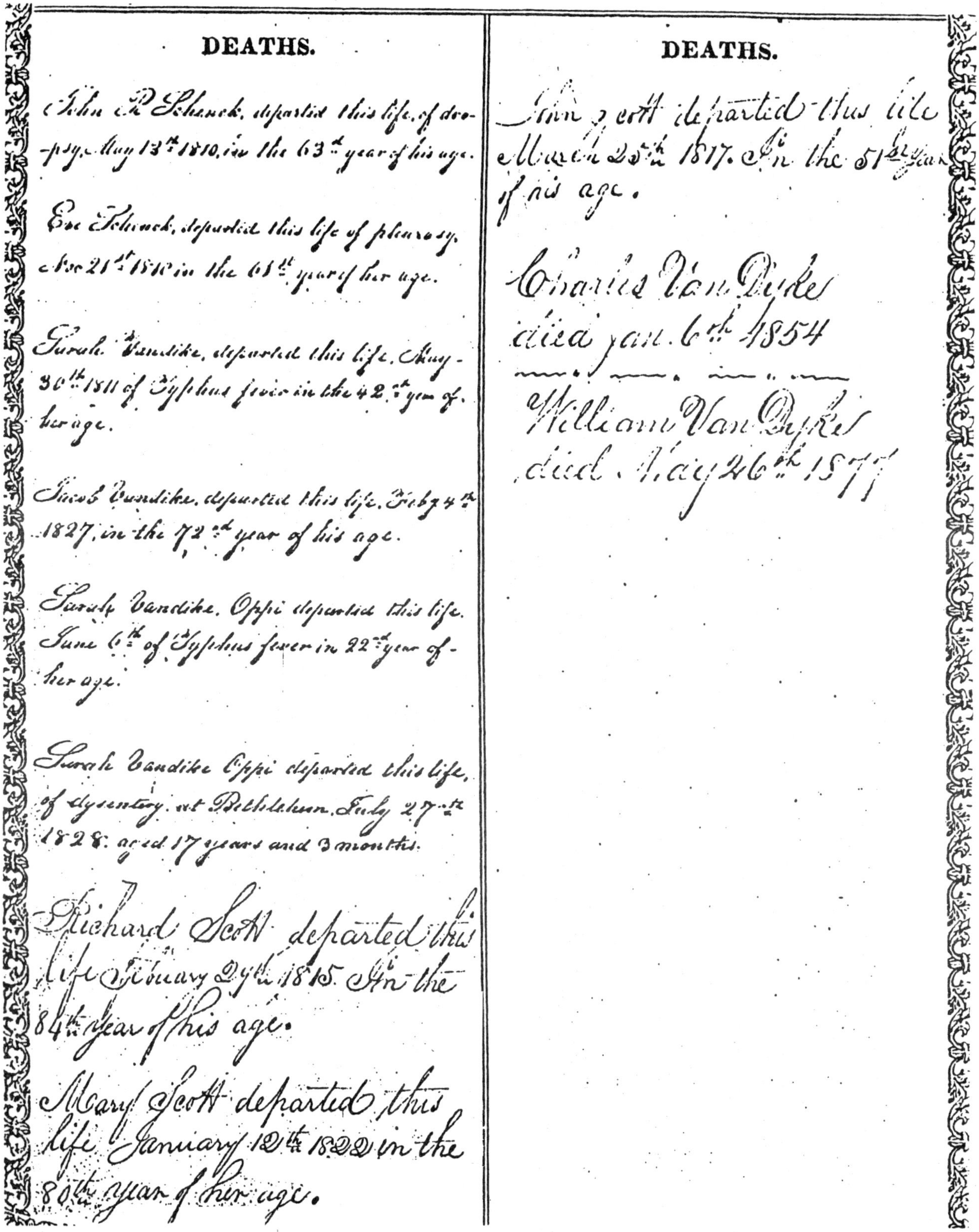

DEATHS.

John R. Schenck. departed this life, of dropsy. May 13th 1810. in the 63rd year of his age.

Eve Schenck. departed this life of pleurasy. Nov 21st 1810 in the 61st year of her age.

Sarah Vandike. departed this life. Aug. 30th 1811 of Typhus fever in the 42nd year of her age.

Jacob Vandike. departed this life. Feby 4th 1827. in the 72nd year of his age.

Sarah Vandike. Oppi departed this life. June 6th of Typhus fever in 22nd year of her age.

Sarah Vandike Oppi departed this life. of dysentery. at Bethlehem. July 27th 1828. aged 17 years and 3 months.

Richard Scott departed this life February 29th 1815. In the 84th year of his age.

Mary Scott departed this life January 12th 1822 in the 80th year of her age.

DEATHS.

John Scott departed this life March 25th 1817. In the 51st year of his age.

Charles Van Dyke died Jan. 6th 1854

William Van Dyke died May 26th 1877

Death records (reduced) in the family bible of Mary Schenck Scott.

Author's possession

every duty. As a citizen, throughout a long life he has enjoyed the confidence and esteem of all that knew him. In an honored old age he has been gathered to his fathers, leaving behind him the memory of a good man's name, better than treasures of wealth or monuments of brass.[2]

Van Dyke Family Bibles

Upon the marriage of Captain Jacob Van Dike and Sarah Schenck in 1786, the lives and fortunes of these two Dutch families were uniquely entwined. Events taking place in rapid sequence could never have been foreseen. As aptly said by Lord Byron, "Tis strange but true; for truth is stranger than fiction." Here, the amazing truth is revealed by two family bibles.

In the year 1804 a large leather-bound bible, beautifully illustrated with engravings, was purchased in New Brunswick,[3] probably by Jacob and Sarah, and made a gift to Sarah's sister, Mary Schenck Scott. A handwritten inscription on the flyleaf reads:

Mary Scott her Book
God give her grace therein to look
bought at New Brunswick 1804

For reasons that will become apparent as our story unfolds, Mary Scott's bible reverted in a few years to the Van Dyke family. Handed down through successive generations of the family, this precious heirloom over the course of a century and a half came into the author's possession (VDFB/Author). Family records penned therein disclose that John R. Schenck and his wife, Eve Houghton, were the parents of two daughters: Sarah born January 24, 1769 and Mary born January 9, 1776. Since they were the only children of the marriage, John Schenck's sole heirs at law were his wife Eve and his two daughters, Sarah and Mary.[4]

Further we discover that Jacob himself owned a family bible wherein he personally recorded his marriage to Sarah Schenck and the birth and death of members of his family (VDFB/Princeton). Purely by happenstance this old book came to light when found in a Princeton storehouse in 1944 and thereupon donated to the Historical Society of Princeton. Obviously a genealogical windfall! Jacob's bible corroborates most of the events recorded in the bible that constituted a gift to his sister-in-law, Mary Schenck Scott, in 1804.[5] The two family bibles confirm beyond doubt the death of Sarah's father and mother in the year 1810. "John R. Schenck departed this life May 13th, 1810 in the sixty third Year of his age" and "Eve Schenck departed this life Nov. 21, 1810 in the sixty-first year of her age" (Jacob's bible). Coupled with these facts are significant provisions in the will of John R. Schenck made October 24, 1807 and probated in New Brunswick May 26, 1810 (SA). As provided by his will, Eve received all his personal property. Extensive landholdings were distributed as follows: (1) "to my daughter Sarah Van Dike the plantation whereon I now live, with the appurtenances, situate lying and being in West Windsor, on Penns Neck"; (2) "to my daughter Mary Scott my plantation, lying on the adjoining Assampink, in the township & County aforesaid, which I purchased of the Executors of Cornelius Hendrickson deceased"; and (3) mindful that no children had been born to his daughter Mary Scott then thirty-one, he directed: "But if my said daughter Mary should die, without leaving living issue, then and in that case it is my will and I do give and devise the same unto the child and children of my aforesaid daughter Sarah Vandike, equally to be divided between them, share and share alike". Mary and John Scott had no children.[6]

Thus by operation of law Jacob and Sarah Van Dike and their children were the beneficiaries of the Schenck family fortune.

Yet even more extraordinary facts, we find, are revealed by the Van Dyke family bibles.

Miserabile Dictu

Monday, December 2, 1811 marked the silver wedding anniversary of Jacob and Sarah Schenck Van Dike.

Sadly, there was nothing to celebrate. In the spring of 1811 tragedy descended on Jacob. His life was forever changed.

On April 29 his son-in-law, Captain Isaac Oppie, died at the age of forty-six.

Eleven days later (May 9) his granddaughter Sarah Van Dike Oppie, died "in the 5th year of her age"

Three weeks later (May 30) his beloved wife Sarah died "in the 42nd year of her age."

One week later (June 6) his only daughter, Sarah Van Dike Oppie,[7] died "in the 22nd year of her age."

Seventeen days later his two brothers, John (Tory) and Frederick, died on the <u>same</u> day (June 23).

Thus in the brief period of eight weeks Jacob lost his wife, his daughter, his first born granddaughter, his two brothers and his son-in-law!

Incredible! Words cannot describe his grief, suffering, bitter agony.

Obviously the scourge was a fatal disease of epidemic proportion. On the continent of Europe and in England in the Middle Ages people died by the thousands from the plague or Black Death, as it was usually called; the cause unknown. Similarly in colonial America, physicians and clergymen[8] expressed bizarre ideas about communicable disease couched in terms of the patient's symptoms; for example e.g throat distemper, distemper of measles, smallpox, yellow fever (Wilkes 32-35). When the dread epidemic struck the Millstone Valley in the year 1811, the doctors could do little more than assign a name to it.

Family bible records assert what the doctor said it was: "typhoid fever" (Jacob's wife); "typhus fever" (Jacob's daughter); "dysentery" (Jacob's granddaughter) (VDFB/Author). It may have been cholera, an acute intestinal disease caused by bacteria in contaminated water prevalent in New Jersey.[9]

To bring medicine out of the Dark Ages, the New Jersey Medical Society was organized in 1766 becoming the first society of its kind in the American colonies. Sixteen "Practitioners of Physic and Surgery", as they called themselves, met in New Brunswick on July 23, 1766 to form a society "for their mutual improvement, the advancement of the profession and the promotion of the public good". Their constitution boldly referred to medicine as a science: "one of the most useful sciences to mankind, and at the same time the most difficult to be fully attained"; and humbly adding: "as every means, therefore, that will tend to enlarge the stock of knowledge and experience of the pursuit of this science, should be eagerly sought after and prosecuted"[10] (Wickes 43-45).

Although this might be termed a step forward, medical practice advanced only at a snail's pace. Under an apprentice system of medical education, progress was sorely inhibited. A student lived in the home of a preceptor for a year or two serving as an assistant, or even a servant, reading such books as were available on herbs and roots regarded as cures for disease. On occasion he would accompany his preceptor on visits to patients' homes affording him the opportunity to observe the bloodletting and tooth-pulling. Bloodletting was standard medical procedure. Doctors, generally men of good character and intelligence, although adherents of medieval practices rooted in superstition and ignorance, saw their patients waste away before their eyes and die. The wonder drugs in their world were calomel, epsom salts, opium and cod liver oil.

It is not difficult to envision the bedlam in Jacob's household in the spring of 1811 compounded by quackery in the form of blood-letting and strange concoctions administered by the practitioners of physic and surgery. Said Fred B. Rogers, M.D. and A. Reasoner Sayre in a History of the Medical Society of New Jersey:

> *The treatment began with "cleansing the prima via", administering the usual jalap or rhubarb, calomel, and opium, then giving consideration to quieting the stomach with soda water, ice, cold water, and spirits of camphor. Dr. Marsh used oxide of bismuth. Patients were kept warm in bed with heated bricks and sandbags, bottles of hot water, friction, sinapisms to the hands, feet, wrists, ankles, and epigastrium. Stimulation made by applying a mixture of cayenne pepper and mercurial ointment was sometimes substituted, and vapor baths were used to promote perspiration. When the reaction came, the wise doctor had lancet, scarificator, cups, and leeches ready. If congestion of the head threatened, leeches or cups went to the temples, and ice or a blister might be applied to the shaved scalp. If the lungs were congested, venesection and antimonials were used" (Rogers/Sayre 86).*

A patient was fortunate to survive the treatment.

Whether or not Jacob fell victim to the scourge is unknown. We do know that he lived to nearly seventy-three, a respectable old age at that time. Comforting him in his affliction were his sons, John Schenck and Jacob, nine and four respectively, and his infant granddaughter, Sarah Mary. Upon them he bestowed his affection and largesse.

Sarah Mary Van Dike Oppie

Jacob's granddaughter born at the outset of the epidemic on March 26, 1811 became an orphan at ten weeks of age. It is remarkable that she survived while the epidemic claimed the lives of her father, mother and five-year-old sister within a few short weeks. Her name uniquely identifies her as a member of the family: SARAH MARY for her maternal grandmother and Aunt Mary; and VAN DIKE OPPIE, surnames of her mother and father respectively.

Jacob saw in his tiny granddaughter whose life was miraculously spared his beloved wife and daughter now taken from him. A warm and tender relationship flourished for years until terminated by his death. Sarah Mary was then a teenager approaching her sixteenth birthday, an impressionable age. What a shock and sobering experience for this young lady realizing that Grandfather Jacob was no longer living or part of her life! Love and affection is reflected in Jacob's will leaving her a bequest of two thousand dollars - not a small sum in 1827 - directing that it "be paid to her at the age of one and twenty."

Yet Sarah Mary never received the legacy! Ironically, as frequently happened in these times of widespread pestilence, death struck another crushing blow.

The final chapter takes us to Bethlehem, Pennsylvania. There, a student at an elite boarding school for girls known as the Moravian Seminary for Young Ladies at Bethlehem, Pennsylvania, Sarah Mary died. She lies in the Old Moravian Cemetery, in an area set aside for "Children and Unmarried Women". What was once a "seminary" for young ladies functions today as a private school for boys and girls. Walking through the tranquil, tree-shaded burial ground adjoining the old Moravian school, one sees long rows of graves uniformly marked by stone tablets on the grass surface. The stone over her grave reads:

In memory
of
SARAH V. D. OPPIE
born March 26th 1811
near Kingston
N. Jersey
departed July 21st 1828
The spirit dwells beyond the skies
The mortal part shall glorious rise

Grandfather Jacob, deceased, was spared the pain and anguish of Sarah Mary's untimely death.

His sons, John Schenck and Jacob, were appointed guardians of her person and property by the Orphan's Court of Somerset County.[11] Wishing to provide her with a sound academic education, they enrolled her in this select private school for girls. A Book of Accounts in the Moravian Archives discloses the tuition, room and board, and incidental charges including special "instruction in music", "washing", a "Doctor's bill", and items relating to "ribbon week", an annual ceremony. Credit is allowed for $35.00 termed "entrance money" received on May 11, 1827, the approximate date of her admission, plus additional credits of $69.50 on September 30, 1827, $56.50 on February 29, 1828, and a final sum of $5.75 on July 31, 1828 (shortly following her decease), hence a total of $166.75 representing the cost of a superior private school education for fifteen months. Even a penny in 1828 possessed real economic value. And a dollar was worth a hundred cents.

A Sterbe Register (Death Register) contained in a Kerchenbuch Der Germeine in Bethlehem (Churchbook of the Congregation in Bethlehem) records July 21, 1828[12] as Sarah's date of death. Another rare and interesting book in the archives narrates the history of the Moravian Seminary for Young Ladies from 1785 to 1870, which includes a moving account of the epidemic that struck the Bethlehem community in July of 1828.[13] The following abstract portrays the tragic episode from the school's perspective:

> *The year 1828 is also memorable for the afflicting dispensations of Providence. It was probably a year of trial and anxiety for the Principal and his wife, when sickness entered the precincts of the school and death a second time laid low two of their charges. With the opening of the warm season a fever of malignant type made its appearance and a number of the pupils in the Seminary were sufferers in common with the inhabitants of the village. On the 21st of July, Miss Sarah V. Oppie of Kingston, New Jersey, fell a victim to the prevailing malady in the eighteenth year of her age, and on the 12th of August, Miss Janette Taylor, of New York, died in the tenth year of her age. The Principal was at this time absent, which heightened the consternation that seized the inmates of the house and spread panic through the town. The physicians declared themselves ignorant of the nature of the disease and the method of its treatment. There were those even who urged the speedy removal of the scholars from Bethlehem until the epidemic should have run its course. It was a severe blow, which fell heavily on the Principal, when, on his return he learned the affliction with which Providence had been pleased to visit his household...*

Bridges and Other Items of Business

Somerset County encompassing 307 square miles is interlaced with rivers, brooks and streams. Examining its early history, we find that its heavily watered, floodplain character was the very reason for carving Somerset out of

Middlesex three centuries ago. The East Jersey Provincial Assembly passed an Act on May 22, 1688 declaring in the preamble: "For as much as the uppermost part of the Raritan River is settled by persons, whom in their husbandry and manuring of their lands, are forced upon quite different ways and methods from the other farmers and inhabitants of Middlesex County because of the frequent floods that carry away their fences on the meadows, the only arable land they have, and so, by consequence of their interests are divided from the other inhabitants of said county, Be it therefore enacted ..."

The early inhabitants of Somerset recognized that not only roads but bridges were essential for commerce and social intercourse to exist. Jacob's civic activities were synonomous with the building, repair and maintenance of bridges. In 1800 there were twenty-four bridges scattered throughout Somerset, which constituted one of the most important items of business at every meeting of the Board of Chosen Freeholders. From 1797 to 1809 Jacob was a chosen freeholder representing Franklin Township located in the southeasterly corner of Somerset. Eight years later, having reached his sixties, he held the same office (SCM). The eight-year hiatus (1809-17) is explained by the tragic loss of his loved ones dramatically curtailing community activities.

At the annual meeting of the board held at the court house on Wednesday, May 14, 1800, ten members were present, among them Jacob Van Dike and his brother-in-law, Henry Berrien (1743-1806), representing the citizens of Franklin Township. There was a full agenda to consider consuming two days of deliberations. A manager was appointed for each bridge for the ensuing year. "Jacob Van Dyck" was named the manager of the "Rockey hill bridge" near his home. Eleven bills for repair and maintenance were submitted for the board's approval ranging from $3.25 for "removing logs and other obstructions at Raritan bridge" and $5.37 1/2 - even a half cent had value - for the "repairs of Harris's bridge" to the sum $45.00 (highest expenditure) for a "bridge having been built by direction of six of the chosen freeholders over a gully near Abraham Van Doren's mill in the Township of Franklin" (SCM 159-162).

The Board of Chosen Freeholders was by no means a rubber-stamp body approving bills for bridge repairs. Exercising its authority concerning two such bills plainly elicited protracted and serious consideration: "Whereas certain orders were issued by the director on the county collector for the repair of bridges in the township of Bridgewater, to the amount of $17.53, and for the repairs of bridges in the township of Bernards to the amount of $39.81, which orders appear to have been improperly issued; therefore ordered that the county collector be, and he is hereby directed to charge the said townships with the said sums respectively in his books; and that the assessors of the said township do assess the same on their several townships in addition to the amount of the county charges which may be agreed upon by the board of assessors at their next meeting". Similarly, they found another bill for repairs that lacked merit: "Thomas Hall presented an account for repairing the abutments to the bridge at Phillips mill on the South branch. Resolved that the same be dismissed" (ibid).

Concerning the aforementioned repairs to Harris's bridge at a cost of $5.37 1/2, the board, after further discussion the next day, concluded that this was merely a stopgap measure and therefore took the following action: "Resolved that Messrs Jacob Van Dyck, Gerretse, Berrien and Wyckoff cause the bridge over Millstone called Harris's bridge to be repaired or rebuilt in such manner as they shall think most conducive to the public good; that they contract with such persons and on such terms as they shall think proper for the performance of the necessary service, and that they certify to the director the sum necessary to defray the expense who is hereby authorized to draw an order on the county collector for the same". Two other bills, unrelated to bridges, were approved: "Joseph Doty, sheriff, presented an account for stationery, candles and fuel for the use of the court, amounting to $5.00, which was allowed ..."; and "Joseph Arrowsmith presented an account for boarding prisoners amounting to $9.40", which was allowed (ibid 162,166).

Another important matter of business coming before the board was the sale of the "old gaol" for $60.00 and the "old court-house" for $240.00. Financing was arranged by the issuance of forty-five interest-bearing certificates to specifically named persons for building a new "gaol and court-house". The sum raised totaled $4,724.45. To this was added $9,644.17 which the "manager has received of the county collector at different times" (ibid 162-164). By Monday, September 1, 1800 construction seems to have been in progress because it is recorded: "Resolved that an order do issue in favour of Aaron Van Doren for $14.06, being for 50 bushels of lime for the court-house which was issued accordingly (ibid 168).

Once again the board found it necessary to call upon Messrs. Berrien and J. Van Dyck for additional help at its September meeting: "It having been represented to this board that considerable repairs are necessary to be done to the Landing bridge, therefore, resolved that Messrs. Berrien and J. Van Dyck be a committee to inspect the said bridge, and if necessary to cause the same to be repaired in such manner as they may judge most advantageous to the county; provided the board of chosen freeholders of the county of Middlesex shall appoint some person or persons with similar powers; that the said committee certify to the director the sum expended in the performance of this service, who is hereby authorized to draw on the county collector for the same". A letter was read for the third time concerning a proposal by Col. John Neilson for the appointment of a committee to confer with a committee of the county of Middlesex on the subject of "building or purchaseing a poor house" for both counties. Following a vote the clerk noted: "It was carried in the negative. Resolved that the clerk of the board forward a copy of this entry to Col. Neilson" (ibid 167,168).

Twilight of Slavery

In New Jersey slavery was a dying institution in the early nineteenth century, a fact self-evident fron the estate inventories and records of manumissions filed in the Somerset County Clerk's Office.[14] It will be recalled that there were eight slaves on the plantation of Jacob's father. While Jacob possessed far more extensive landholdings, he owned two slaves when he died. His estate inventory lists a "Black man named Adam" and a "Time of Black boy named Dave",[15] both undoubtedly farm hands. If Adam or Dave were born after July 4, 1804, freedom was granted them upon attaining twenty-five years of age pursuant to an act of the New Jersey legislature passed February 24, 1821. For female slaves the age was twenty-one (SCHQ 1:275).

Slaves departed the New Jersey scene almost as quietly as they appeared a century earlier.

Notes, Bonds and Leases

In the wake of the epidemic of 1811 Captain Jacob Van Dike, a widower in his mid-fifties, was a sad and lonely man. He was, also, a very rich man. Plainly he would have traded all that he owned for the return of his wife and daughter; in balance, wealth was unimportant.

For miles around friends and relatives called to tender their sympathy. On some occasions, it appears, they were in need of financial help. Creditors were pressing for payment. Time was of the essence; and he, Jacob, could solve their problems.

The record reveals that he was a man of compassion who listened sympathetically to their pleas. It may be said that he was generous to a fault since the indebtedness on notes and bonds at the time of his death totaled $16,600.00, a substantial sum at that time. Of this total, $2,552.02 was found by the court appraisers to be "Doubtful". There were seventy-five personal loans; and in some cases he saw fit to grant the debtor a second and even a third loan although the previous balance had not been paid. Could it be that he looked upon himself as the Good Samaritan, ever ready to satisfy human need?

Two plantation farms or parts thereof in West Windsor Township on the Straight Turnpike were the subject of leases, one to his son John Schenck, as disclosed by his estate inventory:

John S. Van Dyke	$246.00
Glover Applegate	228.44
John Simpson	80.00
Nathanial Phillips	52.50

A Dutch Family Farm

Affluence did not alter Jacob's lifestyle. Like his Dutch forebears he was a farmer to the core.

The principal product of his land was grain. In the winter of 1827 the court appraisers observed "Green grain in the ground" (considered personalty) to which they assigned a value of ninety dollars. Two barns designated "old" and "new", contained abundant stores of grain from the previous season's harvest: oats, "rye in sheaf", "rye in the bushel", wheat, buckwheat, corn, hay, straw and potatoes. Farm animals, always an integral part of a Dutch farm, included ten milking cows, four yearling calves, five two-year old cattle, seven horses, three colts, one yoke of oxen, nineteen sheep, three lambs, six hogs, and a large assortment of ducks, geese and fowls.

Dutch farmhouses with their steep sloping roofs and long overhanging eaves were attractive to the eye while unpretentious and functional. The rooms were moderate in size featuring furniture of simple design, well constructed, exceedingly sturdy, intended to last a lifetime. Treasured pieces eventually became heirlooms. Every Dutchman loved his home. On a cold winter evening he looked forward to a comfortable chair by the fire where he could watch the flames from a burning log and bask in its warmth. There was always one special room where the family gathered at the end of the day - not necessarily the kitchen - for lively conversation and entertainment of their own making. Jacob's dwelling, long since razed, followed this Dutch pattern. Carpeted floors, as shown by the estate inventory, imparted an air of coziness and warmth. Each room contained a fireplace or woodburning stove with a set of tongs, andirons and a shovel. The "family room", as the appraisers called it, was furnished with window curtains, a looking glass, desk and bookcase, tables and stand, chairs; also a "Library and contents of Book Case". Other appointments listed in a fourteen page inventory were candlesticks and mantel ornaments, an eight-day clock, crockery ware, several sideboards, cupboards, chests, and pictures. A "plate" (no further description) valued at ninety dollars was surely a treasured piece (SA).

Jacob's barn contained a full complement of farm equipment, including three plows and harness, four wood sleds, scythe and cradle, forks, rakes, shovels, grindstone, two sets of harness, two wagons, gig and harness, one windmill. Stored in the cellar, usually entered from the outside of the house with an entrance protected by a hatch cover, were apples, lard, butter, tallow, casks, vinegar in a cask and three barrels of whiskey. In the smoke house were casks of beef, pork, mackeral in barrel, and shad in barrel.

Last Will and Testament[16]

After remembering his beloved granddaughter, Sarah Mary Van Dike Oppie, with a bequest of two thousand dollars, Jacob effected an equal division of his estate between his two sons:

> - To John Schenck "my two farms situate in the township of West Windsor" on Penns Neck.
>
> - To Jacob the "homestead where I now reside. Also the fifty acres of land which I purchased of Abraham Quick adjoining the said homestead. Also fifty acres of woodland near the Sand Hills in the County of Middlesex and "the sum of one thousand dollars to be paid to him at the time of my death out of such obligations as he may select" and "all my household and kitchen furniture".
>
> - To John and Jacob jointly "all my horses, cows, cattle, hogs, sheep - all the farming utensils, my waggons, riding chair and waggon and harness - All the hay that may be cut and all the grain that may be gathered at the time of my decease, to be divided between them share and share alike" (SA).

Demise

The Emporium, Trenton newspaper, published the following announcement on February 17, 1827:

> Suddenly, at his residence near Griggstown, Somerset County on the morning of the 4th inst. Capt. Jacob Van Dyke aged 72 years.[17]

The inscription on a white sandstone monument in the Ten Mile Run cemetery reads:

IN
MEMORY
OF
Capt. JACOB VAN DIKE
WHO DIED FEB 4th
1827
AGED 72 YEARS
1 MONTH 9 DAYS

A few feet away lie his grandfather, Jan Van Dike, who donated the land, and his grandmother, Annetje Verkirk Van Dike. If his father's body had been found, he would have been buried here.

I give and bequeath to my son Jacob Vandike all my household and kitchen furniture.

I give and bequeath to my son Jacob Vandike the sum of one thousand dollars to be paid to him at the time of my death out of such of my obligations as he may select.

I give and bequeath to my grand daughter Sarah Mary Vandike Oppie the sum of two thousand dol=
=lars to be paid to her at the age of one and twenty. And if she should die before the age of one and twenty, and without lawful issue, ~~then I give and~~ bequeath the said two thousand dollars to my two sons John and Jacob, to be divided equally.

I give, divise, and bequeath all the rest and res=
=idue of my estate both real and personal to my two sons John and Jacob to them their heirs and assigns forever.

I do here by nominate, constitute and appoint my two sons John and Jacob executors of this my last will and testament.

In witness whereof I have hereunto set my hand and seal this twenty second day of August Eighteen hundred and twenty five. Jacob Van Dike

Signed sealed Published

Manuscript copy of the will (signature page) of Jacob Van Dike (1754-1827) made August 22, 1825 and probated February 15, 1827.

Courtesy New Jersey State Archives, Department of State

Above: **TEN MILE RUN CEMETERY** today is well maintained and still graces the quiet countryside, a symbol of early Dutch habitation. Jan Van Dike of the Fourth Generation who donated the land would be pleased.

Below: Tombstone of his grandson, Jacob.

Photographs 1989

SEVENTH GENERATION

Genealogical Note

JOHN SCHENCK VAN DYKE
B September 25, 1801
D December 3, 1852
M

JOHN SCHENCK VAN DYKE - the surname is now variously spelled van dike, van dyke, Van Dike, Van Dyke - looks Dutch, sounds Dutch and is Dutch. He was the son of Jacob Van Dyke (1757-1827) and his wife, Sarah Schenck.

Beginning with the original Dutch settler, Jan was a chosen name in the family, which inevitably was anglicized and became John. His mother, Sarah Schenck, was the daughter of John R. Schenck (1748-1810) whose remote ancestor, Jan Martense Schenck of Amersfoort, Province of Utrecht, Holland, arrived in New Amsterdam in 1650, two years before Jan Thomasse Van Dyck (SCHQ 5:89, 116). Thus in true Dutch tradition it seemed preordained that Jacob and Sarah should name their first born son John Schenck Van Dyke.

In the family bible his father wrote, "John Skenck Van Dike was born September 25th, 1801" (VDFB/Princeton). His aunt, Mary Schenck Scott, recorded the same birthdate (month, day and year) in her bible (VDFB/Author). He was baptized at Six Mile Run on November 10, 1801 (SCHQ 8:275). The author visited the Penns Neck Cemetery, also known as the Schenck-Covenhoven Burial Ground, located on the former Jewell farm, West Windsor Township, Mercer County, near Princeton, in 1956, and photographed his tombstone inscribed as follows:

In Memory of
JOHN S. VAN DYKE
who died Dec 3
1852
Aged 52 years, 2 mo & 8 days

According to the inscription on the monument his birthday was September 25 in the year eighteen hundred. Could two family bibles and the church records be in error?

We conclude that the evidence weighs heavily in favor of the documents extant and against the stone carver!

William

William Van Dyke was born April 8, 1822 (VDFB/Author). John Schenck, his father, was twenty years old at this time. A marriage was not recorded in the family bible.

Copies of the Van Dyke Genealogy compiled by the author in 1957 were distributed among members of the family including the author's aunt, Pearl Van Dyke Harvey, living in Orlando, Florida. A letter was promptly received reading in part: "Dear Paul, Thanks very much for the Van Dyke Genealogy - it arrived yesterday and I immediately sat down and read it through with a great deal of enjoyment. You certainly did a wonderful job, and I will always keep it as one of my most cherished possessions...I can supply the missing link on my Grandfather.[1] In the early summer of 1821, John Schenck Van Dyke fell in love with a girl by the name of Baker and his father shipped him off to Holland where he lived until his father died.[2] Upon his return he wanted William's mother to come home with him but she preferred to remain at her brother's. She, however, let him take their son to raise. Grandfather used to tell as a boy he had his own pony, and every Saturday, his father would say: 'William, go see your mother'. After William's mother died his father married his housekeeper."

In a letter replying to several queries, Aunt Pearl said that upon John Schenck's return to America he "asked the Baker girl to marry him but she refused as her brother had previously dragged her through the courts trying to make Jacob Van Dyke acknowledge William as his grandson and she felt disgraced. I never heard her first name but they said her brother was mean to her and she evidently died quite young."

Viewed in historical perspective, John Schenck had broken deeply rooted tenets of the Dutch community. In the eyes of the church, he had committed a cardinal sin.[3] For one transgression seemingly beyond redemption, there was a very heavy price to pay. Surely he had envisioned a happy home surrounded by children. Now, suddenly, it was not to be. This incident - unforgettable - left an indelible imprint, a feeling of emptiness and melancholy that haunted him his remaining years. The word quickly spread throughout the community and was on everyone's lips, a source of untold embarrassment to his family and friends. As for Jacob, his father, already deeply saddened by death and grief, it was another burden along the way.

John Schenck, it appears, returned to America very soon before his father's death on February 4, 1827 after the matter had been quietly settled. His signature is on an affidavit taken before the Surrogate of Somerset County on February 15, 1827 in probate proceedings of his father's estate. Social acceptance is a subtle thing. We cannot penetrate the distant past to learn how he was received by the Dutch community upon his return to America. However it may be presumed that, given the moralities of the time, a reasonable measure of forbearance was called upon to reestablish himself and carry on.

He did carry on as the history shows.

West Windsor Township and the Village of Princeton

In 1830 Andrew Jackson (1767-1845) was president of the United States. Two years earlier Jackson defeated John Quincy Adams (1767-1848) who sought a second term, by a two-thirds majority of the electoral vote. Peter D. Vroom (1791-1874)[4] was governor of New Jersey. How John Schenck Van Dyke voted is unknown; however, it is reasonably certain that he cast his ballot at the polls set up in the Red Lion Inn in West Windsor Township (WWTM). With respect to the New Jersey governor and two senators representing the people in the Congress, he had no choice because, as mandated by the state and federal constitutions, these officials were chosen by members of the New Jersey legislature. The term of the governor's office was one year. Conditions were ideal for some intriguing political scenerios.

The population of New Jersey was rapidly increasing. By 1830 Middlesex County counted 23,257 inhabitants. A statistical analysis drawn from tax records assembled by Thomas A. Gordon in his fascinating Gazeteer of the State of New Jersey (1834) brings the demongraphic picture into sharp focus. Proving that cold figures can be interesting as well as enlightening, Gordon informs us that in 1830 Middlesex County was composed of 10,523 white males, 10,487 white females, 904 free colored males, 914 free colored females, 130 male slaves, 179 female slaves, 174 aliens, plus a few others. In 1832 the county contained 841 householders whose tax ratables did not exceed $30, 477 single men, 99 stores, 20 saw mills, 42 run of stones for grinding grain, 2 plaster mills, 2 woollen factories, 7 carding machines, 39 distilleries, 3,684 horses and mules, and 7,675 neat cattle[5] over three years of age (Gordon 178). These tangible items were part and parcel of, and basically supported, a robust agrarian economy. And, it may be added, were of special interest to the tax collector.

In consequence, by the 1830s the Township of West Windsor had grown into a thriving agricultural community with the vast majority of the inhabitants living on farms. Many farms contained several hundred acres with a full complement of servants and hired hands to perform the onerous tasks. Once again Gordon's statistics are most revealing. Within West Windsor's 19,000 acres in 1832 there were were 226 householders whose tax ratables did not exceed $30, 64 single men, 6 merchants, 1 large grist mill with 3 run of stones, 1 woolen factory, 3 distilleries, 496 horses and mules, and 848 neat cattle over 3 years (Gordon 264). Of 383 employed persons in 1840, 266 were engaged in "agriculture" and 73 in "manufactures and trades".[6] Provincial is an apt term to describe the community, rural and rustic in character, its industry and social affairs mainly confined within its borders. A large segment of the people were of Dutch lineage: Beekman, Kovenhoven, Ten Eyck, Gulick, Updyke, Van Hise, Van Ness, Van Sickle, Vroom, Van Dyke, to name only a few (WWTM).

When the federal census taker called at the Van Dyke farm in the summer of 1850, he noted in his report the name of the head of the family (John S. Van Dyke), that he was then forty-eight years old[7] and a farmer. A momentary glance at the countryside would have been convincing that agriculture represented the principal occupation. Horses, cows and sheep were grazing in the pastures. A fruit tree orchard graced the dwelling house. Fields of wheat and corn stretched far in the distance. Looming up in the background was a huge Dutch barn (Estate Inventory, SA; WWTM).

The nearest village was beautiful historic Princeton, originally named Prince Town (NJRM). Located on the north side of Stoney Brook less that a mile away, it had been the site of the College of New Jersey since 1756 when Nassau Hall was erected. A prestigious edifice of dark-red freestone four stories high and 176 feet long, Nassau Hall was one of the largest and finest buildings in the American colonies. Looking south beyond Stoney Brook on a clear day, the students were afforded a charming vista of trees and fields (Wertenbaker 188). In 1846 the College of New Jersey[8] was a century old, having been chartered in 1746,[9] and opened the following year in Elizabeth. Jonathan Dickinson (1688-1747), a Presbyterian minister of the Elizabeth church, was appointed its first president. The first class consisting of eight or ten students was taught by the Reverend Dickinson himself assisted by a tutor (Wertenbaker 24-25). As history proves, it is quality that counts. In the first century of its existence the small college steadily grew consistently fostering and maintaining the highest standard of scholarship; and, in the process, imparting to the village of Princeton the allure and quiet dignity of a college town. Still Princeton retained its distinctive rural flavor evidenced by the fact that of 3,055 inhabitants in 1840, 202 were engaged in "agriculture", 33 in "commerce", 277 in "manufactures and trades", and 76 in the "learned professions and engineers"; hence a well diversified cultural balance.

Additional light is shed on this tranquil rural scene by Peter Kalm, the Swedish professor-botanist who toured colonial America. Travelling along the primitive dirt road from Trenton to New Brunswick in October 1748, Professor Kalm passed through the heart of the Dutch farmland and found the journey a pleasant and rewarding experience. His journal records that during most of the day he saw very extensive cultivated fields on both sides of the road. With evident exuberance he wrote in his journal:

> *Near almost every farm was a spacious orchard full of peaches and apple trees, and in some of them the fruit had fallen from the trees in such quantities as to cover nearly the whole surface of the ground. Part of it they left to rot, since they could not take care of it all and consume it. Wherever we passed by we were welcome to go into the fine orchards and gather our hats and packets full of the choicest fruit, without the owner so much as looking at us. Cherry trees were planted near the farms, on the roads, etc. (Kalm 118).*

Nothing escaped the Swedish professor's discerning eye, especially the cavernous Dutch barns that invited a close inspection; and so he and his companion-servant tarried even longer that day. While seeking rest and refreshment overnight at one of the wayside inns he took pen in hand to recount a "concise description" (his words) of one of the Dutch barns that he examined in depth:

The main building was very large almost the size of a small church; the roof was high, covered with wooden shingles, sloping on both sides, but not steep. The walls which supported it were not much higher than a full grown man; but on the other hand the breadth of the building was all the greater. In the middle was a threshing floor and above it, or in the loft or garret, they put the unthreshed grain, the straw, or anything else, according to the season. On one side were stables for the horses, and on the other for the cows. The young stock had also their particular stables or stalls, and in both ends of the building were large doors, so the one could drive in with a cart and horses through one of them and go out the other. Here under one roof therefore were the thrashing floor, the barn, the stables, the hay loft, the coach house, etc (Kalm 118, 119).

This, then, was the land and the people whom John Schenck Van Dyke knew intimately. Obviously they molded his thinking, his philosophy, his entire life.

Farmer, Judge, Community Leader

John Schenck was a dedicated member of the Princeton Agricultural Society. Active in the 1830s, the society sought a larger field of influence and therefore proposed changing its name to the New Jersey Agricultural Society. Notice was given to interested citizens of the formation of a state society and a meeting to be held for the purpose at Princeton on August 10, 1839. At the meeting a new constitution was adopted. Officers of the new society were elected and included "Abraham Cruser President; Caleb Smith Green, William Gulick, Peter Voorhees, John S. Van Dyke Vice Presidents" (Hageman 259, 260).

A fondness of the soil and its bounty marked only one aspect of John Schenck's personality. Said Pearl Van Dyke, speaking with authority, "John Schenck Van Dyke was called 'Judge Van Dyke' and considered one of the first citizens of the community". Nothing has been found indicating that he was elected or appointed a jurist, and thus we are lead to the conclusion that "Judge" was a title of respect and affection. From the evidence available, it undoubtedly stemmed from his activities as a court functionary; in part, in his capacity as an estate appraiser[10] and a notary acknowledging deeds and mortgages and administering oaths of office (WWTM). An obituary characterizes him as "Judge John S. Van Dyke, a well known citizen of Princeton".[11] Living comfortably with his son William whom he reared and educated on one of the plantations inherited from his father, he made a decision very early in life to devote his time to civic affairs. People turned to him for leadership. On April 9, 1827, only a few weeks after his father's death, he was elected clerk of West Windsor Township, an office he held for twenty-two years. Additionally, from 1836 to 1848, when his health failed, he was a chosen freeholder of Mercer County (WWTM). Fortunately, the minute books of West Windsor Township, for many years in his custody, have been preserved. Two well-worn, leather bound volumes document the history of township government as he personally witnessed it.[12]

Customarily in April of each year a town meeting was held to elect township officials and chosen freeholders of the county. Civic matters were openly discussed and appropriate action taken. Then followed one or more meetings of the Township Committee, the single governing body possessing wide discretionary powers. A final committee meeting was held the following spring principally for the purpose of approving bills and settling accounts. At the annual town meeting the citizens elected a moderator and judge of election, a clerk of the township, an assessor, a collector and overseer of the poor, two surveyors of the highways, two chosen freeholders, five members of the Township Committee, three commissioners of appeals in cases of taxes, two or three constables,[13] seven overseers of the highways, and one or more pound keepers.[14] As will be seen, pound keepers fulfilled an equally essential and important function.

When John Schenck was first elected township clerk, the town meeting was held "at the house of Eli Rogers, innkeeper, at Dutch Neck on Monday, the 9th of April 1827." This was followed a month later by a meeting of the Township Committee "at the Hotel of Asher Temple on Penns Neck on Saturday the 5th of May 1827". High on the agenda was the repair and maintenance of the roads. Each of the overseers of the roads was allotted a budgeted sum for the year. An order entered on April 9 provided that "the sum of two hundred dollars be raised for the use of the roads" and that "the Overseers of the roads do their work previous to the first day of October next ensuing and work out no more than their own tax with their own hands". The care and support of the poor was another important township obligation. John Schenck recorded "the Township Committee at their next meeting raise the 'Poor Tax' and the sum of twenty five dollars be raised for the purpose of educating the poor children of the Township and that the said sum be placed in the hands of the Committee for distribution". At the committee meeting on May 5 it was further ordered that "the sum of five hundred dollars be assessed and collected for the support of the Paupers of the Township"(WWTM).

Dogs, Sheep and Stray Animals

One of the intriguing matters of business coming before the Township Committee each year concerned dogs and sheep. Problems arose because dogs that habitually roamed the countryside would sometimes kill a farmer's sheep. And the particular dog and his owner was usually unknown.

Was this really a community problem?

It was!

Since time immemorial, man's best friend has been a part of the Dutch household. Dutch genre paintings of the seventeenth century, for example, commonly show a friendly canine in the family gathering sometimes wagging his tail and participating in the action.[15] Even today in Holland the dog is welcome with his master on trains, trolleys, boats, and in public places. Hence it is not surprising that on the Dutch sailing ships bringing the settlers to America their dogs shared quarters with them.

A practical solution was obviously needed. And these pragmatic Dutch and other canine lovers found it. An insurance fund, appropriately called the "Dog Fund", was raised each year from dog license fees providing compensation for loss of the owner's sheep. Yes, the dog had rights, too.

The plan worked well for many years modified as experience dictated. On April 10, 1828, we find that twenty-four persons "presented Certificates stating damage to their sheep by dogs unknown". The dog was always unknown! The total sum claimed was $178.50 while the "Dog Tax less Assessor's and Collector's fees with the overplus of the Dog Tax of the last year amounted to $79.52". A deficit was frowned upon. And so compensation was prorated: "The aforesaid persons were paid forty-five cents on the dollar", John Schenck wrote in the minutes for April 10, 1828. Accordingly, at the annual Town Meeting four days later the dog license fees were increased; an order was entered that "the tax on dogs be assessed as follows - The 1st dog $00.50 - The 2nd $2.00 - The 3rd $5.00 - $5.00 for each other dog owned by one person - $5.00 for each slut". The same pattern continued for many years.

In addition to passing upon claims for the loss of sheep, John Schenck received reports of stray animals. This he recorded in the back of the minute book under the heading, "Book kept for the purpose of posting strays". The following are examples:

West Windsor, Nov 8th 1841

Job G. Olden gave me a note in writing stating that there came upon his enclosed land about the first of the present month a dark red steer, two years old last spring with a short tail and long horns - no artificial marks perceptible

John S. Van dyke
Clerk
of West Windsor

West Windsor Nov 24th 1845

William Smith Schenck gave me a note in writing stating that there came upon his enclosed lands on the 8th day of November inst. Two red and white calves, the one a bull the other a heifer, each supposed to be about six months old - the end of the right ears of each cut off, and a notch on the underside of the left ear of each.

John S. Van dyke
Township Clerk

The First Public Schools

The earliest schools, as previously seen, were either church controlled or privately run "pay schools", so named because the schoolmaster was paid a stipulated sum. Consequently, the education of children in colonial times depended upon the availability of a church school conveniently located or a private tutor, if one could be found. Public school education was unknown. One example of a private tutor in New Jersey comes to light in the form of a receipt for services. Cornelius Ten Broeck, living in Montgomery Township, Somerset County, in 1750, and the court appointed guardian of four minor children as directed by the will of his deceased brother, Wessel, secured a teacher, namely, Lewis Charles Faniuil, who signed a receipt for seven shillings and two pence for services. The receipt reads:

> *Received March 31st, 1750 of Mr. Cornelius Tinbrook, Seven shillings and Two pence of money at Eight shillings p oz. In full for schooling and all other accounts [due] me.*
>
> *Lewis Charles Faniuil*

(SCHQ 1:274)

Curiously enough, Faniuil was a schoolmaster in Somerset County twenty years later, it appearing that he submitted a bill to Cornelius Tinbrook for "schooling" three children with a note appended:

Mr. Cornelius Tinbrook Dr. To Lewis Charles Faniuil

To Ballance due at settlement	*L*1.0.4
1769, Decr.13. To 3 mo. schooling, 3 children	1.6.0
1770. To schooling to the time I left the school	0.9.0
	*L*2.15.4

> *Sir: As I expect to move to Milstone in a few days more I send you your acc't, and should be obliged if you'l pay the same before I go. I shall keep school till I have notice from Milstone* (SCHQ 3: 149).

The picture was fundamentally the same in John Schenck's youth when the new republic was feeling its way in the world. At the same time circumstances indicated that a new policy or plan of education was needed. On November 11, 1828 a meeting was held in the State House, Trenton, when a committee was appointed to inquire into the condition of education in the state. The following year it published its findings setting forth, in part, that schoolmasters were left to pursue their own course of instruction with no supervision and more that 11,000 children in New Jersey received no instruction. Based on these findings, an act establishing "common schools" was passed by the New Jersey legislature. From a permanent school fund raised by taxes and other means, $20,000 was divided among the counties, the Board of Chosen Freeholders of each county being authorized to distribute the subsidy among the townships (Thompson 203-205, CMCL).

Thanks to the minutes of West Windsor Township, a factual record exists. In the spring of 1828, prior to the aforesaid legislation, the inhabitants, deeply concerned about children of less affluent families who could not afford a teacher or tutor, inaugurated their own public school system. In keeping with action taken at an annual town meeting at the "house of Eli Rogers innkeeper, at Dutch Neck on Monday April 14th AD 1828", John Schenck entered the following order in the minute book: "Ordered - That the sum of three hundred dollars be assessed and collected for the purpose of employing teachers for common schools - And that the Township Committee divide the Township into suitable districts and on condition that the inhabitants in the several districts, raise by voluntary contributions a sum of money, which by being placed with their respective quotas of the money raised by the Township be sufficient to hire a teacher for the term of one year - Then the Committee shall order the Collector to pay unto the trustees of the several districts their respective quotas of the tax - And in case any district shall neglect or refuse to comply with the above conditions - Then the share of the tax what would have been alloted to them will remain in the hands of the Collector for the use of the Township"

Four weeks later at a meeting of the committee "at the Hotel of Asher Temple at Penns Neck on Saturday the 10th of May 1828", four men were appointed to report at the next meeting the "number of scholars in their respective districts", namely, Rev. Daniel Dewelle for the Dutch Neck District, John F. Hutchinson for the Edinburgh District, David Dye for the Clarksville District, and John S. Van Dyke for the Penns Neck District. At a meeting "at the house of Eli Rogers, innkeeper at Dutch Neck on the 6th of June 1828", the committee reported:

Rev. Daniel Dewelle	*- 40*	*Scholars*
John F. Hutchinson	*- 40*	*do*
David Dye	*- 40*	*do*
John S. Vandyke	*- 33*	*do*

John Schenck recorded in the minutes: *"The Committee upon consideration agree to allow the trustees of the Dutch Neck School the sum of $75.00 and to each district the sum of $60.00 -Provided they receive all the scholars in their districts (those that are not able to pay to be educated gratis). The balance of the said fund - $45.00 [total $300.00] to be appropriated towards building a school house on the parsonage between Penns Neck and Dutch Neck - And in case the inhabitants of that district refuse to build the said school house, then the said sum of $45.00 to go towards educating the children in said district; or a due proportion of it."*

Can there be any doubt that a positive effort was undertaken to provide education for all children regardless of financial circumstances and that West Windsor Township stands in the vanguard of public school education in New Jersey?

The Red Lion Inn and Other Taverns

A tavern in John Schenck's day was variously known as a house ("public house" in early times), an inn or hotel usually identified by the innkeeper's name. In the township minute book, for example, John Schenck refers to the "house of Eli Rogers innkeeper in Dutch Neck"; the "hotel of Asher Temple innkeeper in Penns Neck"; the "house of John Van Hise innkeeper at Dutch Neck"; the "house of William K. Holmes, innkeeper at Assanpink".

Adding a touch of glamour, the taverns displayed colorful signs with imaginative and romantic names. The first tavern in Penns Neck, built when John Schenck was six or seven, was called the Red Lion Inn. In nearby Princeton there was the Sign of the College of New Jersey, and the Sign of the Houdibras and The Kings Arms. There was the Tavern in the Woods (later called the Woods Tavern) in Hillsborough. In New Brunswick there was the famous Indian Queen tavern; in Perth Amboy the Long Ferry and in Trenton the Ship and Castle. With the exception of the Red Lion Inn in Penns Neck, all were engaged in business before the Revolution. Attractive signs hung from a wrought iron bracket extending from the building, and, in some cases, from a post in front where it was more clearly visible (Van Hoesen Chap2&3).

The taverns not only accommodated the tired and weary traveler, but served a secondary purpose, namely, a center for community activities including town meetings and social gatherings, business and political discussions, a polling place for elections both local and national; and, always, a source of the latest news and gossip. John Schenck was acquainted with the innkeepers with whom he made arrangements for the town meetings.

Still another good reason existed for the eye-appealing signs. Not everyone could read; and so, for the illiterate, the tavern was identified by a distinctive symbol. While West Windsor Township endorsed public school education early in 1828, there were thirty-one persons over twenty in a total population of 1,536 in 1840 who could not read and write.[16] Thus a bright red lion represented the Red Lion Inn. The King's Arms, another popular name, was symbolized by a crowned head. Innkeepers, appreciating their commercial importance, often took the signboards with them when they moved to a new location. As more wayside taverns appeared on the scene, some bore the same name. For example, in Elizabeth there was Red Lion Inn. After the Revolution it operated for a time as the Indian Queen, later assuming its original name. In Trenton and in New Brunswick there was an Indian Queen (ibid 55,100,101).

As long as the horse reigned supreme, innkeeping was a highly competitive business. Taverns blossomed overnight along narrow dirt roads cut through the wilderness, especially along the main arteries connecting the principal villages and towns. Philadelphia to New York by way of Trenton and Princeton was a journey of two to three days depending on the weather and the season. The traveler, tired and hungry - sometimes near the point of exhaustion at the end of a long day's journey - craved food and lodging. His horse made similar demands. And so the enterprising innkeeper provided stables for the horses and hay and grain for sustenance. Grooms and stable boys attended them (ibid 28,29).

Above: Entrance and partial view of the stone wall surrounding the Penns Neck Cemetery, also known as the Schenck-Covenhoven Burial Ground, located on the former Jewell farm near Princeton. One of the oldest tombstones marks the grave of William Covenhoven who died October 7, 1777. In the last quarter century the cemetery has fallen into ruin, the result of sheer neglect and the ravages of nature. Currently it is being restored.

Photograph 1988

Below: John Schenck Van Dyke (1801-1852), well known in West Windsor Township and Princeton as Judge Van Dyke, is buried among his Dutch friends.

Photograph 1956

At a meeting of the committee of the Township of West Windsor held at the house of Eli Rodgers innkee-
-per at Dutchneck on Thursday the 5th. day of April 1838. The following members were present viz —

William Post
Ezekiel Rodgers
James McGalliard
James Olden —

The overseers of the highways presented their accounts and vouchers for settlement.

It appeared that Vincent Perrine had expended $34.25

Vincent Perrine	$34.25
Richard C. Mount	86.49
William Stonakar	47.39
	$168.13

	168.13
David S. Voorhees	$34.27½
Charles S. Olden	67.81
John S. Fisher	54.91
Ezekiel Rodgers	74.63½
Elisha Jewell	151.75
William Wiley	24.93
	$581.44

Henry Dye presented his accounts for services rendered as overseer of the poor amounting to $43.01½ which was allowed —

Manuscript copy (selected portions) of minutes of the annual town meeting of West Windsor Township on April 9, 1838 in the hand of John S. Van Dyke.

Courtesy West Windsor Township

The following persons presented certificates stating the damage done their sheep by dog or dogs unknown Viz

Thomas S. Wright	$59.00
James Olden	39.20
John Jamison	15.00
William Wiley	4.00
Thomas B. Hooper	11.00
Charles Updike	9.00
Elias Golden	3.00
John G. Schenck	3.00
Ann Case	3.25
Randolph Chamberlin	1.50
	$147.95

The whole amount of dog tax of the present year after deducting the Assessors and Collectors fees is $75.36

To which add the surplus of the dog tax of the two past years amounting to ——— $" 69.54
Makeing alltogether the sum of ——— 144.90
Which sum paid the different persons claiming pay for damages sustained about ninety seven and three quarters of a cent in the dollar

---

The whole amount of money expended the past year in support of the poor amounts to ——— $427.30½

Leaving a ballance due the township of West Windsor in the hands of Henry Dye collector of ——— $193.62½

John S. Vandyke
Clerk

William Post
Chairman

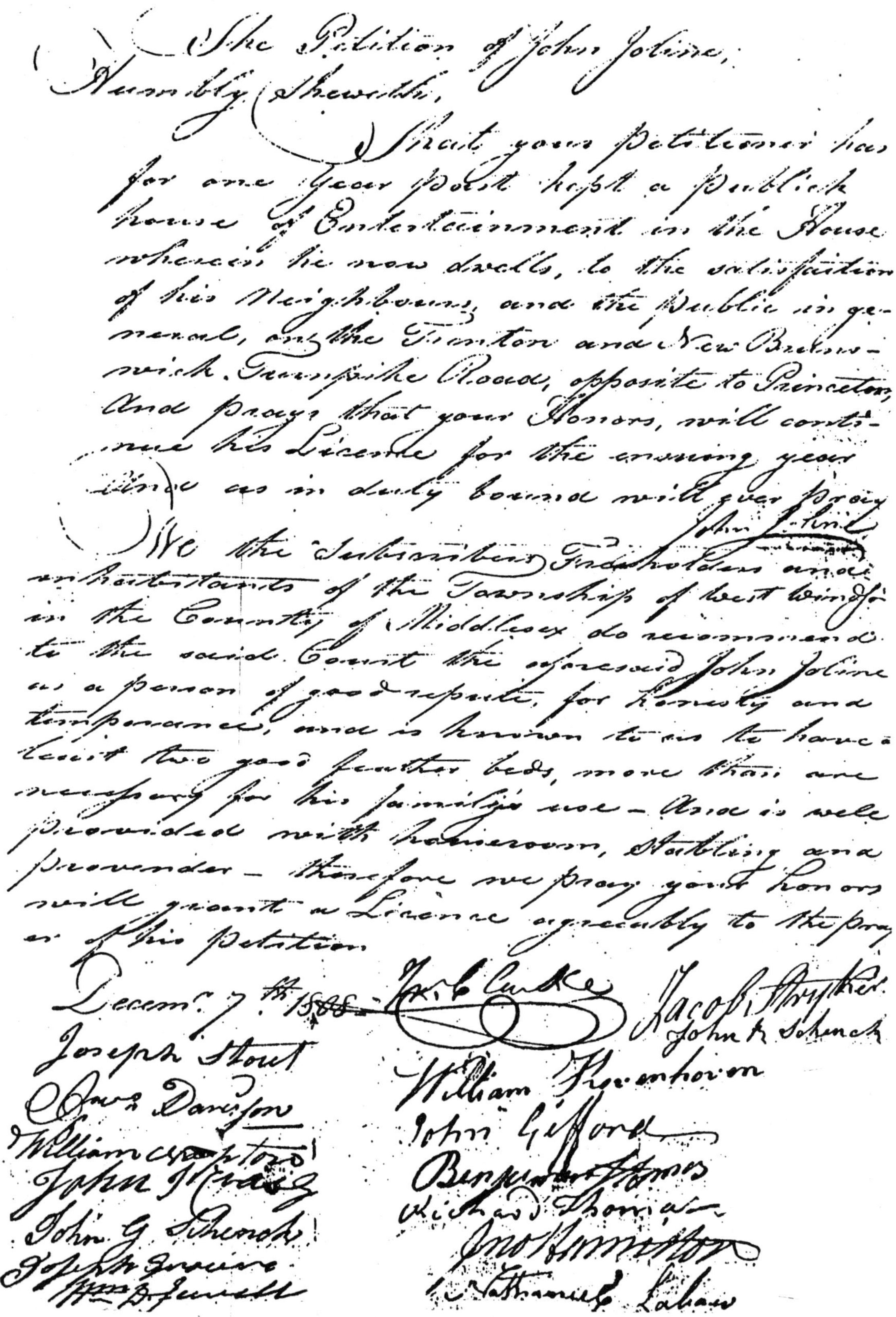

The Petition of John Joline,
Humbly Sheweth,

That your petitioner has for one Year past kept a publick house of Entertainment in the House wherein he now dwells, to the satisfaction of his Neighbours, and the public in general, on the Trenton and New Brunswick Turnpike Road, opposite to Princeton, And prays that your Honors, will continue his License for the ensuing year And as in duty bound will ever pray

John Joline

We the Subscribers Freeholders and inhabitants of the Township of West Windsor in the County of Middlesex do recommend to the said Court the aforesaid John Joline as a person of good repute, for honesty and temperance, and is known to us to have at least two good feather beds, more than are necessary for his family's use – And is well provided with houseroom, Stabling and provender – therefore we pray your honors will grant a License agreeably to the prayer of this petition

Decem.r 7th 1808

Jas. Clarke
Jacob Stryker
John K. Schenck
Joseph Stout
Jas Davison
William Crawford
John Craig
John G. Schenck
Joseph Grover
Wm D. Jewell
William Covenhoven
John Gifford
Benjamin Stones
Richard Thomson
Jno Hamilton
Nathaniel Labaw

Manuscript copy (reduced) of John Joline's petition for a Tavern License in the December Term, 1808, of the Court of General Quarter Sessions and of the Peace held at New Brunswick.

The innkeepers, sometimes referred to as "landlords", were friendly, congenial gentlemen who stood ready and eager to accommodate their guests, warmly welcoming them on arrival - spirits assisting - and wishing them Godspeed on departure. It is not difficult to envision the hospitality lavished upon distinguished personages such as Washington, Adams, and Franklin who patronized the Indian Queen at Albany and Water Streets in New Brunswick in the course of their journeys (ibid 55).

John Joline was the first innkeeper of the Red Lion Inn on the Straight Turnpike at Penns Neck built about 1807. At the December 1808 Term of the Court of General Quarter Sessions of the Peace held at New Brunswick, Joline filed a "petition" for a Tavern License requesting "your honors will continue his license for the ensuing year", signed by sixteen freeholders and alleging that he had "for one Year Past kept a Publick house of Entertainment in the House wherein he now dwells, to the satisfaction of his Neighbours and the Public in general, on the Trenton and New Brunswick Turnpike Road, opposite to Princeton"; and further setting forth that they recommend him "as a person of good repute, for honesty and temperance, and is known to us to have at least two good feather beds, more than are necessary for his family's use - and is well provided with houseroom, stabling and provender." Joline has been depicted as "perhaps the most notable of all the landlords. He was jovial and obliging; he set a good table and kept good horses. When he was at Princeton the temptation for the students to loiter around his tavern and watch the arrival and departure of travelers and the changing of horses - often as many as a hundred standing ready to take the place of the tired ones - was so great that the college authorities passed regulations forbidding the students to be seen there. But in spite of these regulations, or because of them, Joline used to treat the college boys to clandestine suppers and take them for midnight sleighrides" (OPN 69).

Life in Nassau Hall in colonial times was rigid and confining, in consequence calling for some form of mental and physical relaxation, an element not fully appreciated by the faculty and trustees. At five in the morning the boys were roused by the loud blast of a horn outside their dormitory doors summoning them to prayer, roll call, and the singing of a psalm in Prayer Hall. They washed and dressed by candlelight. This was the beginning of their daily routine rigorously supervised by professors and tutors. Latin and Greek were mandatory courses of study, the heart of a gentleman's education. When they happened to engage in a game with balls and sticks on the back common of the college, it was stopped on the theory that it was considered "low and unbecoming gentlemen and students". A rule forbidding sleigh-riding was habitually broken (Wertenbaker 138). Obviously the tavern was a most inviting attraction.

The minutes of West Windsor Township record four township committee meetings in the year 1808 at the "House of John Joline" Saturday, April 23; Saturday, August 13; Wednesday, November 9; and December 6. The jovial and obliging host prominently stands out as a charismatic figure demonstrating a pragmatic knowledge of human psychology astutely blended with business acumen. Success was bound to follow. Having spotted a better opportunity in the village of Princeton, he left the Red Lion Inn in 1810 and managed the Sign of the Houdibras for two years. Thereupon for twenty three years, Joline held forth as the genial innkeeper at the Sign of the College of New Jersey which during his tenure became known as the Nassau Inn, the name it bears today (Van Hoesen 130,Hageman 42)

It is truly amazing that Nassau Inn on Princeton's main highway has been open to the public for over two centuries. Thus it has witnessed an extraordinary series of historic events in our nation's history: among them, the Battle of Princeton in 1777; meetings of the legislature and the Council of Safety during the Revolution; the triumphal celebration for Washington in 1783 when Princeton was the nation's capital; the reception for the very popular Marquis de Lafayette who visited Princeton on his sensational tour of the United States in 1824. Worthy of mention also was the newly arrived freshman bearing a letter of recommendation to the president of the college. Often a journey of hundreds of miles by stage coach and ferry, he arrived tired and a trifle homesick, and engaged a room for the night at the Sign of the College of New Jersey across from Nassau Hall. With trepidation he awaited a meeting the next day at the President's House where he presented his letter and was confronted by the professors and tutors with entrance examinations (Wertenbaker 184).

Another Princeton spectacular of national significance was the reception given that bold and combative soldier-statesman from Tennessee, Andrew Jackson (1767-1845), the president in 1833. John Schenck was thirty-one; his son William eleven. Jackson was honored by Princeton in the true red-carpet tradition. The horsemen and the infantrymen together with the town's citizens plus faculty and students of the college and seminary were on hand, having assembled about a mile out of town, there to escort the president to Joline's tavern (ibid 248)). The next morning Jackson attended prayers in Nassau Hall and toured the college buildings. Similarly the great orator and statesman from Kentucky, Henry Clay (1777-1852), three times defeated for the presidency, found good reason to visit Princeton, namely because Jackson, his political adversary, had been there before him. Clay's famous speech on the Senate floor captivating a large audience in the gallery, as history records, made Jackson a bitter enemy when comparing him by innuendo to Caesar and other despots in history. Jackson never forgave him.[17] Observing that John Schenck and his son William resided on the main highway to Princeton, it is not unlikely that they too joined the cheering throng eager to catch a glimpse of the popular president. It was, of course, a gala occasion typical of the American political scene. Even as in today's world, the festivities were carefully planned and orchestrated: the color guard carrying the flags, the sleek cavalry, men in trim uniforms marching to the beat of the drummer or a brass band, the day's program capped by speeches lauding everyone politically or socially prominent. Princeton could claim its fair share of distinguished men. Personal observations and sallies exchanged between father and son would have been a delight to hear.

Let us leave the Nassau Inn and return to the Red Lion Inn, which first opened its doors to the public when John Schenck was a small boy and John Joline was the amiable landlord who in 1810 sought greener pastures in Princeton. Succeeding Joline was Asher Temple, the innkeeper for many years but a much less popular figure. Temple bought the property in 1819 from William Kovenhoven for four thousand dollars, which is described in a deed as a "certain Tavern house and lot of land in the Township of West Windsor in the County of Middlesex" lying along the "southeast side of the Trenton and New Brunswick Turnpike Road, and on the easterly side of the Road leading from Princeton to Allenton", setting forth the metes and bounds.[18] Between 1827 and

1835 eight meetings were held at the "hotel of Asher Temple", recorded by John Schenck in the minute book. In 1835 the pattern abruptly changed; the last township meeting, we find, took place on May 3, 1835. Temple's sponsorship of horse racing and betting brought him into disfavor with the township fathers.[19] Eli Rogers, the proprietor of a tavern at Dutch Neck, was host to the township on thirty-five occasions.

It is remarkable indeed that the Red Lion Inn at Penns Neck survives today structurally intact. At a critical time in history it found a new purpose and raison d'etre, luckily escaping demolition, the sorry fate of other taverns. The story is well documented and a fascinating one. With the decline of the stage lines in the last half of the nineteenth century, the wayside inns fell on hard times. Noah Reed, in 1873, purchased the property for $4,400[20] and found the business unprofitable. Upon his death leaving an estate heavily burdened with debt, letters of administration CTA were granted by the Surrogate of Mercer County to Isaac G. Waters who, pursuant to directions in the will, placed the property on the market for sale.

The longtime neighbor of the Red Lion Inn was the Princeton Baptist Church whose congregation erected its first church edifice in 1812 on adjoining land (Updyke 12,22). In later years the pastor, trustees and congregation watched with grave concern as social conditions changed and liquor was dispensed to young men in the community causing "no little annoyance to the Church". It was a problem crying out for a solution (Updike 34).

And they found it! The trustees bought the tavern.[21]

The human side is movingly told by the pastor who recorded the history of his nine-year tenure. Said the Reverend L. O. Grenelle:

> *The old hotel property on the corner had long been an eyesore to the Church. I had a big fight on hand and in the start stood alone, but soon had others to aid in the struggle. I distinctly remember that I said in one discourse one of these institutions will go down, either the dram shop or the Church. But the temperance move was on the gain. Some who had been indifferent took a bold stand. The tavern property was not occupied, was under mortgage and was to be sold. To put it short, the trustees bought it at public sale for a parsonage and you ought to have seen the sacrifice of labor of some half dozen men for weeks in papering, cleaning and fitting the property for church use. I moved into it with my family and we lived happily for years in it. A grand good and true sister of the Church let them have means to make the first payments.*[22]

Thus, what was once a busy, boisterous, pulsating hostelry was transformed into a peaceful parsonage which has served the Princeton Baptist Church for over a century.

The Straight Turnpike, the Canal and the Railroad

In discoursing on canal building in America, history books commonly cite as an example the Erie Canal that connected the Hudson River at Albany with Lake Erie at Buffalo. Opened for barge traffic in 1825, it was hailed as a tremendous engineering feat.

The Delaware and Raritan Canal completed nine years later was a comparable engineering achievement. Stretching across New Jersey's waistline, it linked the Delaware River at Bordentown with the Raritan at New Brunswick, a distance of twenty-eight miles as the crow flies but nearly twice that distance traversed by water. Following a circuitous course through farmlands and forests, it adapted to the topography and feeder streams. Various water levels presented problems which were artfully resolved by a series of locks at strategic points. The highest elevation was 56.3 feet at the State Street lock in Trenton (same at Kingston) gradually descending to 5 feet at the terminal lock in New Brunswick. How was it accomplished? Briefly, with meticulous planning by the designers and engineers and backbreaking toil of thousands of men wielding picks and shovels, and horses pulling plows, scoops and other devices. Manpower and horsepower were all that they had to perform major surgery. Both in construction and in operation, the canal was a marvel of age.

At Penns Neck the man-made waterway hugged Stoney Brook and cut through John Schenck's land on the northern border. Invoking the right of eminent domain, the company appropriated approximately an acre of his land. Meanwhile the southern boundary ran coterminous with the old New Brunswick and Trenton road which became known as the Straight Turnpike. Accepting Euclid's axiom that a straight line is the shortest distance between two points, the planners designed the highway to conform to a straight line. "Pike" refers to the bar suspended across the road where the tolls were collected. Completed in 1808 by the Trenton and New Brunswick Company when John Schenck was seven, it was a heavily traveled thoroughfare accommodating all forms of traffic: men on horseback, horsedrawn wagons, carriages, buggies, stage coaches and cattle on the hoof. Tolls were collected at tollgates located ten miles or less apart. According to schedules posted, the toll for a horse and rider or a led horse or mule was one-half cent. For a dozen calves, sheep or hogs the rate was a half cent a mile while a dozen cattle, mules, or horses paid one cent; and carriages paid one cent per mile for each horse up to four, additional horses at two cents. Sometimes the toll collector was confronted with a problem when droves of livestock raised clouds of dust and blocked the way as he tried to count their numbers (PNJHS 54:35,36).

John Schenck was, therefore, an eyewitness to all modes of transportation, both old and new, without leaving his land. As the years passed, he saw the inevitable decline of the turnpike companies and the stage lines and the emergence of the canal and the railroad operating more efficiently and at lower cost. One canal boat could transport a load ten times greater than a four-horse team (PNJHS 54:41).

Historically, the idea of a canal was conceived in 1676 by William Penn who commissioned a survey to determine the feasibility of an inland waterway between the Delaware and Sandy Hook (Cranmer 24,Viet 60). In 1783 George Washington envisioned an extensive system of inland waterways.

Above: Princeton Baptist Church stands today on heavily traveled US Route 1 at Penns Neck. The original structure was erected on this site in 1812 when the highway was known as the Straight Turnpike. Enlarged and extensively remodeled in 1877, it has little changed in general appearance.
Below: The church's neighbor was the Red Lion Inn built around 1807 serving the public traveling between New Brunswick and Trenton. In 1879 the congregation bought the tavern and transformed it into a parsonage.

Photographs in 1989

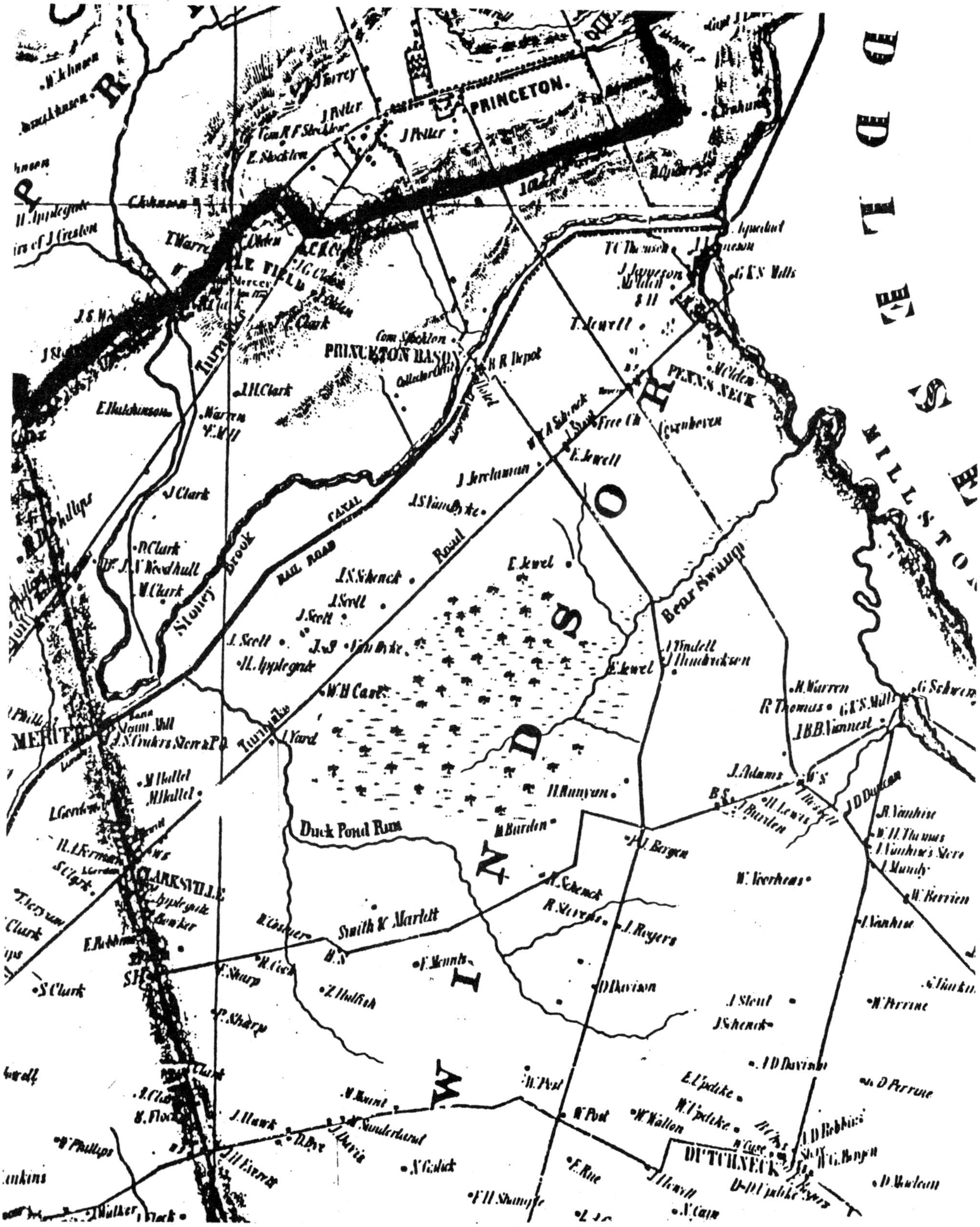

Map of Mercer County (selected portion) published in 1849, original in Rutgers University Library, Special Collections and Archives. The canal and the railroad parallel Stoney Brook, a tributary of the Millstone. Penn's Neck, Clarksville and two farms of John Schenck Van Dyke (J. S. Van Dyke) are seen on the Straight Turnpike connecting New Brunswick and Trenton.

"Prompted by these actual observations, I could not help taking a more contemplative and extensive view of the vast inland navigation of these United States, from maps and the information of others", Washington wrote, "and could not but be struck with the immense diffusion and importance of it; and with the goodness of that Providence which has dealt her favors to us with so profuse a hand. Would to God that we may have the wisdom enough to improve them. I shall not rest contented 'till I have explored the Western Country, and traversed those lines (or great part of them) which have given bounds to a New Empire."[23]

In 1836, after the canal was built, John Schenck was compensated for the taking of "ninety eight hundredths of an acre" of his land lying along Stoney Brook. A deed of conveyance discloses the consideration of "One hundred and five dollars".[24]

Land on the north side of Stoney Brook was held by a prominent Princeton born naval officer, Robert Field Stockton (1795-1866), a man of exceptional talent and versatility. Ironically, he was a college dropout. After matriculating as a freshman at the College of New Jersey at age thirteen and reading the adventures of Captain Nelson of seafaring fame, he decided to leave his alma mater and enlist in the navy notwithstanding that he excelled in mathematics, languages and elocution and could have graduated with high honors. As a mere youth in the navy, he saw action in the War of 1812 for which he was commended by Commodore John Rogers, commander of the flagship, The President, following several important military operations. Later, in the Mexican War, Stockton himself commanded a naval squadron capturing Los Angeles and San Diego, and, amazingly, still found time for self-study and to read the classics including the Bible, Shakespeare, Cicero and Lord Bacon. Resigning his commission in 1850, he served the citizens of New Jersey in the United States Senate from 1851 to 1853. Finally, between naval exploits, he was the president of the Delaware and Raritan Canal Company in which he risked his private fortune (Myers 60;DAB,Vol IX,48,49).

In essence, Robert Field Stockton, a seasoned naval officer harboring a creative mind and an extensive knowledge of marine navigation, conceived the canal as a means of transporting coal from the Pennsylvania mines to New York faster and cheaper than around Cape May. A voyage between Philadelphia and New York depending upon the wind and the weather could take as long as two weeks.

This era also saw the dawn of the steam age witnessed by John Schenck Van Dyke. Inventive minds were at work devising ways of using steam to propel a boat on water and a carriage on rails. John Fitch (1743-1798), successively a clockmaker, brassfounder and silversmith, built a steamboat equipped with paddlewheels, a homemade boiler and a Watt engine that carried passengers on the Delaware between Philadelphia and Trenton in the summer of 1790. Robert Fulton (1765-1815), an American engineer with the assistance of Robert L. Livingston, American minister to France, constructed the Clermont which plied the Hudson between New York and Albany in 1807; and in 1814-15 built the Fulton, a vessel of thirty-eight tons, the country's first steam warship. Not to be forgotten, there was James Watt (1736-1829), a Scottish engineer, who is said to have obtained the first patent on the steam engine. Robert Stephenson (1803-1859), an English engineer, won a five hundred pound prize for his Rocket, a steam engine on rails, which in 1829 was the only engine in a competition to draw a load three times its own weight at 12.5 miles an hour and a carriage with passengers at 24 miles an hour.

From this moment agriculture was destined to play a gradually diminished role. The rural family was no longer directly dependent on the land for survival. Hence John Schenck witnessed the birth pangs of a new era, an industrial economy ushered in by huge canal barges and freight cars on rails moving tons of commodities to cities and towns. Men of vision foretold a vast network of rail lines and canals interconnected, carrying goods, passengers and the mail over long distances. Steam, an alternative energy source, might well complement horsepower, but it would never supersede the horse, so the soothsayers said. In fact more, not less, would be needed as the population increased thereby creating a greater demand. Certainly the horse was essential for local transportation and in the fields, and generally as a draft animal.

How wrong they were!.

As we further glimpse the history of canal building, the driving force was the War of 1812. The British blockade of ports along the Atlantic seaboard made it necessary to move goods overland. Between Philadephia and New York thousands of wagons drawn by teams of horses and oxen - all of this seen by John Schenck in his youth - formed a near continuous stream hauling goods previously transported by coastwise vessels. Freight rates and commodity prices soared. This, in turn, spurred private interests to build the waterway long envisioned (PNJHS 54:36-38). While earlier, several companies had been chartered for the purpose - for neither Congress nor the New Jersey legislature had the money - they failed for lack of sufficient capital (Cranmer 27-68).

Finally, in the late 1820's, two powerful lobbies emerged, one for the canal and the other for the railroad. In near predictable fashion, the legislature resolved the problem: it granted charters to both companies, in fact on the same day, February 4, 1830 (Myers 60). The Camden and Amboy Railroad and Transportation Company was given the right that no other railroad could be built within five miles of the Camden and Amboy without its permission. Similarly the Delaware and Raritan Canal and Banking Company was granted the right that no canal could be built within five miles of the Delaware and Raritan or its feeder. In return for these monopoly grants and in lieu of all taxes the companies were to pay transport duties based on tonnage and the number of passengers carried per mile. One year later, after still more lobbying, the two companies were merged under a socalled "Unity" or "Marriage Act" whereby they combined revenues and expenditures but retained their corporate identities. The reason, publicly announced, was to ensure financial stability and completion of both the canal and the railroad (Viet 63,64). But for whatever the reason, a formidable transportation monopoly was created. Both companies were fabulously successful (Cranmer 313-317). The Sherman Antitrust Law was years into the future.

The Camden and Amboy Railroad and Transportation Company inaugurated a daily rail service in February 1833 between Bordentown on the Delaware River and South Amboy on Raritan Bay. The steam locomotive, still primitive and experimental, might be a little dangerous, the company engineers thought. Hence horses were used initially to pull the carriages on cast iron rails. Gordon's

Gazeteer of the State of New Jersey says, "Until September, 1833, the carriages were commonly drawn by horses; at that time steam locomotives were applied to one of the three daily lines which traverse it" (Gordon 20).

The engineers were right. The steam locomotive was dangerous. Accidents occurred causing death and serious bodily harm all of which generated newspaper publicity triggering a public outcry. Its political impact was palpably felt. The New Jersey legislature, in its political wisdom, passed an act declaring in substance that the operation of a steam carriage at a speed greater than twenty miles an hour constituted gross negligence; and if an accident resulted in the death of a passenger, the manager, conductor, engineer, or company agent was deemed guilty of manslaughter (Princeton Recollector, September 1979). Certainly the engineers had much to learn. It was back to the drawing board.

Property owners along the right of way were also vulnerable to the vagaries of the puffing steam monster. On a windy day in April 1845 a passing locomotive belching flaming embers from its stack set fire to "some 25 or 30 acres of wood land" owned by "John S. Van Dyke, Esq., on Penns Neck", as was reported in the columns of the Princeton newspaper. Fortunately, a town meeting was in progress. The fire alarm sent the town's citizens scurrying to the fire; and they were successful in extinguishing it before any buildings were destroyed. Acknowledging the charitable deed, John Schenck tendered grateful thanks to his fellow citizens who, in his own words, "when his property was in flames rushed to the rescue, and by their cool deliberate judgment, activity and perseverance, saved a great portion of it from the devouring element" (Princeton Whig, Friday, April 18, 1845).

The extraordinary joint venture of private and state enterprise unfettered by competition possessed a bright economic future. John Schenck, noting steady growth day by day from his vantage point, concluded that the canal was here to stay. He bought five shares of Delaware and Raritan stock inventoried and appraised at $700.00 and a bond of the joint companies worth $130.50 (Estate Inventory, SA).

The Stage Lines

A journey by stagecoach from Philadelphia to New York over rough rutted, dirt roads may be described as a bone-jarring experience. Consuming two to three days, the shaken traveler looked forward to a smooth water-crossing by ferry - assuming that the weather cooperated - and by the end of the day, rest and refreshment. No wonder innkeeping was a lucrative industry, not only in colonial times but well into the days of John Schenck Van Dyke when the nation was young.

We envisage John Schenck waving to the drivers of the stages pulled by a team of galloping horses as they swept by his land on the Straight Turnpike. In fact he knew many of the stage drivers. Having observed the stage operation in and about the village of Princeton, he believed it to be a viable business enterprise prior to the heyday of the canal and the railroad. In the company of James S. Green,[25] William Gulick and others, he bought an interest in the popular Nassau Inn (or Nassau Hotel) and its accompanying stage line, it appearing that the two entities were closely associated in catering to the traveling public (Hageman 41).

In a large leather-bound, grossly deteriorated Stage Book (SCA) the names A. D. Degraw, John Joline, Isaac Gulick and Jacob Gulick frequently appear indicating that some or all of them held a proprietary interest, or were in some way actively involved, in this stage line. Perusing its tattered pages, one sees written in beautiful flowing script "William Joline's Book - October 18th 1818" repeated three times. William Joline was the son of John Joline[26] who probably was the penman who wrote the title headings, namely: Princeton March 23, 1817; Princeton Stage Book; Post Chaise Book; Exchange Line. This may not have been the sole ledger employed since the records relate only to the years 1817-19 and 1826, the latter year recording fares from the Exchange Line "commenced running April 1st, 1826."

Margaret Nevius Van Dyke in her memoirs casually refers to this stage operation. The days of the stagecoach were then slowly fading. Alluding to her happy childhood, Cousin Margaret said, "After the Camden and Amboy Company bought out the Stage Route from the Gulicks, Bayles and Van Dykes the old stages, some of them for years, were in the wagonhouse and we children played staging and the hens laid their eggs in them, and we, hens and children, had fine times" (Princeton Recollector, January 1979).

In marked contrast to the canal and the railroad which enjoyed powerful monopolies with the state's blessing, the stage lines operated in a free economy. For them it was unbridled capitalism. In true entrepreneurial style every owner-operator sought to convince the public that his transportation service was the most dependable, the fastest, the cheapest and the best. Among advertisements appearing in newspapers we find:

- John Argue of Somerville began running his Coach in 1827 between Somerville and New Brunswick "for the season," and advertised that "as he intends to spare no pains to accommodate them, solicits a continuance of patronage. The Coach will leave Somerville every morning at 9 o'clock and arrive in time for the steam-boat for N. York; returning, will leave Wm. Mann's hotel at 4 P.M. Fare 50 cents. Passengers who may be ready at the time of starting, will be provided with an extra conveyance, should the stage be full. J. A. will keep a light wagon for the conveyance of such of his passengers as may wish to go to any part of the country - to whom charges will be moderate" (SM,April 5, 1827,RUL).

- Wm. Van Derveer and John Edgar doing business as the Old Swift Line announced the running of a "Stage between Centreville & Elizabethtown Point being a continuation of a line through from Philadelphia to New York. Passengers by this line leave New-York by the steam-boat Bellona at 10 o'clock A.M. on Mondays, Wednesdays and Fridays, and Centreville each following day at 4 o'clock A.M. and arrive at N. York at 2 P.M. - passing through Somerville, Boundbrook, Plainfield, Scotch Plains, Westfield etc. They have provided themselves with good horses and carriages; and for way-passengers going to New York this is much the shortest and cheapest route. Fare through from Philadephia to New York, $3.50 - from Somerville to the latter, $1" (SM,February 8, 1827,RUL).

Steamboat passenger service was advertised with equal fanfare and zeal:

- Lewis Carman, president of the New-Brunswick Steam Boat Ferry Company, on March 3, 1825 announced the procurement of a "superb Boat, which is allowed by competent judges to be excelled by none for accommodation, speed, and safety," and providing a new service headlined "The New, Elegant, Fast & Safe Steam-Boat Legislator, Capt. I. Fisher" which "Leaves New-York at 6 o'clock A.M. and New-Brunswick at 2 o'clock P.M. every day (Sunday excepted) for the moderate fare of 12 1/2 cents - Breakfast 37 1/2 cents - Dinner 50 cents," and while previously "it was almost impossible (although boats in abundance) to have a horse or any kind of carriage taken" his company includes the transportation of "Horses, Gigs, and light Carriages taken at reasonable rates for the accommodation of their friends and customers who may wish to visit Long-Island and the Eastern states, with their families, and their own carriages" (SM,March 3, 1825,RUL).

One of cousin Margaret's earliest memories was greeting the passengers in the stagecoaches at noontime: "When about three years old I went to Princeton to go to school ... held in Captain Stockton's house, in a back room ... I must have been between five and six when all the Van Dyke Fathers put their money together and built a school-house on the Straight Turnpike, the old Stage Route, between Abram Anders' farm and Jacob Van Dyke's. They then hired a young woman, Anna Louisa Napton, to teach us, and I studied under her many years. Our noon spell commenced at twelve o'clock. At a quarter before, the twelve stages swept each way past the school House. I always tried to get out to bow to the passengers" (Princeton Recollector, January 1979).

Margaret loved an audience.

Van Dyke Diaries

Diaries survive of two Van Dyke members:[27]

- Mary Dix Strong Van Dyke of New Brunswick wife of John Van Dyke (1807-1878),[28] a great grandson of Jan the Fifth.

- Rachel Van Dyke, of New Brunswick, a daughter of Frederick Van Dyke (1751-1811), and a first cousin of John Schenck Van Dyke.[29]

The family of Judge John Van Dyke moved to Washington, D.C., in 1849 following his election to the House of Representatives. Mary Dix Strong, his wife, much enamored of the Washington social scene was moved to keep a diary commencing November 20, 1849 upon their departure from New Brunswick for Washington. Sketchy entries made during the last eight months of the administration of Zachary Taylor (1784-1850), who died in office in July 1859, consisting primarily of scattered bits of trivia - the purchase of a new hat, attending a tea, Senator Miller who called leaving his card, etc. - are largely unrevealing.

The diary of Rachel Van Dyke, born February 28, 1793, is of a different genre; she offers a vivid portrayal of life in New Brunswick transporting us back to the years 1810 and 1811. Reared in an urban home in a family rich in Dutch heritage and only one generation removed from the land, Rachel, with forthright and uninhibited prose, reveals herself as a charming young lady blessed with every cultural advantage and luxury, yet unspoiled. Her personality is marked by distinctive Dutch qualities - independence, candor, wry humor. Frederick (1751-1811), her father, son of Jan the Fifth (Cook 22) who served in the Revolution and married at twenty-seven, left the Van Dyke homestead at an early age and was one of the first of the Van Dyke family to forsake the land and pursue an occupation in the commercial world. It is said that he "kept a store for some time at Van Dyke's Mills on the Lamington" (tributary of the Raritan) and thereafter removed to New Brunswick where he was a merchant and lived on Albany Street where he died (SCHQ 6:189,190). As a member of the merchant class, he prospered and provided handsomely for his children. Rachel was the youngest of six children of Frederick and Lydia Cole Van Dyke. Her brother, Frederick Augustus (1790-1875), grandson of Jan the Fifth and one of the first of the family to attend college and enter the professions, rose to be a successful and well known physician.[30] At seventeen and eighteen Rachel poured into her "journal" (as she called it) her innermost thoughts and emotions, emerging as a charming and mature young lady with a zest for learning, unusual sensitivity and refreshing candor. Not only does she divulge her true innerself, but additionally conveys a remarkable insight into the life and culture of New Brunswick in these early times. Customarily at the midnight hour in the solitude of her room when the candle was burning low, she took pen in hand to record the day's happenings. And now, the long years have transformed her intimate narrative into a delightful history that is at once warm and moving.

Between five and six o'clock in the morning Rachel arose and by eight o'clock was on her way to a select girls' school within walking distance of her home. One academic subject was Latin taught by a young Yale graduate. Many hours were spent in her room upstairs translating Virgil; and if she had not become enamored of her learned male tutor, a fact she declines to admit but becomes quite apparent, she would not have studied nearly so hard. In addition she mastered the genteel art of sewing, needlework, singing, and playing the piano. Her father's will bequeathed "to my daughters Lydia and Rachel the Forte [piano] heretofore purchased by me for them" (SA). On Sundays she attended church at least once, sometimes twice, a custom that frequently elicited a candid and forthright opinion not only of the content of the sermon but the preacher himself. In short, people, places and things encountered daily were subjects for critical review and frank appraisal, often in the form of a short composition although not so intended. Two such essays abstracted from her journal merit quoting more extensively to preserve their color and poignancy. Their relevancy is obvious.

An epidemic of cholera (possibly typhoid), it will be recalled, invaded the Millstone Valley and the family of Jacob Van Dyke (Sixth Generation) in the spring of 1811 with devastating effect. It was no mere coincidence, as we examine the facts, that Rachel's father died in the spring of the same year, very likely of the same disease. His death occurred not long after April 13, 1811 (date of execution of his will and prior to July 18, the date of probate) wherein he declared "being sick and weak in body". There can be little doubt that water in the family wells was contaminated as a result of a violent storm that ravaged New Brunswick and the entire Jersey countryside in the fall of 1810 causing widespread flooding. In the words of Rachel Van Dyke:

> *November 10, 1810 - Saturday A dark stormy day - I rose quite late. After dinner I set Sylvia [a servant] to work scouring my room - then hunted some carpenter tools and shingles - and climb[ed] up into the little garret above - and worked hammered and tried to stop the water from running down below - but I did not do much good - the rain still beats in and leaks through the ceiling of my room ... Sunday, November 11, 1810 - With all my haste last night it was long after twelve ere I had visited my pillow - When I awoke this morning I saw no signs of clear weather - I could scarcely summon sufficient resolution to rise ... This is a most dreadful storm I don't think I have ever seen its equal - The river has been very high all day and appears to rise higher every hour. Much property has undoubtedly been lost this day - and it is probable much more will be lost this night - Wood railings, apples, pumpkins, potatoes and other such things in abundance have been continually floating down the river. The inhabitants of the houses down town that stand nearest the shore are obliged to forsake the first story for the second - many of their shore house grounds have been destroyed and they fear that even the storehouses will not be able to withstand the fury of this Tempest ... My room leaks in twenty places and with all my pans dishes cups I cannot keep my floor dry - But I scarcely think of this now I tremble for the poor mortals who are now exposed to more important and serious misfortunes - - I have just been downstairs. It is eleven o'clock but the family are yet up - I have been looking out of the door and upper windows - a dreadful prospect presents itself all around - The river is now running before our windows and people are going through the streets in boats - Some moving their goods - some their friends - some their cattle and all doing what they can to prepare for the worst -- How strange it is to hear the waves dashing in the streets - The clock now strikes one - I have been leaning out of my window listening, reflecting, shuddering - It rains incessantly - the wind blows furiously - and the noise of the men, the cries of fowls, horses, pigs the barking of dogs - the water - the boats - all add to the horror of the night - We, I believe are not in much danger without the water rises a great deal higher - But, Oh my God! how many of my fellow mortals may this night breathe their last - If it is so bad here - what - say what must it be on the wide boundless ocean. Oh horrible! horrible! [At this point Rachel laments those who may have perished at sea] ... I have been down stairs again - The water has risen higher still - It is*

like a river 4 or 5 houses above us - Assistance has been offered to us - but as yet we do not need it - The water can only do injury to the cellars of our house - Our first stories are so much higher than our neighbors ... I have already heard that several lives have been lost at the Landing many houses carried away - - and all of them in great danger - Oh Great Creator of all be merciful unto us - Tho' we are sinners deserving thy wrath - Thou art a present help in time of need - In thee I always put my trust--It is past three o'clock - I have been half sick all day - but now feel worse still. I don't want to go to bed - there is no use in it ... Monday, November 12, 1810 - I rose this morning at nine o'clock with heavy eyes and an aching head ... The streets were still filled with water as much as four houses above us - and in the street facing us entirely down to the Market house. Instead of carriages - boats were passing our windows trees - boards - rails - masts - and much heavy lumber laid around - and the people from other parts of town came flocking together to view the sight - About one o'clock the river began to fall and now again the pavements are bare ... I am almost stupid for want of sleep It is now twelve o'clock and I think I had better go where all in the house now are - - I could work a great deal tonight but Oh Mercy I am so sleepy - I can scacely keep my eyes open - I have not learnt any Latin these four days.

In a much lighter vein but with no less sensitivity, Rachel recounts a week's sojourn with her uncle and aunt in New York. There was but one transportation medium between New Brunswick and Manhattan Island, namely the sailing ship. Depending upon the weather, the wind and the tide, it was a voyage of four to five hours to reach the southern tip of Manhattan. Added to these uncertainties was another unpredictable factor: the Captain's decision whether to sail at all, doubtless related to the number of passengers aboard his ship, as Rachel would soon learn. Small wonder, then, that the traveler faced by these obstacles might succumb to frustration, as Rachel's journal demonstrates.

With sparkling humor, Rachel provides a rare glimpse from real life experience. Early in the morning of Wednesday, March 20, 1811, before breakfast while sitting in the parlor reading by the window, she saw approaching the front door her Uncle Tallman. His home was on Broadway directly opposite Bowling Green[31] in New York. Said Rachel, "Almost the first words Uncle said to me, were 'Come you must get ready to return home with me' I should like very well to accept his invitation for it is more than two years since I have been at New York - He has again told me that he shall go on Friday - and says that he has orders both from Aunt and Maria to bring me along with him - Mama has no objections". It was arranged that her brother Augustus would accompany her to New York and she would return home with him.

And so Rachel packed her trunk fully prepared to leave for New York on Friday morning. Yet she entertained some misgiving: "The wind blows, the sky is darkened by thick clouds, and there is every appearance of an approaching storm - It is my opinion that my Ladyship will not be able to leave Brunswick tomorrow". Early Friday morning her trunk was taken to the dock by a servant. "After walking more than a mile, and having arrived at the new dock, we found that the tide was then at the highest, but the boat was not half loaded and therefore would not go in some hours. We were all vexed then, and still more so when after sitting in a smokey cabin for more than an hour, the Captain declared that he would wait for the evening tide ... Uncle and I packed away our things and we all marched home", calling forth this soliloquy: "Surely there is nothing more disagreeable, vexatious, and teazing than to be ready, expecting every hour to set off on a journey, and then at last after passing the day in suspense to be disappointed and obliged to wait till the next day. The next day perhaps you may go; of if you don't you may pass it in the same delectable manner in which you did the former". A few hours later, she continued in her journal, "The Captain came this afternoon, and told us he had concluded (bless his conclusions, I wish he would make one final conclusion) it would be better to wait till morning, and he would then sail at seven o'clock".

Awake before six on Saturday, Rachel "rejoiced to hear that the wind blew fair, and to behold the brightness of the morning sun". Finally aboard the boat basking in the sun's warmth and savoring the cool morning breezes as they sailed smoothly down the Raritan to New York - all vexations now behind her - she seized the opportunity to record a few observations: "We are now six miles from New Brunswick, and are still going very rapidly - There is but one woman on board besides Eliza [a servant] and myself - and a number of men, but none of a very genteel appearance - It is a delightful day - the air is not very cold, the banks look so green and beautiful, and the birds are singing on either side"

A pleasant week was spent in New York with Uncle and Aunt Tallman seeing friends, promenading on Broadway, visiting museums, churches and bookstores. However, this is another episode which we shall pass. The return voyage is typical of the discomfort borne by the traveler in inclement weather here tersely recounted by Rachel with a tinge of irony: "We had a very quick, rough, disagreeable passage. For the first hour I was very sick but soon recovered, when Augustus took me out in the air - After tossing in the wind [and] rain, four hours, we arrived in Brunswick - We dined in New York and drank tea at Brunswick - very expeditious traveling."

Thank you, Rachel.

A Country Squire

Rachel Van Dyke and John Schenck Van Dyke, eight years younger, were grandchildren of Jan the Fifth and first cousins. Both possessed substantial wealth. But beyond this their lives were world's apart. Rachel ultimately settled in New York, married an Englishman, and, we may reasonably assume, found a niche in the New York aristocracy (SCHQ 6:190).

John Schenck was acquainted with aristocrats, too, although seen by him in a somewhat different light. In his eyes wealth and social status were irrelevant. Sitting in the legislative councils of Mercer County, he exchanged pleasantries with distinguished colleagues, men in the learned professions and business. As the record shows, he was an advocate of public schools for all children, rich and poor alike, at a time when education was the exclusive domain of the well-to-do who could afford to pay a teacher or tutor to instruct their children. In the village square he was warmly greeted as "Judge" by people in all walks of life, the common folk with whom he had a special rapport.

However, it was in the solitude of a his home on several hundred acres in rural surroundings where John Schenck found what he most longed for, serenity and peace of mind. Compelling testimony springs from an extensive inventory of personalty[32] gracing a sixteen room house of which the following is representative:

- In the "Parlor":[33] a sofa, 9 fancy back rush bottomedichairs, carpet on the floor, fire rug, 1 foot stool, 4 venetian blinds, 1 looking glass, 1 pair glass lamps, 5 candlesticks, 1 card table, 1 breakfast table and cover, 1 work stand, contents of closet on south side, lot of books, andirons, shovel and tongs, snuffers and tray.

- In the "Front Bedroom": bed, bedstead and bedding, 1/2 dozen rush bottomed fancy backed chairs, carpet on the floor, 4 pictures, 2 dressing glasses, 1 wash stand with pitcher and basin, lot of white curtains, 6 sheets, roll of linen, 1 white counterpane, 1 set bed curtains, 1 double coverlet, 6 silver tablespoons, 8 silver tea spoons.

- In the "Sitting Room": dining table and cover, tea table and cover, workstand, writing desk (portable), 6 rush bottomed chairs, carpet on the floor, looking glass and pictures, 1 pair brass andirons and bellows, contents of large closet, contents of small closet, lot of books.

- In the "Bar Room": an eight-day clock, looking glass and pictures, 2 driving whips, candlestand, sideboard and contents, demijohns and carpet.

The principal focus of the court appraisers was, of course, monetary evaluation. Hence precious books, records and documents were relegated to vague catagories designated "contents", "lot" (number of things), "residue", concealing the facts we would like to know. Clearly his home was his castle, a retreat from the outside world of government and politics. While he enjoyed good fellowship, he savored even more the tranquility permeating his home. The socalled "lot of books" in two rooms, "workstands", "writing desk", and "contents of office" plainly evidence hours of pleasure derived from reading, writing and contemplation. Analyzing all the evidence, John Schenck emerges as a quiet, introspective man.

Hunting and fishing may be counted among his hobbies. In the "Mens Room" he kept a double barreled shot gun, a single barreled gun, two game bags, powder horns and shot bags. In the "shop" were steel traps, fish nets, a crab net, grindstone, chest of tools, work bench and similar items. A tour of the storage areas and outbuildings bespeaks a passion for the land: the products of the soil, farm animals and all living things. The "North Cellar" contained apples, potatoes and turnips. The "Store House" held two barrels of cider, a barrel of vinegar, a lot of whiskey, a lot of scales, weights and funnels,

A true and perfect inventory of all and singular the goods and chattles rights and credits of John S Vandyke late of the township of West-Windsor in the County of Mercer and State of New Jersey deceased that came to our hands for appraisment Dated December 16th 1852 —

	Apparel		$ 20 00
	Purse		133.11½
	Gold Watch		4 00
	Parlor		
	Sofa	4 00	
9	Fancy back rush bottomed chairs	5 00	
	Carpet on the floor	5 00	
	Fire rug	75	
	Foot-stool	50	
4	Venitian blinds	4 00	
1	Looking glass	3 00	
1	pair glass lamps	40	
5	Candlesticks	60	
1	Card table	2 50	
1	Breakfast table and cover	3 00	
1	Work stand	2 00	
	Contents of closet on South side	1 00	
	Lot of Books	50	
	Andirons shovel and tongs, snuffers & tray	1 25	33 50
	Amt Carried forwd		$ 190 61½

Manuscript copy (three of fourteen pages) of the Inventory of the Estate of John S. Van Dyke (1801-1852) deceased.

Courtesy New Jersey Archives

Garret

	The one equal undivided half part of		
9	Silver table spoons		
1	do Sugar tongs		
1	do tea pot		
1	do Soup ladle		
1	do Butter Knife		
1	pr do plated Candlesticks	15 50	
	Residue in the Garret	75	16 25
	Bar room		
1	Eight day Clock	1 00	
	Looking glass and pictures	2 00	
2	Driving whips	75	
	Candle stand	1 25	
	Sideboard and Contents	7 00	12 75
	Demijohns and Carpet	75	
	Sitting room		
	Dining table and cover	4 00	
	Tea do	2 00	
	Workstand	1 00	
	Writing desk (portable)	75	
6	Rush bottomed chairs	2 50	
	Carpet on the floor	2 25	
	Looking glass and pictures	1 75	
1	Pair brass andirons and bellows	50	
	Contents of large closet	3 00	17 75
	Amt carried forwd		~~$ 281 36½~~
			$ 294 21½

13

	I V D Joline's bond dated Oct 1st 1847 payable Oct 1st 1851	250 00	
	Interest	78 10	328 10
	I V D Joline's bond dated Oct 1st 1847 payable Oct 1st 1852	250 00	
	Interest	78 10	328 10
	I V D Joline's bond dated Oct 1st 1847 payable Oct 1st 1853	250 00	
	Interest	78 10	328 10
	Jno W Barklow's bond dated Apl 1st 1850 Due on principal	200 00	
	Interest	8 50	208 50
	Bond D & R Canal & C & A R R Co	120 00	
	Interest	10 50	130 50
	Jas H Jones Com bills		99 32
32	Shares Princeton Bank Stock with dividend due		732 80
5	do Delaware & Raritan Canal stock (Hypothecated to I N Woodhull)		700 00
	Note Doubtful		
	C H Burroughs agt Note dated Feb 21st 1848 payable one day after date	7 00	
	Interest	2 03	9 03
			~~$ 4608 50½~~
			$ 5088 98

Appraised by us

D K Schenck
James H Everett

and a large chest of salt. In addition there were other buildings including a "Milk Cellar", a "Hot House", a "Steam House" and an "Ash House" (for making soap) equipped for their special functions.

Of necessity there was a "Wagon House" with "three wagons": a farm wagon, a large top wagon, and a small top wagon. And a "Stable" with three horses, a brown bull, three cows, plus large quantities of hay, straw, corn, oats, wheat and buckwheat to bed and feed them. Farming, we conclude, was a cherished avocation for his personal enjoyment. He carried a gold watch valued at four dollars. In his purse was $133.11 1/2.

He was a country squire.

Demise

On April 13, 1846 John Schenck was elected a chosen freeholder for the tenth and last time. He continued, however, to serve as the township clerk through 1847 and for a brief period the following year. On April 29, 1848, shortly after his election, he attended a township committee meeting for the last time (WWTM). And so after twenty-two years his clerkship duties abruptly ended. His health was failing. He could no longer carry on.

He died at his home on December 3, 1852 after a long illness. The Daily True American, a Trenton newspaper, on Monday, December 6, 1852, published the following notice:

> *Judge John S. Van Dyke, a well known citizen of Princeton died on Friday night in the 52nd year of his age. He had been suffering from ill health for a long time.*

He once said to his son, "William, I am leaving you well provided for" (PVDH).

The court record shows an intestacy and a renunciation by the widow of her right to administer the estate[34] in favor of John Schenck's brother, Jacob, whom the court appointed administrator.[35] A will was never found.

EIGHTH GENERATION

Genealogical Note

WILLIAM VAN DYKE
B April 8, 1822
D May 26, 1877
M May 25, 1848

WILLIAM VAN DYKE, the only son and lineal heir of John Schenck Van Dyke, was born April 8, 1822 in Rocky Hill, Somerset County (VDFB/Author,VS/NJ).

William was the great, great, great, great grandson of the pioneer settler Jan Thomasse Van Dyke who struggled to survive in an environment firmly linked to agriculture. Now - two centuries later - budding industries spurred by remarkable inventions were making sweeping changes in the economy. Dependency on the land was one step removed. Doors opened to other occupations for those who aspired to lead a simpler life. While aware of the transition offering a more comfortable lifestyle, William did not choose to follow that course.

Early Years

Reared in the home of a loving and caring father, William received everything that a growing boy could wish for. Nor was his formal education lightly passed over or neglected. His father, active in promoting public schools in the Township of West Windsor, would have been seriously concerned about his son's education. An obituary characterizes William as a "man of considerable reading and intelligence".[1]

It is sometimes said that boys are prone to accident. And so it seems with William. In his youth he sustained a bone fracture that was negligently treated, a classic case of malpractice by a doctor who, even in that time, should have possessed greater medical skill. Said Aunt Pearl, "Do you know why grandfather didn't serve in the Civil War?[2] It seems he broke his upper arm when a boy and the doctor set it backward - the elbow on the inside so that it was difficult for him to raise his hand to his head" (PVDH).

The Jewell Family

In addition to strong atavistic elements implicit in his Dutch ancestry, William's marriage into the Jewell family may have influenced his decision to remain on the land.

William Jewell (1727-1784), son of Richard Jewell (1703-1757), was born near Dutch Neck, then in Middlesex County, and purchased large tracts in West Windsor Township. He was the progenitor of one of the most prominent families in the area (Lee 609). His sons and grandsons, prosperous farmers and landholders, held offices in the township government. In part, his son, William Dey Jewell (1765-1839), was an overseer of the highways for three years (1801-1804), a constable for eighteen years (1798,1804-1820), and later a moderator and judge of elections for four years (1827-1831); and his grandson, Elisha Jewell (1800-1873, son of William Dey Jewell) was a member of the township committee for ten years (1838-1847) (WWTM).

John Schenck Van Dyke and Elisha Jewell were friends and neighbors residing on adjoining tracts. Serving together as township officials for many years, they shared common interests. On January 26, 1827 the first child of Elisha and his wife, Mary Mount, was born, a daughter whom they named Elizabeth Ann. In this setting there was ample opportunity for William to meet Elizabeth Ann.

It was love at first sight. "Grandmother was very pretty", said Aunt Pearl who had visited her many times. "She showed me a daguerreotype of herself which I would have loved to have ... Grandmother was the oldest of thirteen children and she told me that when Grandfather came a-courting, she was tending one baby on her knee and another in the cradle so she decided she would marry grandfather and have her own children." Plainly tongue-in-cheek! Elizabeth Ann Jewell entertained a much better reason, as the facts prove, for marrying Grandfather. It would have been a delight to meet this charming and vivacious lady. Aunt Pearl, born in 1890, was seventeen when her grandmother died in 1907 and she harbored fond memories of her.

Marriage and Children

William Van Dyke and Elizabeth Ann Jewell were married on May 25, 1848[3] significantly enhancing the ties of friendship between the Van Dyke and Jewell families. The marriage, presumably taking place on the Jewell farm, was attended by the officiating minister, the Rev. D. D. Gray, and the parents of the bridal couple joined by members and friends of the respective families.[4] At that time it was the custom to hold the wedding ceremony and festivities at the home of the bride's parents, as was the case years later upon the marriage of William's daughters, Alice and Mary.

Five children were born of the marriage:

Alice	B December 17, 1848, D January 10,1912 M October 18, 1871, Voorhees Stryker, infra
Mary	B March 16, 1850, D September 8, 1919 M October 18, 1871, Luther C. Van Zandt, infra
Frank	B December 11, 1851, D July 30, 1895 M July 4, 1875, Emma Cox, infra
Charles	B December 27, 1853, D January 6, 1854
John Schenck	B May 23, 1857, D August 8, 1906 M ca 1881, Anna Reed, D June 21, 1947 (NINTH GENERATION)
	(VDFB/Author)

A Nation in Crisis

William lived through an era of extraordinary political and social unrest. He witnessed a nation in crisis.

In September of 1850 California was admitted as the thirty-first state. It was still a young nation, less than a century old. The North and South were split over one overriding issue: slavery. A civil war was on the horizon. "These are the times that try men's souls" - monumental words of Thomas Paine (1737-1809) - were as relevant then as they were when penned in 1775 by the Revolutionary pamphleteer. Congress could do nothing save engage in verbal combat and effect political compromises as new states - slave and nonslave - were admitted into the union. Only one man on the national scene came face to face with the facts. "A house divided against itself cannot stand", said Abraham Lincoln quoting Scripture (Mark 3:25): "I believe this government cannot endure permanently, half slave and half free ... it will become all one thing or all the other." These were the opening words of Lincoln's "House Divided Speech" delivered before the Republican State Convention in Springfield, Illinois, on June 16, 1858. His Republican friends and supporters strongly counseled against it; too radical, politically unwise. Lincoln saw no reason to change it. He hated slavery to the marrow of his bones. The famous "House Divided Speech" was published in full in the daily and weekly newspapers throughout the country which served to make Lincoln nationally known. We may assume that William read all or part of it and certainly concurred in its message. Neither he nor his father owned slaves. In fact, early in the nineteenth century the majority of people in Somerset, as well as in other counties, opposed "human thralldom", as they called it, and began to manumit their slaves aided by legislation enacted for the purpose.

Yet now, at mid-century, the nation was being torn asunder, steadily driven toward a bloody conflict over one festering moral issue that the peoples' representatives - and their Constitutional Fathers before them - had struggled to resolve and failed. Why must this come to pass? Is there no other solution? These were some of the thoughts that entered the mind of William and Elizabeth Ann. There is no doubt how William voted in the national election of November 1860.

Happy Farmer

When the decennial census was taken in West Windsor Township, Mercer County, requesting the name, age and occupation of the inhabitants, William responded that he was a "farmer" (Federal Census 1850,1860,1870). To this terse characterization should be added that he was a farmer in the true spirit of his Dutch forefathers who cleared the land and made it productive. A member of the Mercer County Grangers, William was wedded to the soil.[5]

In the fields surrounding his home in June 1877 were crops in various stages of growth: Four acres of wheat, five acres of rye, seven acres of corn near the house, nine acres of rye in new ground, 840 potato hills, one acre of potatoes, lot of grass along the road, lot of grass by the house, sixteen acres of oats, half a lot of Hungarian grass, twenty-two acres of corn, ten acres of oats, two acres of wheat, seven acres of rye, as more fully set forth in his estate inventory.[6] Lush fields of grain carefully managed were a source of pride as well as the primary support of the family. In July 1870, the Van Dyke household consisted of William, age forty-eight, his wife Elizabeth, forty-five, their oldest son Frank, eighteen, designated a "farm agent", two daughters, Alice and Mary, twenty-one and nineteen respectively, and John Schenck, thirteen, "attending school"; also a female servant, Martha Plant, born in England, and a male laborer, Charles Mitchell, born in New Jersey (Federal Census July 11, 1870).

Other hired hands were employed to assist the laborers on the premises, particularly at planting and harvest time. The growing season, as every farmer well knew, made critical demands depending upon temperature and rainfall; sometimes grossly excessive precipitation and at other times a dismal drought. Patience was called upon as well as hard work. A bountiful harvest responsible for their wealth was the reward of countless hours of toil from dawn to dusk, plus good soil management and animal husbandry; and also a measure of Dutch frugality born of pride - a deep inner pride. Adrian C. Leiby, referring to the simple houses and spacious barns of the Dutch farmers, aptly summarizes it: "Dutch self-denial, as much as hard work, was responsible for their wealth. Too proud to complain of an empty purse, they were not too proud to do the things that kept their purses full" (Leiby 111).

William's home and furnishings appear quite modest, solely in keeping with the character of the Dutch farmer. Every room was carpeted. The dining room contained six Windsor chairs, a freezer, extension table, andirons for the fireplace, lamps and shades, one clock and two arm chairs. In the sitting room was a settee and cushion, a stove, books, and looking glass. The family slept in goosefeather beds. Compared to the handsomely appointed rooms in the home of his late father, William's home was unadorned, if not a bit humble; still it was comfortable and served the family purpose. They could live happily without white counterpanes, window curtains and venetian blinds.

The barns and outbuildings were large and spacious, several times the size of the dwelling house. Ample space was needed to provide shelter for the farm animals including the horses, mules, cows and hogs, and fodder and hay to feed and bed them; to store the large volume of grain at harvest time and seed for the next planting; and, lastly, to hold the extensive array of farm equipment: wagons, a carry-all wagon, a broad-tread wagon and a narrow-tread wagon, lumber, bar posts, shovels, forks, knives, two cradles, bench tools, axes, hedge shears, buck scythe, crosscut and buck saws, grindstone, hoes, plows, picks, harrows, two furrowing sleds, windmill, mowing machine, reaping machine, carriage, sleigh, two sets of double harness, Rigg's plow, in addition to sundry other articles in the Wagon House and Store House. Every item of farm equipment had its own story to tell. Viewed dispassionately, they mirror the myriad activities taking place on the Van Dyke acres at Penns Neck in the last century.[6]

Proud Father

Tilling the soil and harvesting the grain was a labor of love exceeded only by the love for his family. The evidence points to a warm and tender marriage. Devoted husband and proud father, William was a happy man.

On an October afternoon in 1871, a double wedding ceremony took place on the Penns Neck farm for daughters, Alice and Mary. "Grandfather [William] gave each a outset costing $1,000.00" (PVDH). The wedding invitation reads:

Mr. & Mrs. Wm Van Dyke
Request the pleasure of your company at the
Marriage Ceremony of their Daughters

Alice	Mary
to	to
V. D. Stryker	L. C. Van Zandt

Wednesday Afternoon, October 18th, 1871
At 1 o'clock
Penns Neck, N. J.

When his son Frank was married[7] "Grandfather said 'Shaw, $1,000.00 isn't much for a boy' and gave him $1500.00" (PVDH). If he had lived to see the marriage of his son John Schenck, he would have been equally generous.

William never sought to be the township clerk and fill the void left by his late father. If so invited, he would have politely declined. A few months after his father's death, however, he agreed to serve on the township committee. The minutes of the annual meeting of April 6, 1853 held at the home of William K. Holmes in Assanpink discloses that he was elected to this office which he held for four years (1853-1857). In later life at a township meeting on March 11, 1873, he was elected a Commissioner of Appeals, a committee of three members (WWTM). Unlike his father, government and politics were not his forte.

Untimely Death

In March 1877 Rutherford B. Hayes (1822-1893), a Civil War general, took the oath of office as the nineteenth president of the United States. The outgoing president was the renowned Civil War hero, Ulysses S. Grant (1822-1885), dubbed "Unconditional Surrender Grant". When piloried by his enemies for insobriety, President Lincoln said, "I can't spare that man - he's a fighter."

The following month, on April 8, William Van Dyke, in apparent good health, celebrated his fifty-fifth birthday. Seven weeks later, on May 26, death struck suddenly and without warning. "I do know the cause of Grandfather's death", said Aunt Pearl in response to the author's query. "He was a heavy-set man, taking after the Bakers and was out on the farm when one of his colts got out of the pasture. He chased the colt and after catching it, went up to the house and sat down on a bench in the outside shed and leaned over with his head in his hands. My father[8] sat down on the bench and put his arm around his father - then Grandfather fell over on Father and they both fell to the floor. When picked up Grandfather was dead from a brain hemorrhage" (PVDH).

His son John Schenck was the only witness. Elizabeth Ann was doubtless engaged in household duties and unaware of what had happened in that brief tragic moment. Her grief, understandably, was overwhelming. In a letter to friends, John Schenck conveyed the family's deep sorrow: "I take upon myself the painful duty of writing to inform you of the serious loss which has befeld us, our beloved Father has been taken without a moments warning away, and we can but trust in a 'Higher Power' for consolation in these hours of deep distress. He attended as usual to his duties at home until six o'clock when he died in an instant. The funeral will be on Tuesday at 2 o'clock at the house to which you are respectfully invited".[9] Dr. McCorkle of the Second Presbyterian Church of Princeton and the Rev. L. O. Grenelle of the Princeton Baptist Church officiated.

Following the funeral service attended by family members and friends, a long funeral cortege of carriages solemnly proceeded from the Van Dyke farm in Penns Neck to the Princeton Cemetery about a mile away. "Grandfather was well liked in the community," said Aunt Pearl, "and neighbors came from miles around to his funeral - there were fifty carriages in his funeral procession" (PVDH). Standing at the graveside for the final prayers and benediction with her children by her side was the grief-stricken widow.

Elizabeth Ann Jewell was fifty. She never remarried.

Elizabeth Ann Jewell Van Dyke

William never expected his life to be cut short in his fifties and had not made a will. Accordingly, the intestate laws dictated that his personal estate be advertised for sale in order to make distribution. It is probable, however, that a public sale was averted by a family settlement or similar arrangement.

The Van Dyke acres remained a working farm and the home of Grandmother Elizabeth Ann. In June of 1880, we find her residing there with her son John Schenck, twenty-three, in the capacity of farm manager, her daughter, Alice Stryker, thirty-one, with her two minor children, a "servant" and "farm laborer" (Federal Census 1880). The daughter of a wealthy family living on productive land, her life was reasonably comfortable although very lonely. Her father died in January of 1873 leaving an estate of substantial worth.[10] In January 1875, she received $5,825.03 in final distribution (HSP).

At length the time came when Elizabeth Ann could no longer supervise a large farm operation. The problem was enhanced when her son John Schenck married and departed, the story recounted in the Ninth Generation. In consequence she was faced with a compelling decision: sell the Penns Neck farm.

Leaving forever the marital home in the beautiful New Jersey countryside was difficult; indeed heartrending. She moved to nearby Princeton where she spent her remaining years. The quaint college town with its attractive tree-lined streets evidently held a certain appeal; the locale was tranquil and not far from the open land she knew and loved. Prominent among her treasured memories were the fertile fields and green pastures bathed in the warm sunshine and the intimacy of the family homestead surrounded by her children.

Grandmother Elizabeth dearly loved her children and grandchildren. Once again cruel fate intervened. Only a mother understands the mental stress and torment. Both of her sons died prematurely: Frank in 1895[11] and John Schenck in 1906,[12] a profound shock. She died at her home 112 Mercer Street in Princeton on April 3, 1907 (VS/NJ), eight months after the death of John Schenck.

"Grandmother was very proud of her thirteen grandchildren of which I was the youngest," said Aunt Pearl. "She left me a legacy of $100.00 which is the only money I ever received which I didn't work for" (PVDH). Her will bequeathed:[13]

- $100.00 each to May Van Dyke and Grace Van Dyke (daughters of Frank) and Pearl Van Dyke (daughter of John Schenck).

- $50.00 each to William Van Dyke and Raymond Van Dyke (sons of Frank) and Carl Van Dyke and Jewell Van Dyke (sons of John Schenck).

- The "old hall clock" to Alice Stryker, daughter.

- The "old side board made by my father's brother" to Mary Van Zandt, daughter.

- "Beds and bedding and my wearing apparel" to be divided between daughters Alice Stryker and Mary Van Zandt.

- Residue to daughters in equal shares.

112 Mercer Street

Grandmother Elizabeth's home in Princeton claims a place in history and merits comment. In contrast to the customary historic structure plainly identified explaining its association with a prominent person or great event, one does not find at 112 Mercer Street a sign or plaque. Tourists receive no handouts. The reason is clear when we examine the facts.

A deed of conveyance to Elizabeth Ann Van Dyke dated February 1, 1896 for a consideration of $2500 describes a property 50 feet wide on Mercer Street, Princeton, extending in depth 448 feet, 6 inches.[14] On this site stands today - just as it did in Grandmother's day - a two story, white wood-frame house with clapboard siding and shutters accenting the windows, Victorian in style and unpretentious. Four square columns topped with ornamentation support a porch roof. A small lawn and privet hedge separate the house from a pedestrian walk in front. Four steps lead to the porch and front door. The number "112" appears to the left of the doorway above a mailbox. This is where Pearl Van Dyke visited her paternal grandmother and from whose lips she learned many things about the Van Dyke family.

At the turn of the century there was living in Zurich, Switzerland, a young German scientist who was applying for Swiss citizenship. A graduate of Zurich Polytechnic Institute, he was looking for a job at university level and could find none. He was so depressed that his father, deeply concerned, wrote a solicitous letter on his son's behalf to help him find employment. Again without success. He had alienated most of his professors. One professor rebuked him saying, "You won't let anyone tell you a thing". At the age of fifteen he was a school dropout. He strongly rebelled against rote learning in general, and Latin and Greek in particular. A teacher of Greek predicted that he would never amount to anything and chided him, "your mere presence spoils the respect of the class for me". He was a loner and a dreamer; a child who disliked games, sports and military parades. As a young boy of four or five ill in bed, his father gave him a magnetic compass which instantly thrilled him. Why did the needle, totally enclosed, always point to the north? Years later he wrote, "I can still remember - or at least I believe I can remember - that this experience made a deep and abiding impression on me".

This passionately curious young man - if not readily apparent - was Albert Einstein (1879-1955). Tragic events in Nazi Germany forced Einstein to flee the country. We find him in October 1933 living in Princeton, celebrated, honored and revered throughout the world; for by then the theory of relativity revolutionizing Newtonian physics was no longer the subject of bitter criticism and ridicule, the vocal critics having fallen by the wayside as experimental findings confirmed the humble scientist's conclusions. On July 24, 1935 the two story white, wood-frame house at 112 Mercer Street became the home of Albert Einstein.[15] Here he resided simply and quietly, shunning publicity, until his death on April 18, 1955. Here he continued his work in theoretical physics and received notable public figures including Prime Minister Nehru of India, Bertrand Russell, William Faulkner and Marion Anderson.

Grandmother's second floor rear bedroom was converted into a study. A large picture window was installed so that Einstein could look out upon the flowers and trees as he contemplated problems in physics or in lighter moments

PUBLIC SALE

OF

PERSONAL PROPERTY

The Subscriber, Administrator of William Van Dyke, deceased, will sell at Public Vendue,

ON TUESDAY, JUNE 26, 1877

At the late residence of said deceased, in West Windsor, on the Trenton and New Brunswick Turnpike, between Penns Neck and Clarkesville, the

PERSONAL PROPERTY

of said deceased, consisting of Horses, Mules, Cows, Hogs, Fowls, Wagons, Sleigh, Mowing Machine and Reaping Machine, Plows, Harrows, Hoes, Spades, Shovels, Harness, Roller, Sled, and a variety of other Farming Utensils; also, growing Wheat, Rye, Corn, Oats and Grass, 9 Hives and Bees, together with a variety of

Household Goods & Furniture

Such as Beds, Tables, Chairs, Carpets, Stoves and Dairy Fixtures, with a number of other articles too tedious to mention.

Sale to commence at 10 o'clock A. M. on said day, when attendance will be given and conditions made known by

JAMES B. COLEMAN,

Dated June 9, 1877. **ADMINISTRATOR.**

Copy of a broadside advertising personalty of William Van Dyke (1822-1877) who died intestate. The original measures 12 X 18.5 inches. It is unlikely that the public sale took place.

Albert Einstein found peace and seclusion in this unpretentious Victorian home - 112 Mercer Street in Princeton - in his last twenty years. Earlier, in 1896, Elizabeth Ann Jewell Van Dyke bought the property and lived there until her death in 1907. The purchase price was $2500. It could not be bought at any price today.

These monuments crafted of metal mark that graves of William Van Dyke and his wife in the Princeton Cemetery. Elizabeth Ann Jewell by her will specifically directed the purchase of a "headstone similar to the one I erected over my husband's grave".

Photographs 1989

read letters, a large number from children asking interesting questions and moving him to reply .

Einstein's devoted wife Elsa died at 112 Mercer Street after a painful illness. His stepdaughter Margot lived there until her death in 1986 when, in accordance with the provisions of his will, the property descended to the primary beneficiary, the Institute of Advanced Study. It will remain, as Einstein wished, a private residence for its scholars.

Only after great difficulty did Grandmother's attorney and executor succeed in selling 112 Mercer Street after her death for $4,000 more than a year later. A full account is contained in the court documents.[16]

Final Resting Place

The opening paragraph of Elizabeth Ann Jewell's will provides: "My will is and I do hereby direct that all of my just debts and funeral expenses, including a headstone similar to the one I erected over my husband's grave, be paid by my executor..." (MCSC).

Identical monuments mark their graves, side by side, in the Princeton Cemetery symbolizing a marriage nurtured by love and devotion.

The inscriptions read:

ELIZABETH
ANN
JEWELL,
WIFE OF
WILLIAM
VAN DYKE,
BORN JAN 26, 1827,
DIED APRIL 3, 1907.

WILLIAM
VAN DYKE,
DIED
MAY 26, 1877,
AGED
55 Y'RS 1 MO.,
16 DAYS.

NINTH GENERATION

Genealogical Note

JOHN SCHENCK VAN DYKE
B May 23, 1857
D August 8, 1906
M 1880/81

JOHN SCHENCK VAN DYKE, the fifth and last born child of William Van Dyke (1822-1877) and Elizabeth Ann Jewell (1827-1907), his wife, was born on May 23, 1857 at Penns Neck, West Windsor Township, Mercer County. He was the author's grandfather. Given the name of his grandfather was appropriate for, as it developed, he mirrored much of his character.

John Schenck was innately curious, an attribute exhibited as a boy growing up on the Penns Neck farm. An inquiring mind was constantly asking questions and seeking answers. His zest for knowledge explains a lifelong habit of saving papers of all kinds - personal notes, letters, newspaper clippings, boyhood compositions - sufficient material for a definitive biography. Imbued with optimism and the perception of unlimited opportunity in a wide wonderful world, John Schenck rang down the curtain on the Dutch farm tradition.

Early Years

Examples of medical ignorance have been seen previously. By the mid-nineteenth century very little had changed. In large measure the practice of medicine still resembled the fads and quackery of the Middle Ages.

Grandfather John Schenck was fortunate to survive infancy. The fact that his life was spared was due to the loving care and determination of his mother rather that the expertise of the family physician. Said Aunt Pearl: "Uncle Charles died when ten days old, and my father was also sickly when born and the doctor told Grandmother that she wouldn't raise him but she made up her mind that she would and she kept him alive by feeding him whiskey."

His formal education was in the public schools of West Windsor Township. It will be recalled that his grandfather, following his election as township clerk, played an important role in inaugurating the first public schools in West Windsor Township. Soon these schools were called "grammar schools". The name was appropriate because reading, writing and grammar were emphasized and taken very seriously. Letter writing and compositions constituted a significant part of the course in English. John Schenck neatly copied in ink in a large bound notebook a number of his class assignments demonstrating that he, also, took the study of English seriously. "My Dear Teacher," he wrote on April 28, 1868 at nearly eleven, "This is the first letter I ever tried to write plese excuse all mistakes and improper spelling I do not think it will be long for I hardly know what to say as I see you everyday ... Good night Dear Teacher."

In another dear-teacher letter the following month he wrote, "I now sit down to write you a few lines this afternoon. Mother and sister have gone to Trenton they started this morning. I hope Mother will bring me home something ... We are planting corn this afternoon, but we have a field too wet. Papa thinks we can Friday if it does not rain. Sister Alice has got the flower seeds planted she did not plant them very early on account of the wet weather I remain your true friend." A subsequent effort is more effusive. "Beloved Teacher," it begins. Then declaims, "What a beautiful morning it is ... Papa and Mother have just gone to the Square to take a cousin of ours home - she went to the Commencement with us; she was very much pleased with the speaking. I had such a good time. Papa went to the Museum with me; he told me a great deal about the birds, snakes; and other things that we saw, that I never knew before, it was quite interesting. I cannot write you a very long letter this morning. I must learn my lessons." Humbly closing, "From your obedient scholar, John S. Van Dyke."

Examining compositions written for the teacher the following year, we find such prosaic titles as "Summer", "Farming" and "The Horse". "Summer is the warmest season of the year", wrote the obedient scholar. And continued, "It is then that all the fruit gets ripe. Such as apples, peaches, pears and cherries and many other kinds, and the farmers are so busy cutting and gathering their grain and laying up their store for Winter ... we can go out in the orchards and see the trees loaded with the fruit and the limbs almost ready to break down." The same enthusiasm permeates the farm boy's description of a horse depicted as "a very useful animal ... Some are very wild while others are very kind and gentle. This noble animal is useful to man for plowing and a good deal of other hard work he should be treated with kindness and should not be ill used."

The End of an Era

At this point the record indicates that John Schenck was destined to follow in his father's footsteps continuing the Dutch farm lifestyle spanning seven generations of the Van Dyke family in America. For five generations of the family in New Jersey the Dutch culture flourished reaching back to Jan the Fourth (1682-1764) who left Long Island to settle in the Millstone Valley. It thus appears that John Schenck of the Ninth Generation would raise his family on his father's fertile acres deriving pleasure from the things touched upon in his boyhood essays.

But it was not to be.

As he matured and grew to manhood, other forces came to bear. He discovered newspapers, magazines and books. Reading awakened his interest in subjects not taught at school. Another significant factor was the premature death of his father at only fifty-five years of age. Sitting on a bench with his arm around his father, he witnessed his death "in an instant", as he said, whereupon management of the farm was thrust upon him, literally overnight. While he assumed the responsibility, it was a traumatic and unnatural transition. Paternal guidance was gone and in its place, dread emptiness. At this time he needed his father's companionship and counsel more than ever.

A vest pocket diary for the year 1879, worn and frayed, contains faded notes in pencil. On the first page is a personal commitment: "it is the intention of the writer to make this little volume a cyclopaedia of my business transactions together with all the news of interest and should I fail in this my <u>resolution</u> it will not be for want of faith which I place in Him from whom cometh every good and perfect gift". The diary entries, in sharp contrast, are impersonal, couched in short pithy phrases. A few scattered examples: "Sunday, April 20 Was home all day - went to church in the evening - Tuesday April 22 Planted potatoes W. Grove(?) came over from [Princeton] to live Stephen Wedden was here working - Friday April 25 Mr. Malin sowed my oats and we harrowed it in the afternoon - Thursday May 15 Was planting corn in the afternoon finished the field by the ice House - Friday May 16 Was at home went over to Aarons to furrow his corn rained in afternoon sold calf to Reed - Friday June 13 Hauled hay all day - Saturday June 14 Hauling hay to Basin all day Went to [Princeton] in the morning and had my horse shod in the afternoon C. Bennett helped [Mother]."

Although limited to terse statements of mundane matters, the small volume does not entirely lock in secret his innermost thoughts. During the first six months in 1879, we find that he visited Princeton thirty-five times, Trenton on twenty occasions interspersed with journeys to other towns and villages. When in Trenton, he records that he listened to lawyers try their cases and argue points of law. This may have been the time that he bought a set of the Encyclopaedia Britannica subsequently handed down in the family.

In sum, the cumulative evidence persuasively points to a growing restlessness and disenchantment with life on the farm. What were his personal thoughts when he planted potatoes, corn and oats, harrowed the fields, and hauled hay all day? He does not specifically say; however, action speaks louder than words. At twenty-six years of age he set off from the Van Dyke acres in Penns Neck. The decision to leave his boyhood home terminated the farm lifestyle that brought his Dutch ancestors into the Millstone Valley of New Jersey.

It was a complete break with the past; the end of an era.

Marriage and Children

On or about 1880/1881 he married[1] Anna Reed.[2] Four children were born of the marriage:

Jewell	B July 21, 1882, D May 25, 1953
	M1 October 20, 1909 Mattie Clayton (1876-1913)
	M2 October 24, 1915 Mabel Crossman (1888-1979)
Oliver	B January 20, 1885, D June 22, 1941
Carl	B March 13, 1888, D April 25, 1967
	M October 9, 1912 Mabel Virginia Clothier (1887-1978)
Pearl	B January 4, 1890, D July 6, 1965
	M January 29, 1944 David Harvey (1871-1958)

Mining for Gold

"Go west, young man" was a slogan made popular by Horace Greeley (1811-1872) journalist - politician, clearly words familiar to Grandfather John Schenck.

He did just that.

In the fall of 1883 he packed his trunk entertaining visions of grandeur and a new exciting life, and set out on a long trek to the Colorado mountains. On October 31 he signed a lease for a dwelling in Gilpen County, Colorado, described as "One half of a certain House, known as the Leavenworth House". The lease called for payment of eight dollars a month. Shortly before Christmas he was joined by his bride and infant son Jewell. "[They] have stood the long journey so well", he wrote in one of his letters. "I am proud to think Anna had the courage to make such a trip alone, none but a brave women would have done it."

Anna indeed possessed courage. In the 1880s Colorado was wide open, virgin country with scattered mining camps and few inhabitants. In 1876 it was admitted into the Union as the thirty-eighth state. Wagon trains brought the first settlers in 1858 attracted by the discovery of gold in the plains of the tributaries of the South Platte River near Denver. In 1860 the population was 33,000 men and 1,500 women, a ratio of twenty-two to one. Hence, Colorado epitomized the "Wild West", which exhibited all the social conditions and problems common to a mining community including land title disputes, crimes of violence and bizaare methods of administering justice. At the famous Palace gambling hall and theatre in Denver fortunes were won and lost in a night.

This was not exactly the picture painted by a journalist in an article appearing in a St. Louis newspaper on Tuesday, July 10, 1883, which came into the hands of John Schenck. Entitled "THE FAR WEST" and subheaded "A Delightful Letter From the Mountain Region, Correspondence, St. Louis Republican, Denver, June 20", a mountain town in Colorado is portrayed in grandiose terms enhanced by hyperbole. Claimed the writer:

never expected to be quite as near heaven as I was in Leadville ... In this mountain town it is nearly always cool, for it is surrounded by snow-covered ranges, and the fleecy clouds seem very near, floating in the measureless space of ethereal blue ... Of late years the social world of this mining town has compared favorably with that of other western towns. A very fine class of people are to be found in Leadville, and many pretty residences grace the principal streets ... Leadville by gaslight is a revelation to one unaccustomed to the strange life of these western mining camps. Harrison Avenue, the main thorofare, is brilliantly illuminated from one end to the other, and from the hotel windows we can look down upon throngs of people. The street is fairly lined with pedestrians and handsome turnouts, and fast horses make the boulevard lively. What this town must have been in '78 I cannot imagine when it is so full of life now.

The same lively treatment is accorded the mineral wealth:

A visit to most of the principal mines proves that the rich leads are still pouring wealth into the pockets of speculative owners. It is estimated that Leadville receives an income of one million and a quarter dollars from the mines monthly, which is not bad indeed for those who get the benefit of it. But here, as elsewhere, it is the few and not the many who hold the key to the earth's treasure.

The caveat may have escaped Grandfather's notice. As it turned out, he was not one of the lucky ones to unlock the hidden treasure.

William Dey Jewell, (1832-1886),[3] his uncle, was doubtless the source of that lurid piece. But whatever the fact, it was he, not Horace Greeley, who inveigled him to "go west". A garrulous, pleasure-seeking man of substantial worth, he roamed the country looking for ways of increasing his fortune with minimal effort. He bought a cattle business in Denver denominated the Jewell Cattle Co., and, hoping to strike it rich, invested in a mine in Russell Gulch, Gilpen County, near Denver. He was also not averse to making empty promises. Consonant with this philosophy, he induced his nephew to journey west to operate the mine on the strength of a promise guaranteeing the financing. The promise was kept. But for a limited time only. What he did not tell his nephew was that the Leavenworth mine had never shown a profit, that the cost of extracting the ore exceeded its market value, and that he had not paid his manager at the mine site for services for many months. His real intent, the evidence discloses, was to keep the mine in operation hoping to find a buyer and salvage a bad investment.

After a few months the euphoria wore off, as the true facts unfolded, and his uncle's financial support reduced to zero. Yet, even then, Grandfather remained loyal to his uncle and worked the mine, apparently responsive to another empty promise that he would share the proceeds when the mine was sold.

The end of this fiasco came dramatically. In the spring of 1885, late at night, the building and mining equipment were sabotaged. Their lives were placed in mortal danger. "I have gone out of the mining business as it has become too dangerous to hang on any longer", he wrote home in April of 1885. "It succeeded in burning nearly all the building over the machinery; after the fire was put out by a number of us, we found the engine and boiler had a number of sticks of giant powder all capped and put over them so as to blow everything to pieces, it was a miracle that we did not get a dose while fighting the fire but fortunately not one went off ... "

In short, he was victimized by his uncle.

Returning east with his family by way of the state of Kansas, they arrived in Wyandotte, a small settlement near Kansas City.[4] There he found needed employment to support his family. By midsummer of 1885 with the scorching sun beating down on the Kansas plains - "some days it is 93 degrees in the shade", he wrote - homesickness set in. Further he wrote, "Anna has been nearly two years away, and moving around in rented houses she seems to be very anxious to have a place she can call home ... I could find employment in the east as well as out here"

Not a little depressed as he looked back on the Leavenworth mine in the Colorado mountains, he referred to it in one of his letters as "that miserable place called a mining camp" where everything was "so very dull", a far cry from that heavenly spot he once read about in the St. Louis newspaper where "fleecy clouds" float in the "measureless space of ethereal blue and a very fine class of people reside with handsome turnouts" in a mining town called Leadville.[5]

From the beginning of this misguided venture, his mother was gravely concerned. She knew, of course, her brother's habits, his character. Moreover, she had heard stories emanating from the western frontier reputed for violence and lawlessness. There was good reason for apprehension. More importantly, she was his mother. And a mother's love is enduring. From infancy to manhood she lavished tender loving care upon him and proved false the doctor's prophesy that she would not raise him. Each day brought anxious moments; and as the days stretched into weeks and the weeks into months, periods of anguish and despair.

Late in the year of 1885 her wandering son returned. More than two years had elapsed. She welcomed him with open arms.

The long nightmare was over.

From the Mountains to the Sea

In the aftermath of the Leavenworth mining disaster you might think that John Schenck would reconsider his decision to abandon the farm. Was farming not a healthy and respected occupation as it had been for generations of the Van Dyke family? Were not the hours in the fields rewarding? Could he not recapture the enthusiasm of his boyhood?

The answer is "no", assuming that these questions ever entered his mind. He was determined <u>not</u> to be a farmer.

But what was he to do? Where would he go?

Letters written from the west offer a clue. In the hot, oppressive summer of 1885 in Wyandotte, Kansas, he refers in a letter to Asbury Park as a "desirable" place where property would "increase in value". The same letter notes that he entertained no such views concerning property in the west: "Anna and I in our wanderings have never seen a place in the West we would want to invest $1,000".

If it were not for James A. Bradley, a wealthy New York brush manufacturer who decided to spend the summer in Ocean Grove in the year 1870 to restore his health - his doctor having recommended "sea air" - Grandfather would not have known of Asbury Park. James A. Bradley was the founder and developer. A visionary as well as a successful business man, Mr. Bradley saw potential in the land north of Wesley Lake (originally Long Pond), a lonely stretch of sand dunes, briars, thickets and scrub pines. Sixteen years later when the Van Dyke family arrived in Asbury Park, a noticeable transformation had taken place, although the town was still in the early stage of development. The birth of Asbury Park where Grandfather permanently settled, bought a house and ultimately founded his own business, is an intriguing story that merits retelling.

Travelling from New York City to Ocean Grove in the year 1870 was an arduous journey in three stages: first by boat to Port Monmouth on Sandy Hook Bay; secondly by railroad to Eatontown; and finally by horse and carriage to Ocean Grove. Mr. Bradley described the route from Great Pond (Deal Lake) to Ocean Grove as "one of the worst roads that could be well imagined." But instantly he fell in love with Ocean Grove and its surroundings, so much so he said, "that I purchased the first lot ever sold there, the premium being eighty-five dollars" (Ellis 864).

Reaching Ocean Grove at nightfall with his black companion, John Baker, they secured their horses under a shelter and hastened to erect a tent. The Ocean Grove Campmeeting Association building was partially constructed without a roof, and since it was then too dark to get the poles, they hung their tent over the beams. "Soon after lunching on some crackers", they fell asleep, their heads "resting on carriage cushions". Mused the wealthy brush manufacturer, "I left the hum of the busy city behind, to become an inhabitant of the wild woods, where my wearied body and brain might rest lulled to sleep by the murmuring sea at night, and awakened in the morning by the songs of the birds in the pine-trees surrounding my couch." If he could be lulled to sleep so pleasantly by the murmuring sea and his health restored, why could not others enjoy the same benefits?

John Baker did not adapt so easily to this Robinson Crusoe existence. Continued Mr. Bradley: "In the morning Baker sighed and said, 'Mr. [Bradley] this is a wilderness place.' He was homesick; for, let the reader, who, perhaps, has been in the same spot during the busy summer season, and heard the continuous click of the telegraph instrument and seen the vast throng of men and maidens call for their letters when the mail arrives, remember it was far different on the morning of which we are writing; although it was the 10th of June, not a soul was within hearing distance of us. I cheered him by saying: 'Oh! don't be cast down,' and soon we were eating our morning lunch. That finished, we proceeded to my lots on the lake, and pitched our small tent on the ground now built upon and owned by Rev. Alfred Cookman's widow. My large tent was erected on the lot now owned by William P. Brecht, Esq., and so we began our Crusoe life" (Ellis 864).

During the campmeeting in August, there was frequent inquiry about ownership of the "land on the other side of the lake". James A. Bradley immediately saw an opportunity and did not let it pass. "One day Rev. William B. Osborn and myself went over", he said, "and at the risk of having our clothes torn from our bodies, worked our way through the briars until we reached Sunset Lake." Finally, when it was determined after mutual discussion with the trustees of the Ocean Grove Association that they did not wish to purchase the land, he bought it. On January 24, 1871, he purchased three tracts containing a total of 658 acres, including a tract of 387 acres which became Asbury Park, bounded by Great Pond (Deal Lake) on the north, Long Pond (Wesley Lake) on the south, the New Egypt and Farmingdale Railroad on the west, and the Atlantic Ocean on the east (Ellis 865,866).

Yet this was only the beginning for James A. Bradley, a mover and shaker. Through his energy and initiative, Asbury Park named in honor of Bishop Francis Asbury (1745-1816), was incorporated as a borough by the New Jersey legislature on March 4, 1874. The act contains a proviso reflecting the moral precepts of the founder and member of the Ocean Grove Campmeeting Association, namely a stipulation that intoxicating liquors of any kind may not be sold "within one mile of the Wesley Lake Bridge at Ocean Grove and Asbury Park ... except for medicinal purposes, at regular drug stores" (Ellis 866).

Asbury Park's growth was fostered by the railroad, a factor not overlooked by the founder. A timetable of the Pennsylvania Railroad for its New York Division effective November 29, 1885, found in Grandfather's effects, contains the passenger schedule between New York, Trenton and Philadelphia and shows the excellent service afforded. Trains operated daily and on time. The remarkable steam-powered locomotive had at last come into its own. Stations were built for the convenience of the public in practically every town, village and hamlet along the line. Between Perth Amboy Junction and Trenton, a distance of 36.7 miles, there was daily train service to Avenel, Edgar's, Woodbridge, Spa Spring, Perth Amboy, Hautenville, Iselin, Menlo Park, Robinvale, Metuchen, Stelton, East Brunswick, New Brunswick (Suydam Street), Millstone Junction, Voorhees, Clyde, Middlebush, East Millstone, Adams, Dean's, Monmouth Junction, Kingston, Rocky Hill, Schalk's, Plainsboro, Princeton Junction and Lawrence. By the 1880s aggressive railroad companies had made the stage lines and taverns obsolete, marking the dawn of a new era between the stage coach and the automobile. Employing macho expertise and steam power, the railroads exerted an enormous impact on American industry and society. In New Jersey the rail lines crisscrossed the state in all directions linking the principal population centers. A number of lines ran to the coastal areas crossing the salt marshes, bays and inlets, spurring the growth of the resort communities. Cheaper fares on weekends and holidays, known as excursions, were popular. The tried and true horse and carriage provided taxi service to and from the stations. "If you want to get there, take the train" was a common expression.

John Van Dyke wanted to get there. The facts indicate that he and his family boarded a train at Princeton or Princeton Junction with their bags and baggage. Every passenger train was equipped with a baggage car for trunks and bulky articles. The train schedule in the spring of 1886 discloses a Jersey shore route that originated at Monmouth Junction and Jamesburg where there was a "connection" to Sea Girt, passing through towns and hamlets in the heart of the state. Many are now forgotten but some are still well known. Proceeding eastbound: Lower Jamesburg, Hoffman, Trasex, Englishtown, Tennent, Freehold, Howell, Fairfield, Yellow Brook, Farmingdale, Allenwood, Manasquan (Squan), Sea Girt, thereupon proceeding north along the Atlantic coast to Long Branch.[6]

The train chugged and puffed over the rails meanwhile tooting its whistle, shrill and piercing, approaching the highway crossings. At full throttle the monster locomotive generated a speed of twenty-five to thirty miles an hour. High speed in those horse and buggy days. From the train windows a magnificent panorama opened up to the passengers: a breathtaking expanse of land and water, stretches of glistening white sand and sand dunes, sea grass waving in the breeze, scrub pines, and in the distance the open sea.

When the conductor called out "Asbury Park and Ocean Grove", they knew they had arrived. A thrilling moment in their young lives.

37 South Main Street

Asbury Park was a world apart from Russell Gulch in the Colorado mountains and the parched plains of Kansas - friendlier, more civilized. Seeing the Atlantic ocean for the first time and feeling the cool sea breeze - the "sea air" that so inspired the founder - was a pleasant experience; moreover, a welcome change from the dismal mining camps and lawless society of the western frontier.

And so Grandfather John Schenck once again unpacked his trunk. Still naive but a bit wiser, he was ready to move on with his career, whatever it might be. In this he was not entirely alone, for looking about he saw inhabitants of Dutch ancestry who, not long before, had left a rural environment to settle in this resort town. Prominent Dutch names such as Conover, Dehart, DeGrout, Polhemus, Ten Eyck, Van Cleve, Vanderslice, Vanderveer abound in deeds, tax records, wills and, of course, in the newspapers and on cemetery monuments.

The top priority was finding a place to live. Nothing in Asbury Park could be found at an affordable rent, that is to say a sum within his means, since that disastrous mining experience in the far west had left him financially drained. If familiar with Benjamin Franklin's adage, "Experience keeps a dear school, but fools will learn in no other", he would have humbly confessed that he was a living example. Two years in that expensive school had taught him a lesson that he would never forget: agreements and business transactions should be reduced to writing and signed. Thereafter when paying rent, he obtained a receipt written by himself and handed to the landlord for his signature.

At 37 South Main Street, in an area known as "West Grove", he found a house for rent, a six room wood-frame dwelling owned by George Slocum. At this time West Grove was part of Neptune Township that encompassed a large territory extending south from Deal Lake (Duck Pond) to Shark River (excluding Ocean Grove bordering on the east) and west to Hamilton about five and one-half miles. West Grove was the center of political and business affairs as well as social activities. The Neptune Township Committee held its first organization meeting on March 15, 1879 in the fashionable Lake View House at the head of Wesley Lake. Later the committee rented quarters at 47 South Main Street (HNT 6,7). Near Ocean Grove's "Main Gate", opposite the Slocum dwelling, was a wood-frame schoolhouse, originally the first church building of St. Paul's congregation. The congregation sold it in 1882 to the Board of Trustees (Board of Education) of the Neptune Township Schools and in the same year the board converted it into an eight room school. The school enrollment was 120 pupils (HNT 42,51,52).

Traffic on South Main Street consisted of horse-drawn wagons, carriages, buggies and carts intermixed with a few pedestrians and men on horseback. There were no paved walks. Everyone moved at a leisurely pace. Trolley cars first appeared in 1893 pulled by horses. In 1901, the township supervisors, concerned about vehicular accidents as the volume of traffic increased, passed an ordinance limiting the speed of trolley cars to six miles an hour. In the same ordinance they decreed a maximum speed for automobiles of ten miles an hour (HTN8; Eid,Chapter III).

In May 1886 when Grandfather signed a lease for the Slocum property for a monthly rental of $12.50, there were no public utilities on South Main Street. A hand operated pump in front of the house supplied the water. In this era pumps were a common sight. All members of the family shared the daily chore of filling the water bucket and carrying it into the house. Society lacked the normal conveniences taken for granted today. The housewife and mother toiled long hours in the home dramatized by that anonymous couplet, "Man may work from sun to sun, but woman's work is never done". Business in sharp contrast, was an exclusive male domain and only male citizens went to the polls to exercise the voting franchise, subject to the poll tax. John Hubbard, Tax Collector, on September 22, 1887, issued to "John S. Van Dyke" from his office in the Post Office Building, Asbury Park, a bill in the amount of one dollar designated "Poll Tax". A footnote reads: "All taxes must be paid on or before Dec. 20, 1887" or the tax will be returned to the Justice of the Peace for collection with added penalties. We may speculate whether this act was ever seriously enforced. The poll tax was abolished in 1915.

The lease for 37 South Main Street is the epitome of brevity. Handwritten on a small piece of paper, both sides, it reads:

> *Ocean Grove May 2,nd/86 This is to certify that George Slocum of the above Named place doth agree to let unto John S. Van Dyke My House Situated on Main St. Opposite Ocean Grove Gate. Six Rooms for the sum of $12.50 Twelve Dollars and one Half with the Privilege of holding the Same by the Said John S. Van Dyke for one year. And the Said George Slocum to Paint and Paper the two lower rooms of the Said Home an(d) to Change the Pump from the front of the House to the Rear Yard ...*

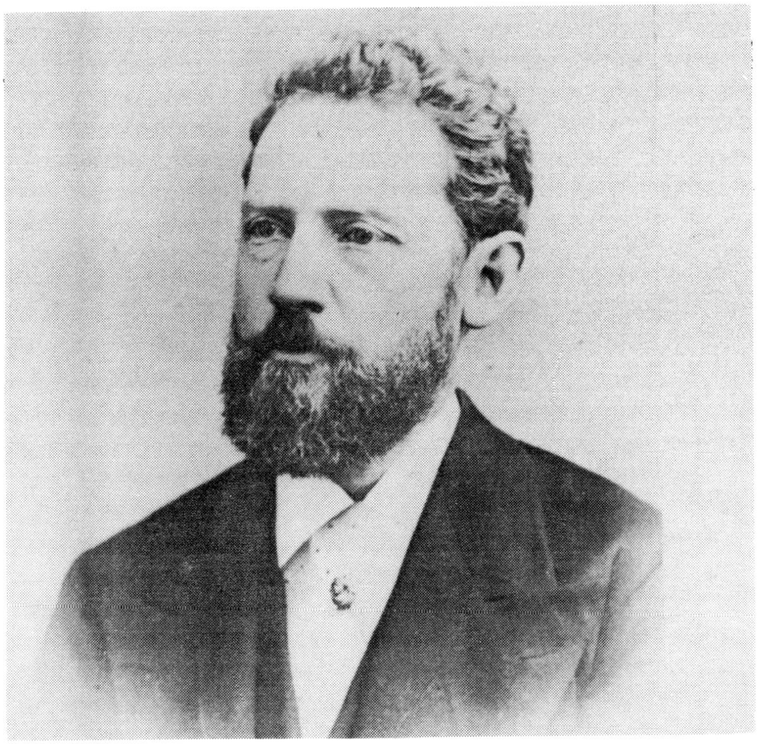

James A. Bradley (1830 - 1921), New York brush manufacturer and founder of Asbury Park.

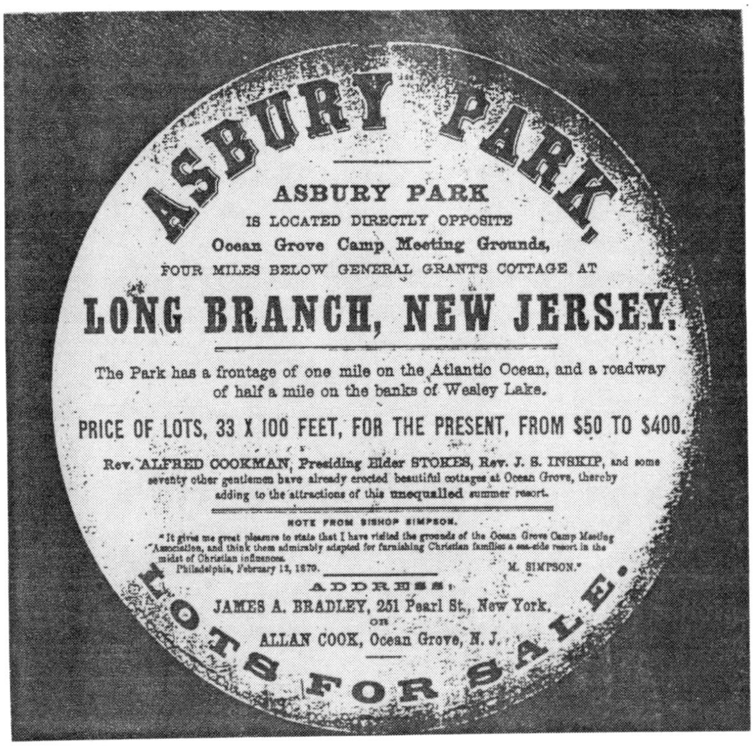

Photocopy (reduced) of a sign posted by James A. Bradley in public places intended to draw a good class of people to Asbury Park. This sign, currently in possession of Frederick A. Smith, Jr., Interlaken, New Jersey, is probably the only one extant.

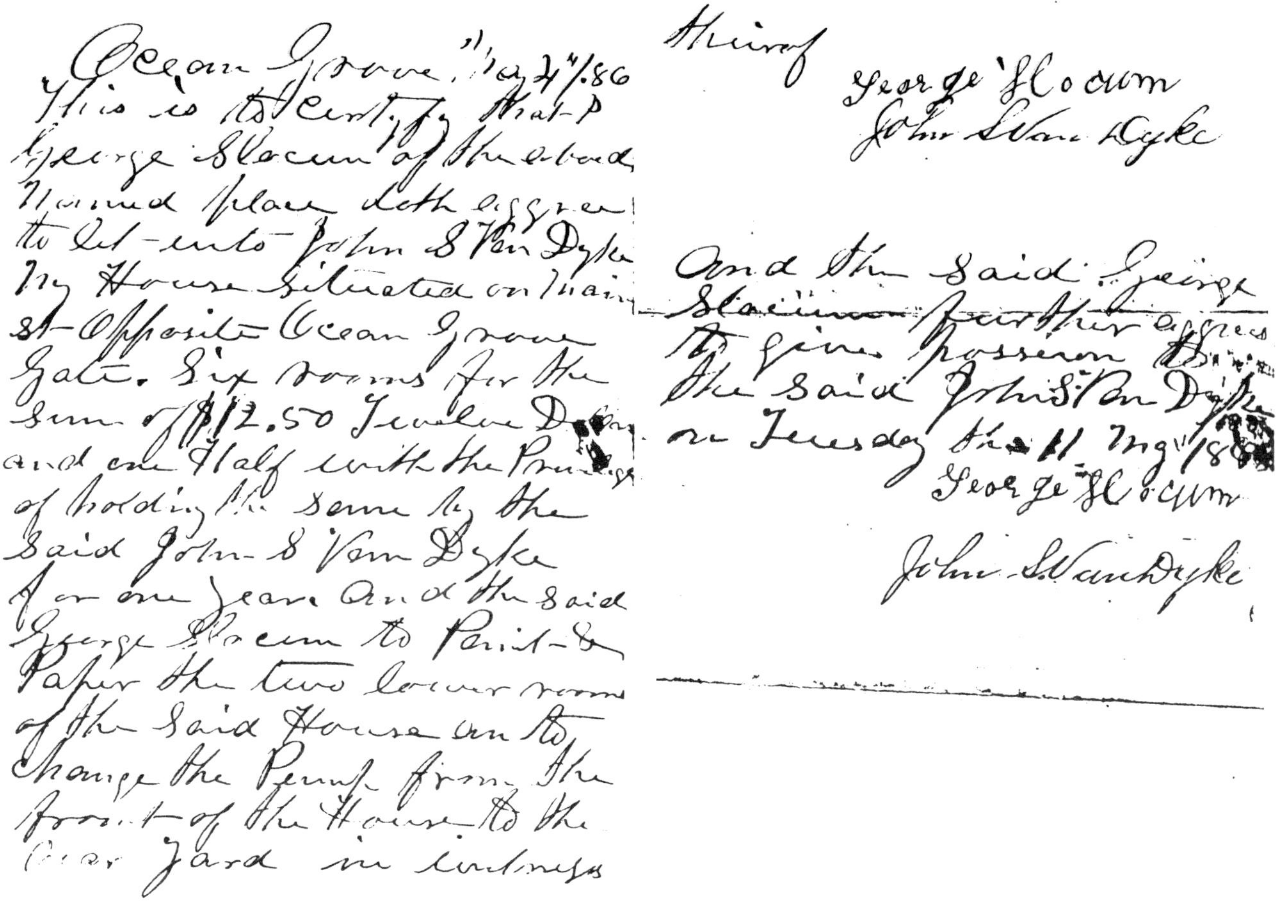

"Ocean Grove" Aug 4/86
This is to Certify that I George Slocum of the above Named place doth aggree to let unto John S Van Dyke My House Situated on Main St Opposite Ocean Grove Gate. Six rooms for the Sum of $12.50 Twelve Dollars and one Half with the Privilege of holding the same by the Said John S Van Dyke for one year. And the said George Slocum to Paint & Paper the two lower rooms of the Said House an to change the Pump from the front of the House to the rear yard in witness thereof

George Slocum
John S Van Dyke

And the Said George Slocum further aggrees to give possession to the Said John S Van Dyke on Tuesday the 11 Aug 188

George Slocum
John S Van Dyke

Photocopy (reduced) of lease of a house known as 37 South Main Street opposite the Ocean Grove's "Main Gate" from George Slocum to John S. Van Dyke.

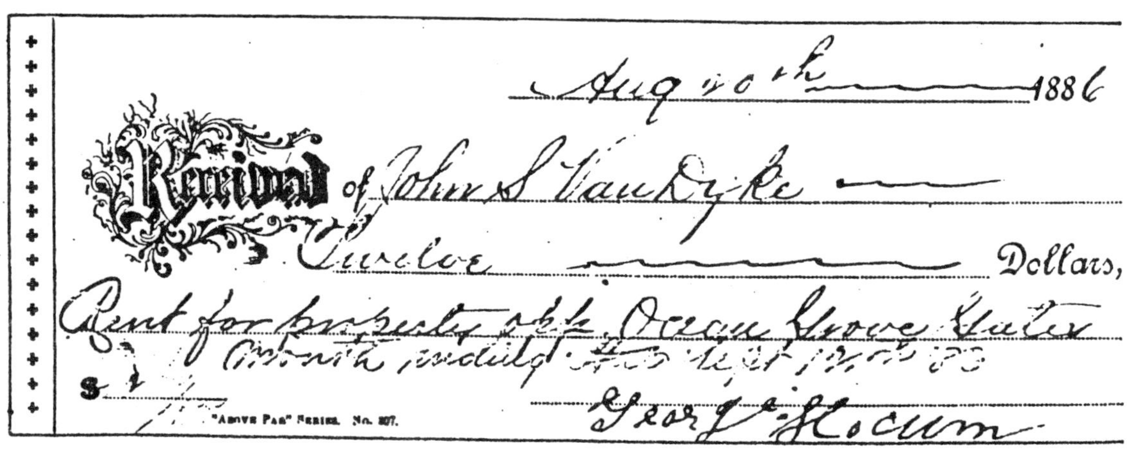

Aug 10th 1886

Received of John S Van Dyke

Twelve Dollars,

Rent for property opp. Ocean Grove Gates one month ending Sept 10/86

$

"Above Par" Series. No. 207.

George Slocum

Photocopy (reduced) of rental receipt in the hand of John S. Van Dyke for one month's rent. For reasons unknown fifty cents was deducted from the agreed rent.

And the Said Geoge Slocum further agrees to give possession to the Said John S. Van Dyke on Tuesday the 11 May 1886

The Slocum house was within easy walking distance of stores on Cookman and Mattison Avenues in Asbury Park constituting the principal business section of the town, and clearly bore no resemblance to shopping malls seen today. Stores and shops were relatively small one and two story wood and brick structures. The streets running in front were a composition of sand, clay and gravel, a surface difficult to maintain. Horse-drawn vehicles plus the elements took a heavy toll creating ruts, depressions and pot holes. A team of horses pulling a heavy load could splash water a long distance or raise billowy clouds of dust in dry weather. Since traffic moved slowly, the pedestrian was reasonably safe. One of the more serious hazards was the splattering of mud on a suit of clothes or a lady's new dress. The rules of etiquette at this time dictated that the gentleman walk on the street or curb side and offer the lady his arm to assist her in crossing the street. Perhaps it should be added that this chivalrous custom was not unique to Asbury Park or the era. Its origin may possibly be traced to medieval times. While sojourning in Philadelphia in 1748, Peter Kalm observed:

> *Itwas a custom in Philadephia, upon meeting a woman on the street, to let her go on the side nearest the houses. To make her walk on the outside was considered boorish and unrefined. I have mentioned before that the streets here are like those in London, with pavements for pedestrians and wooden posts that prevent driving upon the people. Similarly, when walking with a lady, she must be allowed the side next to the houses ... I have seen men so vain in this effort to give honor to another that they have constantly shifted from the right to the left side of a person, depending upon the number of times they crossed the street together. The custom is supposed to have arisen from an attempt to protect the walking companion from the filth of the street, hence, the side next to it is held to be less honorable (Kalm 34).*

Residing on South Main Street, Grandfather John Schenck witnessed the Jersey shore's commercial development. Newspaper advertisements in 1889 graphically depict a broad spectrum. A few examples: Ferguson's Coal, Wood & Charcoal, Geo. E. Farmer, Proprietor; James H. Bird, Best Meats, Finest Poultry, Smoked Meats, Superior Corn Beef; S. Hemmenway, Flags & Burgees, Tents, Awnings, Wagon Covers; John A. Githens & Co. Mattresses, Bedding, Feathers, etc.; D. Enright Stoves, Hardware, Tin Roofing, Ready Mixed Paints; L. McNally, Ladies' and Gentlemen's Fine Shoes; Rogers & Rogers, Millwork; Stauffer "Unique" Portraits, Patent Applied For; Geo. W. Truax, Licensed Auctioneer; N. E. Buchanon & Co., First Class Building Materials; Milan Ross, Real Estate & Insurance; Steinbach Brothers, Leading Merchants of New Jersey; D. Crawford's Palace of Music, Pianos, Organs, Musical Instruments, Books, Sheet Music; James H. Sexton, Cabinet Maker & Undertaker; Coffins & Burial Caskets of Every Approved Style Furnished on a Moment's Notice; First National Bank, Capital $50,000, Surplus $235,000, Organized February 1886, and the Asbury Park & Ocean Grove Bank, Capital $50,000, Organized January 1889 (APJ, June 8, 1889). Opportunity was ripe for an enterprising business man and investor in this period of phenomenal growth. Nevertheless, the community retained much of its pioneer flavor.

Grandmother, recalling those horse and buggy days, said that when walking along Cookman Avenue prickly thorns and burs caught in her skirt.

One store patronized by Grandfather was operated by M. L. Bamman, grocer, situate on the corner of Main Street and Cookman Avenue. A grocery bill addressed to "Mr. J. S. Van Dyke" dated November 28, 1887 lists "5 lbs Gr. Sugar" at 35 cents, "2 lbs Butter" at 56 cents, "Bag Flour" at 85 cents, "1 lb Coffee" at 25 cents, "1/2 Dz Eggs" at 15 cents, and "1 Broom" for 30 cents. Below Bamman's name and address on his billhead appears the words, "Telephone Connection". But no telephone number! The instrument was a curious gadget that people talked about rather than into. James H. Sexton, Cabinet Maker and Undertaker, claimed in June of 1889 that his office was "open day and night" and had "Telephone connections with principal hotels and stores in Park and Grove". This no doubt was an exaggeration because not a single hotel advertising in the same edition of the newspaper listed a telephone (APJ June 8, 1889).

A New Beginning

John Schenck arrived in Asbury Park with little money in his pocket and with no friends or sponsors. His formal education did not extend beyond the three Rs, scarcely sufficient credentials to qualify for worthy employment in an urban community. But this was not the way he viewed the matter. In his eyes Asbury Park offered unlimited opportunity. Anyone reasonably intelligent, he believed, could be an entrepreneur and earn a living.

He did, in fact, assume the role of an entrepreneur, however humble, as the proprietor of a lunch stand at the Asbury Park and Ocean Grove railway station. On March 22, 1888 he entered into a written agreement with Leonard Romain to lease "the ground now occupied by the Lunch Room opp. the New Jersey Depot, and adjoining the feed Store (Known at present as Rynn's Lunch Room, Space to be 10 X 10 ft. in size - for the sum of $50.00" payable in two installments for the term of one year.[7] The venture proved successful since he leased the same space for another year at twice the rental. Romain was evidently looking on. A lease dated April 1, 1889 drawn in the office of Milan Ross, 725 Cookman Avenue, is more imposing than the first. It recites an agreement "Between Leonard Romain of the First Part and John S. Van Dyke of the Borough of Asbury Park New Jersey of the second part" and describes the premises as "opp[osite] the New Jersey Depot and adjoining the Feed Store a building known at present as Van Dykes Lunch room with the appurtenances for the term of One year"; further providing that the lessee shall have the "privilege of running the building back from the rail road twelve feet and the said building to be left on the premises", and conditioned further that the premises shall not be used "in any other manner than as [a] Fruit Stand & Lunch room".

The lunchroom business continued to thrive since a lease for a third year was negotiated encompassing not only the original one hundred square feet but an adjoining area of one hundred and twenty square feet. Although this document has not been found, it is confirmed by Romain's formal notice to vacate the premises by April 1, 1891.[8] Thus it appears that a fair rental figure could not be agreed upon and suggests that Romain may have decided to operate the luncheonette himself.

With the loss of the luncheonette in this devious manner, he was disappointed but undismayed. Assessing the alternatives, he noted that huge crowds arriving in Asbury Park during the spring and summer months flocked to the beach where they spent most of their money. Would it not be possible to rent a site for a refreshment stand near the beachfront?

Entertaining this thought, he approached Samuel B. McIntyre, proprietor of the Oriental Hotel on Asbury Avenue. The Oriental provided summer guests with superb accommodations claiming on its stationery:

> *Accommodations for 300 guests. An ocean view from every window. Orchestra engaged by the season. Conducted in a liberal and first class manner. Comfortable rooms, careful attendance, and superb table ... The best location in Asbury Park.*

Records reveal that Grandfather negotiated a three year lease with McIntyre on February 16, 1891 for "a piece of ground 10 by 15 feet on the south side [and] opposite bay window of Oriental Hotel Cottage", the rent for the first season to be fifty dollars, the second season sixty-three dollars, and the third season seventy-five dollars. An unexpected problem arose concerning the set-back of the stand from the curb, the result of a complaint initiated by several self-interested business men. McIntyre was cooperative and ordered a survey of the property and stand in relation to the curb, and the issue was finally resolved. A receipt in Grandfather's hand was signed June 13 by McIntyre for the "balance in full for rent of property adjoining Hotel on South side by bay window rented by Van Dyke of me". Meanwhile he had squirreled away whatever money he could spare, looking forward to the day when he would no longer be obligated to pay rent to anyone.

The Schlossbach Family and Other Friendly People

South Main Street in West Grove was an enclave unique in every respect. People were caring, hardworking, and of necessity frugal. They were never too busy to lend a helping hand to their neighbors. Diverse occupations and trades were conducted in or near the home. Thus it was not unusual for a dwelling to serve a dual purpose: the family living quarters occupied the second floor while the family business - not infrequently a retail store - operated on the ground floor. Nor were they sensitive about bartering goods, especially when family funds were low. There was no false pride. Personal problems, mutually shared, bound them together akin to a large family.

This merely epitomizes the charming portrayal of life on South Main Street by Isaac Schlossbach (later US Navy Commander Isaac Schlossbach) who was born at 37 South Main Street in 1891. No one can speak with greater authority. Living in the "Bowery", as it was commonly called, Isaac Schlossbach knew everyone intimately. He was one of them.

John Schenck also knew them and was fortunate to live in their midst. Adopting their frugal precepts, he conceived the idea of subletting part of the Slocum dwelling thereby effecting a modest saving of the rent that he was obligated to pay each month. Whether by word-of-mouth or an apropriate sign posted on the property, a tenant was obtained. Three rooms on the second floor were rented for six dollars a month to William H. Hallman, according to a handwritten lease which provided that the second floor be "entered by a side entrance through yard to back of portico and thence up stairway to said rooms". This pattern was repeated when the Van Dyke family moved to a two-story house of Mrs. H. Gravatt, whereupon he subleased to one John Boyce "Two Back Rooms - one on the lower and one on the upper floor" for four dollars a month payable "in advance on the first of each and every month", this clause having been inserted in a formal lease agreement.

Mrs. Gravatt's property, as the lease describes, was "on Main St. West Grove back of the "Coal Office of S. G. Polhemus" who operated a coal yard by the railroad. Nearly every town had a railroad siding with coal and wood for sale, the only energy source. In the kitchen of every home was a coal range for cooking the family meals and in another room the popular potbellied stove. Stoking the fires was a routine family chore along with removal of the ashes. At night the householder religiously stoked the fire and turned down the damper. Upon awakening to a frigid house with white frosted windowpanes on a cold wintry morning, he hastened to open the damper and shovel coal on the dying embers. A comfortably heated home required considerable time and effort.

The Van Dyke family might have resided even longer at 37 South Main Street if it had not been sold. In 1888 Abraham and Martha Schlossbach, Russian immigrants temporarily living in New York, decided to settle in Neptune, New Jersey, and bought the Slocum property. There they resided happily, conducted a drygoods business and raised nine children, five boys and four girls.

Isaac was their second child, born on August 20, 1891. A quiet, shy, serious boy, Isaac attended school in the old wooden schoolhouse across the turnpike road (Main Street) near Ocean Grove's "Main Gate". In his retirement he warmly reminisced about his boyhood days. There was plenty to do both in work and in play: milking the cows on the family farm in the rear of the house, cutting wood for the fires, caddying at the Deal Golf and Country Club, grooming horses for the carriage trade that met visitors at the Asbury Park and Ocean Grove Railroad Station; also ice-skating in winter on Wesley Lake, treading for clams in the Shark River channel by the railroad, playing basketball in the ice house on South Main Street before the ice was cut for storage.

Ike, as he was known to his friends, remembered that he "could fall out of bed at the first school bell in the morning, grab his clothes and run across the street and up the school steps before the late bell rang". This was probably the exception rather than the rule. As a member of the Neptune High School class of 1909 totaling <u>twenty-nine</u> graduates, he had fond memories of "Lady Doren" (Miss Lida Doren). An "excellent principal", he said.

The stores stretching along South Main Street, so familiar to Ike as a boy, also invoked cherished memories. The first floor of the Slocum dwelling was transformed into <u>Schlossbach's Dry Goods Store</u>, as it was known, and the second story became the family living quarters. His mother managed the store where, he said, "farm and work clothes were often bartered for hay and fresh fish". Meanwhile his father labored as a farmer, a butcher, an operator of a hay and feed store, and in other productive occupations to support his large family. On the north side of Schlossbach's Dry Goods Store was Mrs. Snyder's Boarding House. Mrs. Snyder who was the "local midwife" frequently lent assistance to Dr. Johnson from Asbury Park, the only available doctor, who came in a horse and buggy to attend his patients. The birth of a baby on South Main Street was of course an exciting event. The news spread rapidly.

On the south side of Schlossbach's store-dwelling was Hurley's Tinsmith Shop followed by the Goodenough Restaurant displaying "eyewatering homemade pies". Then came Bob Hatfield's Vegetable and Fruit Store that sold "freshly roasted peanuts" outside and "delicious fudge made inside on a marble slab"; then Becker's Candy, the Township of Neptune and Farmer's Coal Yard. Proceeding further south was Johnson's Blacksmith Shop located a short distance down the alley; then Klein's Music Store, the United Ice Company, Consumer's Coal Yard, Charles Lewis Lumber Yard and Gravatt's Bakery at the corner of Corlies Avenue and South Main Street.

"Everyone on the street knew everyone else and looked after each other", said US Commander Isaac Schlossbach. "It was the era of horses for transportation and work, potbellied stoves, hand water pumps and outhouses. Neighbors were very close and friendly and if a boy were seen smoking corn silk or was hurt, the news traveled fast and his parents would know about it before he arrived home."[9]

On South Main Street or the "Bowery" people were people. There was no coverup. John Schenck must have enjoyed their company.

1011 West Cookman Avenue

In the years 1886-90, a period of scrimping and saving, he had accumulated enough money for a down-payment on a home. The time had come to bid farewell to his neighbors in the "Bowery". In April 1890 he purchased a three story, Victorian style home at 1011 West Cookman Avenue, one of the early homes in Asbury Park.[10] The property was subject to a mortgage of one thousand dollars, a tidy sum for one in his financial position. His mother generously loaned him three hundred dollars secured by a second mortgage. At long last he was the owner of a home, albeit subject to two mortgages.

But it was _his_ home.

It was a happy moment when both mortgages were satisfied. The loan from his mother was repaid in 1893.[11] Surely he breathed a sigh of relief when he paid the full sum of one thousand dollars to the holder of the first mortgage, R. H. Eastburn, proprietor of the Quaker City Whisk Broom Works on Arch Street, Philadelphia. A letter addressed to Eastburn (November 28, 1893) reads: "I am in receipt of enough money to pay my mortgage of $1,000. - will you be so kind as to send the papers to Monmouth Trust and Safe Deposit Company of Asbury Park, N. J. ... I thank you for the kindness shown me in the past, I wish to save cost of next month's interest. I was not aware until today I could meet the payment."

Meanwhile, an amicable relationship had developed in a curious way. Reminded by Eastburn that he had not received the first interest payment, John Schenck extended an apology: "In reply to your favor of 28th would say it was entirely to the misunderstanding with the business men at this place that the payment of [interest] was delayed ... I never saw the original mortgage or transfer and did not know your name until receipt of letter ... I have since found out by consulting the records that it is made semi-annually so you are entitled to the money - I payed Mr. Beegle this morning by certified chk. 30 - to July 1st 90."

In acknowledging a receipt of mortgage interest on January 2, 1891 Eastburn wrote, " ... glad to hear of your improvement & hope it is quite satisfactory to yourself - I will see it first opportunity - hope you have had a prosperous year, & you have my best wishes for the future". The "improvement" was undoubtedly a new building erected in the rear of his property and an adjoining lot purchased in October of 1890,[12] the future site of his electrical contracting business.

The Gay Nineties

January 1, 1890 ushered in the last decade of the century, a period frequently referred to as the "gay nineties". William McKinley (1843-1901) was president. The country had come a long way since George Washington, a century earlier on April 30, 1789, took the oath of office at Federal Hall on Wall Street, New York. Americans were enjoying unprecedented prosperity and were far more mobile. A carefree spirit filled the air. Living proof is seen in the thousands of pleasure-seeking visitors descending on Asbury Park in the summer engaging rooms by the day, week, or month at luxurious hotels.

John Schenck's future looked brighter, too. For the first time in an uneven career his family was settled in a home that he owned, not the landlord. He had broken free from the painful duty of paying rent every month. In his position as property owner, tender of mortgage interest did not disturb him.

The gay nineties saw a building boom in the twin cities, Asbury Park and Ocean Grove, now permanently on the map. Replacing the old wooden school house by Ocean Grove's Main Gate on South Main Street was the Neptune High School, a handsome building erected in 1898 accommodating all grades, kindergarten through high school. In a relatively short time public school education had made spectacular gains. If John Schenck had been born a generation later, he would have devoured a high school curriculum. A high school diploma was a coveted, hard-earned document received with pride and celebrated with great fanfare. Thus we find that the commencement exercises for the class of 1906 held on Friday evening, June 22 in the large auditorium received full coverage in the Asbury Park Evening Press, displaying a photograph of the class, all twenty graduates - ten boys and ten girls - dressed in their Sunday best. The Asbury Park Journal similarly announced in bold headlines, "TOWNSHIP GRADUATION - The Commencement Exercises - FINE SHOWING - One of the Largest Classes Ever Graduated There" followed by a detailed account of every phase of the program, even quoting at length the eloquent address of the honorable Walter M. Chandler, an orator from New York, commenting that he was "a treat to hear and whose words made a deep impression upon every listener." Lofty oratory eulogized Washington and his brave soldiers and "all the nameless dead, who ragged, starved, and bleeding, in Freedom's holy name, followed with martial step and hearts that beat like kettle drums, the illustrious Virginian to glory, to victory and to death, let us this day bring our offerings of gratitude and tears"; and extolled liberty and justice for which those "ragged revolutionary continentals fought and died"; and concluding with a peroration denouncing American greed - "Our national passion for accumulated wealth, for colossal fortunes". It was oratory at its best, an art of the past. "The big auditorium was crowded to its fullest extent", the Journal reported, and "President Stout of the Board of Education and Miss Doren ... occupied chairs on the platform with the class, board of education and speakers". It was, perforce, a lengthy program that evening lasting "almost three hours, but very few left until the close".[13]

Ellwood P. Wright, Commission Merchant

On the west side of the railroad tracks in Asbury Park between Cookman and Mattison Avenues, facing the station, stood a two story, wood-frame warehouse. A porch extending across the front of the building served as a showcase for articles on sale. A large sign read, "E. P. WRIGHT & CO., SHORE BAZAAR". The term "bazaar" perfectly described the business with its heterogeneous collection of chairs, tables, beds, mattresses, rugs, parlor stands, pianos, sewing machines, stoves, roller chairs, baby carriages, wash bowls, pitchers, commodes; in short, virtually every household commodity known at the time. A casual observer would have been impressed by the mere sight of this unusual assortment of goods and wares. Ellwood P. Wright, a genial, rotund man in his forties known in the community as a commission merchant and auctioneer, was the proprietor. And he, too, was unusual.

Not far from Wright's Shore Bazaar by the railroad was another large wooden structure where Leonard Romain conducted a feed, hay and straw business and from whom Grandfather leased a small space for a luncheonette. Plainly he entertained no interest in feed, hay and straw. However the Shore Bazaar having once caught his eye was compelling. Soon he and Wright were engaged in lively conversation on a variety of subjects, not the least of which was that extraordinary inventory.

There is no evidence that Wright ever asked John Schenck, "Can you fix it?" Nevertheless there is little doubt that this question was posed innumerable times because, in fact, he fixed many things. High on a post in front of the building was a sign in the shape of a padlock bearing the name "J. S. Van Dyke", announcing services as a locksmith and suggesting that this craft supplemented his earnings from the luncheonette which fell sharply in the winter months. Hence mutual interests brought the two men together. But beyond this, they instinctively liked one another and before long there developed a father-son bond that endured for years until severed by Wright's death.

Buoyed by Wright's kindly manner and encouragement, he proceeded to investigate some of nature's laws whenever time permitted. Of major interest was electricity motivating him to perform experiments with batteries, bells, chemicals, electrical circuits, and a new invention called the telephone. Happy moments were spent in his private laboratory set aside in Wright's building tinkering tirelessly and experimenting.

Wright's Shore Bazaar, strategically located, offered the perfect opportunity. In addition to repairing locks he soon acquired other skills which he offered to the public. A second sign posted on the building reads:

LOCKSMITH &

GENERAL REPAIRER

ELECTRICAL WIRING

BELLS BATTERIES

Ever since Alexander Graham Bell (1847-1922) exhibited the telephone at the Centennial Exposition in Philadelphia in June of 1876, Bell's novel instrument intrigued him. How did electricity transmit the human voice over a wire? He wanted to know the secret. Assembling his own telephone device, he ran a wire from Wright's building to his home approximately three blocks away.

Thus it is not surprising that his mind inevitably turned to invention. What a thrilling moment when a new idea suddenly dawned with Wright looking on like a proud father! An invention that apparently received a patent was a split drill point, a tool capable of reaming the inside edges of a hole drilled in a well pipe. In the days when private wells supplied the water, a letter addressed to Wright in April of 1897 refers to it: "Enclosed you will find the letter referred to. I am glad you offered the same to John Van Dyke and hope he may have much success. My good wishes are with him and I shall always do my very best in helping him push the patent along."

Ellwood P.Wright died intestate on October 12, 1899 at the age of fifty-nine.[14] An administrator's sale on a December morning was a heartbreaking experience for John Schenck, an appraiser of Wright's estate appointed by the Monmouth County court. Serving as clerk of the auction, he was an eyewitness to the final dissolution of the Shore Bazaar.

He had lost a dear friend and mentor.

The John S. Van Dyke Electric Co.

In 1892 the John S. Van Dyke Electric Co. was founded with its headquarters in Wright's warehouse by the railroad announcing readiness to install the incandescent electric light and submit estimates. Wright must have

John S. Van Dyke is standing at the entrance of his Luncheonette located opposite the Asbury Park & Ocean Grove Railway Station. The space was leased for use as a "Fruit Stand & Lunch Room" from Leonard Romain whose feed store is in the background.

Photograph ca 1890

Storage building and warehouse of Elwood P. Wright, commission merchant and auctioneer, the fourth man from the left in this photograph. Wright encouraged John S. Van Dyke in electrical experiments performed in this building, the site of the Van Dyke Electric Company.

Photograph 1895

ADMINISTRATOR'S SALE

Being a continuation sale of the lot of Household Goods, late the stock of Elwood P. Wright, deceased, of Asbury Park, consisting in part of a majority of the best goods in his place, viz:

Four second-hand Pianos, 2 new Roller Chairs, 1 new Baby Carriage, 1 new Lunch Cupboard, 12 French Plate Looking Glasses, 1 second-hand Sideboard, 3 new Parlor Stands, 2 new Refrigerators, 1 Marble Top Stand, 2 new Rugs, 1 new Iron Bed, several new Wooden Bedsteads, 2 new Cotton Mattresses, 4 new Excelsior Mattresses, 1 Safe, 1 Office Desk, 4 Baby Chairs, 2 dozen new Dining-room Chairs, lot of Cot Pads, single and double; lot of new Bed Springs, lot of new double Cots, 1 Vapor Stove, nearly new, 1 second-hand Sewing Machine (Wheeler & Wilson), 1 second hand Extension Table, lot of new Kitchen Tables, 1 Barber Chair, 1 Folding Bed, 2 second-hand Roller Chairs, Baby Carriages and Go-Carts of every description, new and second-hand; 1 Earthen Commode, 1 Emery Wheel, 2 rolls new Matting, lot of new Oil Cloth, lot of new Washbowls and Pitchers, 1 French Plate Mirror, 2 Bureaus, second-hand; 1 second-hand Parlor Desk, Ice Coolers, Mats, Cribs, Chairs, Books, Show Cases, and many other things which will be sold to the highest bidder.

Sale to take place at his old store, opposite Asbury Park and Ocean Grove R. R. Station,

WEDNESDAY, DECEMBER 13, 1899.

Sale to begin at 10 O'Clock. Terms Strictly Cash.

AUGUSTUS C. WRIGHT,
Administrator Estate E. P. Wright.

JACOB C. SHUTTS, Auctioneer.
JOHN S. VANDYKE, Clerk.

Daily Press Printery, Asbury Park, N. J.

Elwood P. Wright, a commission merchant, died October 12, 1899 at the age of fifty-nine. He was a friend and mentor of John S. Van Dyke, seventeen years younger, one of the estate appraisers appointed by the court. The items listed above graphically reflect the era of the "gay nineties".

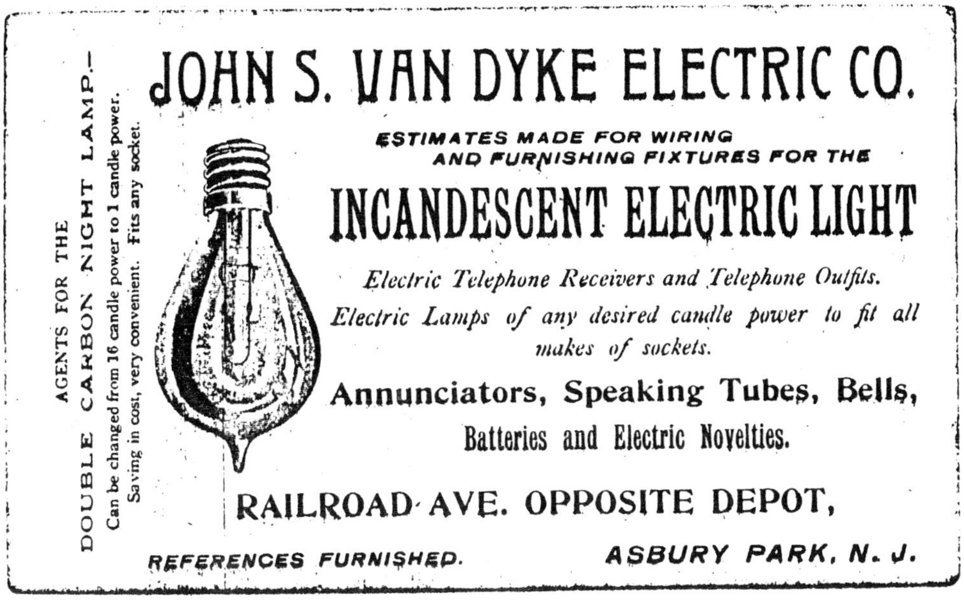

John Schenck Van Dyke founded his electrical contracting business in 1892 in Wright's warehouse across from the Asbury Park and Ocean Grove Railroad Station evidenced by his business card.

By the year 1902 he moved his business to 1011 West Cookman Avenue, Asbury Park.

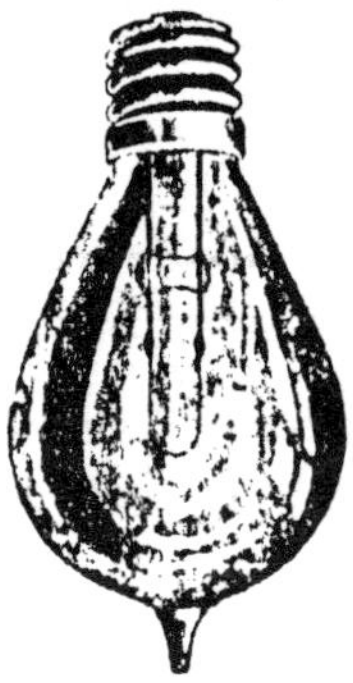

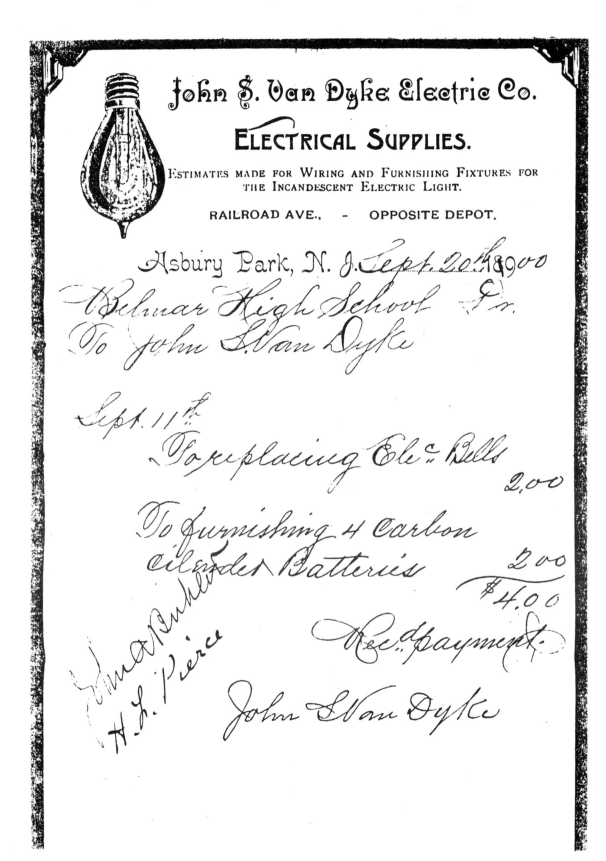

John S. Van Dyke Electric Co.

ELECTRICAL SUPPLIES.

ESTIMATES MADE FOR WIRING AND FURNISHING FIXTURES FOR THE INCANDESCENT ELECTRIC LIGHT.

RAILROAD AVE., - OPPOSITE DEPOT.

Asbury Park, N. J. Sept. 20th 1900

Belmar High School Dr.

To John S. Van Dyke

Sept. 11th

To replacing Elec. Bells 2.00

To furnishing 4 Carbon cilender Batteries 2 00

$4.00

Rec'd payment.

John S. Van Dyke

John A Bucklew

H. L. Pierce

Bill for electrical services of John S. Van Dyke

been as pleased as his young protege, now at last a true entrepreneur embarked on a promising career.

What motivated John Schenck to establish an electrical contracting business?

The short answer is that electrical phenomena, like the magic seemingly flowing from the magician's wand, was irresistible.

The gay nineties heralded new technologies. Electricity hovered on the horizon. To the ordinary citizen electricity was generally perceived as a mysterious force. And dangerous, too! Electrically charged wires installed in the walls of buildings, it inevitably followed, could be hazardous. Yes, even wires for bells and telephones! Are bells and telephones really necessary? So people asked who were quite content to use the speaking tube that was simple and safe. As for long distance communication, the United States Government provided excellent mail service. If a message were urgent the Western Union Telegraph Company was ready to transmit it almost anywhere, whereupon a telegraph messenger boy on a bicycle speedily delivered a tersely worded telegram to the front door.

When John Schenck resided in the Slocum property in the 1880s, South Main Street was plunged in darkness with the last rays of the setting sun. Two generations earlier, it will be recalled, Rachel Van Dyke wrote moving accounts of New Brunswick's social life and studied Virgil by the wavering light of a candle. Looking back to those tiny Dutch settlements, New Amsterdam, New Amersfoort, Breukelen and New Utrecht were cast in total darkness at nightfall, as were other colonial towns, with the exception of the light from an occasional hanging lantern in the village square or the flickering flame of the night watchman's lantern while making his rounds. In sum, all artificial light since antiquity was produced by fire.

In 1895, three years after the Van Dyke electric company was established, the Neptune Township Committee granted a franchise to the Consolidated Gas Company to lay gas mains along South Main Street (FANT 6). Gas illumination was the wave of the future. Or so many people thought, especially those who had invested in the powerful gas industry. But as the history shows, the handwriting was on the wall. One man led the way: Thomas Alva Edison (1847-1931), unmistakably John Schenck's idol. In the famed inventor he saw a charismatic personality and a superb creative mind; a man who was self-driven and practical; a man whose enthusiasm inspired his coworkers, as he liked to call them, and in fact everyone he met.

And, it so happened, John Schenck Van Dyke whom he never met.

The talking machine or phonograph, as it soon came to be called, was exhibited by the great inventor before the American Academy of Science at the Smithsonian in April 1878, a time when his reputation was already well established. The demonstration fortuitously turned into a public relations coup impelled by an invitation from the White House by President Rutherford B. Hayes (1822-1893) for a second demonstration the same evening. In consequence, the phonograph became a sensation overnight receiving full coverage not only in the nation's newspapers, but in England and on the continent of Europe. Small wonder, then, that as soon as he could afford it, John Schenck bought one of the first models. Briefly described, it consisted of a revolving cylinder approximately the size of a glass tumbler turned by a spring motor and a stylus attached to a diaphragm that received the vibrations from an embossed record. A large metal horn mounted on top amplified the sound produced mechanically. How marvelous! Years later this unusual machine, an heirloom handed down, found a place in the author's family attic. On occasion it was brought downstairs, dusted off, reassembled, the horn suspended from an upright bar, and the spring motor wound to the proper tension. Lo and behold, discernible words and music were heard exactly as in Edison's day!

Still greater things were to come. Within two years the Wizard of Menlo Park gave the world the incandescent electric light. How thrilled Grandfather John Schenck would have been in the company of those skilled technicians working in the Menlo Park Laboratory under Edison's direction set upon a single goal, the invention of an electric lamp affordable to the public for common use. After thousands of experiments, night and day, over thirteen months - SUCCESS! Very briefly, a carbonized cotton thread was inserted in a glass bulb, the air exhausted to one-millionth of an atmosphere, and a small current turned on. In awe they watched the primitive glass bulb produce a steady glow for the thirteen and a half hours. The year was 1879.[15]

John Schenck was then twenty-two years old living on the Penns Neck farm, which he managed for his mother, seemingly a contented farmer in the mold of his late father. But, in truth, his mind was far away pondering other things. And asking questions. What is electricity? How is electricity transformed into light? The seed was sown. We can, of course, only imagine his thoughts and dreams in the ensuing years.

The first structure wired for Edison's electric light was his own home. To ensure current at all times he installed a dynamo powered by a steam engine.[16] Coal obtained from the coal yards on the railroad siding supplied the fuel. In consequence, 1011 West Cookman Avenue was one of the first residences in Asbury Park to be illuminated by electricity and probably the only residence possessing its own generating station.

For the greater part of the nineteenth century gas lit the streets, homes and factories in the major cities of America and the industrial centers. By the year 1892 when John Schenck founded his electrical business in Asbury Park, the gas industry was still firmly entrenched. Gas illumination was seen as practical and convenient, ready at the strike of a match. Electric light, on the other hand, was less dependable. Frequently the light would flicker and fade or sometimes die out. Problems associated with the power lines or at the power station constantly confronted the engineers. In Asbury Park the little light bulb produced no light in the late evening and early morning hours since the generators at the power station were shut down.

Ten years later the Atlantic Coast Electric Light Company located at Second and Railroad Avenues inaugurated a new policy intended to make electric power universal. In a series of newspaper advertisements appearing in the summer of 1902 the company announced:

CONTINUOUS ELECTRIC CURRENT
The Atlantic Coast Electric Light Company now
furnishes electric current for
LIGHT AND POWER PURPOSES

The announcement pointed out the advantages of electricity over gas:

> Twenty-four hours a day, three hundred and sixty-five days in the year. With the inauguration of this continuous service electricity now becomes practicable for all power as well as for lighting purposes. It is safe, cool, convenient, noiseless, economical and
>
> ALWAYS READY
>
> [Company name and address]
>
> Electric fans will keep you cool
> and keep the flies away.[17]

Meanwhile the John S. Van Dyke Electric Co. had been growing steadily. By the year 1901 the business moved to 1011 West Cookman Avenue, Asbury Park. Erected in the rear of the property and lot adjoining was a new building containing a garage for several vehicles, a workshop and storage area for electrical equipment. John Schenck's reputation in the new industry spread along the Jersey coast as far north as Long Branch and communities to the south as he responded to customer requests. Recently come to light is a receipted bill in his hand addressed to the Belmar High School. Dated September 20, 1900, it sets forth services for "replacing Elec. Bells" and "furnishing 4 Carbon Cilander Batteries". Total charge was $4.00.

One interesting preoccupation growing out of countless experiments in Wright's building was electroplating. On his billhead he designated himself "ELECTRO PLATER ... In Gold, Silver, Nickel, Copper and Oxydizing". As public demand for services mounted, particularly wiring for electric light, little time was left for electroplating. At length he decided to rent the section of the building associated with this phase, evidenced by a formal lease containing a caveat that the equipment "be used for nickel plating purposes only".[18]

Other documents extant similarly point to an active and prospering business. In 1901 he purchased the tangible assets including all the stock in trade of an electrical supply store in Asbury Park. The bill of sale records "Speaking Tubes, 600 ft conduit, Asbestos, 3000 [ft] No 14 Wire, 100 porcelain Ins. No 5 1/2, 1000 tubes NO 012" and store fixtures consisting of counters, Shelves, chairs etc.[19]

In a relatively short period of fourteen years his electric company was firmly established and a respected part of the business community. Through the many day-by-day activities promoting good will, he received untold pleasure and personal satisfaction while, at the same time, bringing electric light and power into homes, offices, hotels and business establishments. Then, totally unforeseen, death laid its hand. Thereupon the business was conducted by his sons, Jewell and Carl, followed by his grandson, Henry Everett Van Dyke, to the present.

The estate inventory contains an authoritative record of tangible assets shedding considerable light on the new technology when electricity was beginning to gain public acceptance. A partial list is singularly revealing: two automobiles; grinding, buffing and emery wheels; pulleys, porcelain compounds, carborundum, tumbling barrel, drill press, brazing furnace, air pump, baking oven, scales and weights, electric fans, iron and wooden tanks; also volt and ampere meters, three shelves of chemicals, copper and nickel solutions, brass pipe, key sockets, keyless sockets, Hubbel Pull sockets, weather-proof sockets, porcelain sockets, receptacles, tubes, fuses, switches, insolating joints, shades and shade holders, plug cutouts, 500 electric lamps, several thousand feet of wire, batteries, battery jars, bells, buzzers, gongs, speaking tubes, annunciators, telephones.

A curious incident associated with the Double Carbon Night Lamp is another example of the strong Edison influence. Curious to learn the energy consumption, he visited the office of the Atlantic Coast Electric Light Co. with one of Edison's lamps from his stock. The utility, presumably equally interested, conducted a test. The result must have been highly pleasing. "Dear Sir" the manager wrote in a letter, "The Edison night lamp which you handed us for testing comsumes 30 watts which makes it cost a trifle more than one half cent an hour".[20]

We need look no farther than his business card for the most telling evidence. Prominently featured is a picture of Edison's carbon filament lamp with the words:

ESTIMATES MADE FOR WIRING
AND FURNISHING FIXTURES FOR THE
INCANDESCENT ELECTRIC LIGHT

His business card eloquently reflects the transition between gas and electricity. We are informed that he can furnish and install electric fan motors and exhaust fans, fire and burglar alarms, telephones, call bells, annunciators, batteries and electric novelties. And for those people who are still apprehensive of electricity or for other reasons wish to pursue their traditional ways, he is prepared to furnish and install gas lighting attachments and speaking tubes.

Demise

Sadly and tragically, a budding career abruptly ended. In attempting to start the engine of his automobile stalled on Ocean Avenue, Asbury Park, the gasoline tank exploded. Flaming fluid enveloped his body inflicting second and third degree burns that proved fatal.

Death came to John Schenck Van Dyke on August 8, 1906 at the age of forty-nine (VS/NJ).

EPILOGUE

If other Dutch ancestral lines were explored in depth, as here, reaching back to the days of Peter Stuyvesant and New Netherland, the story would embody the same underlying themes. The Dutch colonizers of the New World were true adventurers. Pulling up roots in their native Holland to come to America called for a full measure of fortitude, faith and hope. Venturing into the wild interior of New Jersey fraught with danger and hardship was a test of their resolve.

What motivated them? What was the driving force?

Observing the settlement history generation after generation, two elements preponderate, the family and the land.

Bound by strong family and cultural ties, these Dutch pioneers planned methodically and exceedingly well. They acted in concert as one large family and shared a common goal. All sought a new and better life for themselves, their children and grandchildren. The second element - land - is the other side of the coin. Land was wealth, the key to survival - everything. Ever mindful of their children, they bought more and more land to provide for them and their progeny. In an agricultural environment they, perforce, looked to the land to supply their needs - food, clothing, shelter. This, too, was a family matter wherein every member played an important role, father, mother and children.

Finally, there emerges a third element coming to the surface over the years, a counterpoint to the first two. Ever since The Netherlands, in 1648, won freedom from the tyranny and oppression of Spain after a long bitter struggle, the Netherlanders have been known for tolerance, individualism and learning. Hence it comes as no surprise that their descendants in America, more especially those living on plantations in the valleys of the Raritan and the Millstone, were avowed patriots from the moment of the first strident chords resounded heralding a Revolution. They abhorred government by fiat wherever it existed. Above all, they valued personal freedom, the right to make their own decisions and lead their own lives.

Thus when the nation's economy in the nineteenth century shifted from agricultural dominance, they did not hesitate when they deemed the time appropriate to effect the transition from rural surroundings to business and the professions. Frederick Van Dyke (1751-1811), son of Jan the Fifth, as the family history records, became a successful merchant in New Brunswick after the Revolution, and his son Augustus (1790-1875) rose to be a leading physician in Philadelphia. Further tracing this collateral line, Henry Jackson Van Dyke, son of Augustus, was the father of the well known Henry Van Dyke (1852-1933), beloved Presbyterian minister of the Brick Church, New York, author, poet, popular after-dinner speaker, and in later years professor of English literature at Princeton University. These are but a few examples.

In other families with Dutch roots stemming from the pioneer settlers, similar scenarios have been repeated again and again. Interesting stories of cultural assimilation still remain buried in archival documents waiting to be discovered. On the land only scattered traces exist of their presence, usually in isolated places unknown to the average tourist. As the history shows, commercial inroads with wholesale destruction have exacted a heavy toll of Dutch antiquity. Huge tracts once plowed by horses and oxen yielding rich grain harvests have long since vanished from the scene. Among them is the Penns Neck farm where John Schenck Van Dyke of the Ninth Generation toiled out of a sense of duty in his youth while his mind pondered other things.

By the twentieth century nearly all the decendants of those hearty Dutch farmers had found a niche in American society and were Dutch in name only.

APPENDIX A

PREFACE TO THE "VAN DYCKS" COMPILED BY RICHARD WILSON COOK (1903-1981)[1]

The Van Dycks have been prominent in America for three hundred years, but, like others of a similar age and standing, much of their early history has been lost. Those who have written up the family genealogies have been greatly handicapped due both to the absence of information and to the confusion in such records as still exist. Errors have crept in and been repeated so often that many people today believe such errors now to be facts. This state is most unfortunate as it has led to many wrong conclusions.

After much research and study the following information has been assembled to be used, it is hoped, as a guide by many students of the Van Dyck families. It too may have errors, but it is believed that the way has been pointed toward a clearer understanding of the various families of Van Dycks who settled in New Amsterdam, and of their many descendants who came to New Jersey. Included are the Van Dycks of Long Island, of which there appears to have been three distinct branches, who probably had as their common ancestors one Thomas van Dyck; and the two Van Dycks of New York, the family of Frans van Dyck, and Henricus Van Dyck, the Fiscal.

Abbreviations are those used by the Genealogical Society of New Jersey (GMNJ 24:57).

Flatbush Church Records (Fl CR) are from the Frost Collection in the Long Island Historical Society.

The following genealogical works were consulted and used with caution but are not referred to as they were not considered in general as being satisfactory source material for this compilation.

Bergen: Early Settlers of Kings County
Aitkin: Beekman-Van Dyke Genealogy.
Rev. James R. Whalen Van Dyke &
Rev. Joseph Smith VanDyke: Van Dyke Genealogy.
John C.Van Dyke: The Raritan - Notes on a River and a Family
Holland Society Year Books

APPENDIX B

PURCHASE OF MANHATTAN ISLAND

Peter Schaghen's letter of November 5, 1626 to the States General is the only document extant specifically referring to the purchase of Manhattan Island from the Indians, and hence merits careful analysis against the background of known facts. The statement "they have purchased the island Manhattes from the Indians" instantly raises questions. Who bought the island? When? What are the facts?

The famous purchase took place under one of two Dutch governors: William van der Hulst (Verhulst) appointed provisional director of New Netherland who came with a group of settlers in January 1625 or Peter Minuit who arrived in the colony on May 4, 1626. The settlers were given a choice of residing on the South River (Delaware) or the North River (Hudson) since the West India Company was undecided at that time where the best location was for a trading post to conduct a fur trade with the Indians. This is manifest from the instructions given to Verhulst on April 22, 1625. Verhulst, assisted by Cryn Fredericxsz, a surveyor, was directed to:

> *investigate which is the most suitable place, abandoned or unoccupied on either river, and then settle there with all the cattle and build the necessary fortifications. And finding none but those that are occupied by the Indians, they shall see whether they cannot, either in return for trading-goods or by means of some amicable agreement, induce them to give up ownership and possession to us, without however forcing them thereto in the least or taking possession by craft or fraud, lest we call down the wrath of God upon our unrighteous beginnings ... (Weslager 35,42,43).*

These directions, it may be fairly said, are important in appraising the evidence.

When Peter Minuit arrived in the Dutch colony on May 4, 1626, he found Verhulst in disgrace. Having been charged with converting company goods to his own use, Verhulst was tried, found guilty and banished from the colony, leaving with his wife on September 23, 1626 on a Dutch sailing ship, the same ship carrying the news of the island purchase back to Amsterdam, Holland.

Peter Schaghen's letter is also interesting in asserting that "their women, also have borne children there" and "they had their grain sowed by the middle of May", inferring that these early Dutch settlers on the island had inhabited it for some extended period of time before Minuit arrived. Whatever the period of habitation may have been, clearly the opportunity existed to trade goods with the Indians and obtain possession in a friendly manner.

Did Verhulst follow his instructions?

Why did Schaghen, who must have known the facts, not name the purchaser?

C. A. Weslager, author and Dutch historian, in A Man And His Ship: Peter Minuit and the Kalmar Nyckel suggests, as one hypothesis, that Peter Schaghen may not have wanted to give credit to the banished director and therefore declined to name him (Weslager 38). This has the ring of truth.

Peter Minuit, an able leader, stands in sharp contrast. Held in the highest esteem, he was chosen to head the New Netherland colony replacing the disgraced Verhulst. Would not Peter Schaghen in making the announcement have specifically referred to Peter Minuit, the new director, if Minuit had in fact negotiated the purchase of the island from the Indians?

Michael Kammen, a leading authority on American colonial history, in his comprehensive survey, Colonial New York, assigns full credit to William Verhulst and calls the Minuit purchase a myth (Kammen 30).

APPENDIX C

PROFILE of JACOB LEISLER

Jacob Leisler (1640-1691) considered himself the legitimate head of the New York province in the absence of Nicholson relying upon a letter of the King's Secretary of State to Nicholson empowering him (Nicholson) to preserve the peace and welfare of the King's subjects or "in his absence to such for the time being take care for Preserving the Peace and administering the Lawes of our said Province in New York in America." And Leisler was indeed in charge preserving the peace and administering the laws. It is therefore ironic that he should be charged with committing treason and forthwith tried, convicted, and executed on May 16, 1691. There can be no doubt that a political faction opposed to Leisler was responsible for this gross miscarriage of justice. An act of parliament in 1695 recognized Leisler as the legal governor of New York and absolved him of all wrong doing; and his estate which had been confiscated was awarded to his heirs. With respect to the socalled "rebellion", scholars have disagreed not only on certain conclusions but the facts. A number of facts, nevertheless, are clear. Jacob Leisler, the son of Frankfurt-am-Main's French Reformed minister, arrived in New Amsterdam in 1660 at the age of twenty as a soldier in the employ of the Dutch West India Company. There he married a merchant's widow. By 1689 he had risen to become a prosperous merchant and had served as a justice of the peace, a captain of the militia and a commissioner of the court of admiralty. While well known and highly respected in the colony, he was not accepted by many of the Anglo-Dutch elite. During his short regime (1689-91), he dissolved James II's grants of monopolies to towns, apportioned taxes more equitably and fostered a more representative government.

The Leisler affair paralleled an era of great turmoil in England as well as unrest in her colonies. And for good reason. The colonists in New York were infuriated when in 1688, they learned that their colony had been annexed to the Dominion of New England by an edict of James II. It was a period in England known as the Glorious Revolution, as the English liked to call it. In 1689, James II was overthrown and succeeded by William of Orange, the famous Dutch prince, and his wife Mary, the eldest daughter of James II and a protestant. In this heated political climate Leisler stirred the passions of his enemies who, it appears at the first opportunity, sought revenge.

Dr. David William Voorhees, a Research Fellow at New York University and an eminent authority on Jacob Leisler, is currently editing some three thousand Leisler documents that have survived, a fact remarkable in itself since Leisler's enemies made every attempt to destroy his correspondence and other writings. Dr. Voorhees finds that Leisler came from a very prominent European family. His name first apppears in Dutch documents as an "Adelborst", a gentleman soldier. Religion occupied a major role in the controversy. It is fortunate indeed that the true facts concerning Jacob Leisler and this transition period in history from Dutch to English is now being brought to light.

In a letter to the author Dr. Voorhees said:

There is little to indicate that Leisler was working from democratic concepts. Current studies indicate that the contest between Leislerian and antileislerian was more between two equal parties for power and prestige in a still unstable pioneer society. My own thesis focuses on the religious aspects, but economics, interfamilial feuds, and other factors all played a part. That Leisler's execution was a travesty of justice seems pretty clear, as the Parliamentary hearings in 1695 showed, but to his followers he died as a "martyr" for the House of Orange and the Reformed religion not for democracy.

APPENDIX D

WILL OF JAN JANSEN VAN DYCK (1648/49-ca 1736)

IN THE NAME OF GOD AMEN

I JOHN VAN DYCK of New Uytrecht in Kings County on the Island Nassau in [ye] province of New York yeoman being of perfect health both in Body & mind but knowing the certainty of Death & uncertainty of the Time of its approach Do make my Last Will and Testament in manner and form following

first I bequeath my soul to God who gave it my Body to the Earth from whence it came to be decently Interred at the Discretion of my Executors hereafter named in Certain hopes of a Resurrection & the Union of my Body & Soul at the last day and of Eternal Life through the sole merrits of my Blessed Saviour Jesus Christ and as to what worldly Estate God hath pleased to Bestow upon me and that shall belong to me at the time of my Dec'se after my just debts and funeral are paid and satisfyed I give Devise and Bequeath of the same manner and form following.

Imprimis I give and Bequeath unto my loveing Children John Van Dyck Mattys Van Dyck Catherin Widow of Daniel Hendrickson Jannet wife of Capt Rutgers Van Brunt Angennetje wife to Simon DeHart all my personal Estate which I have within the province of New York or Elsewhere for them their heirs and Assigns forever to be Equally Divided share and share alike that is to say after the Legacies are paid to some of my Grant Children hereafter named to which I have Bequeathed in manner following

Imprimis I give and Bequeath unto my Grant Son John Stephens the sum of five shillings Currant money of New York to be paid to him by my Exers hereafter named within six months after my Decease which sum is to be his full share & proportion of my Estate whatsoever.

Item I give and Bequeath unto my Grant Daughter Teuntje being the widdow of John Sleigh Deceased the sum of twenty five pounds Currant money of New York to be paid to her by my Executors hereafter named within six months after my Decease which sum is to be in full share and proportion of my Estate whatsoever.

Item I give and Bequeath unto my Grant Children of my Daughter Catleyntje Deceased which was the wife of Garret Ketteltas they are in number Three Sons & Three Daughters each five shill Currant money of New York to be paid Them by my Exers hereafter named within six months after my Decease which sum is to be in full share & proportion of my Estate Whatsoever.

Item I give and bequeath unto my Great Grant Son John Van Buren being the son of my Grant Daughter Teuntje Richon Deceased which was the wife of Doctor John Van Buren Junr The sum of Fifteen pounds Current money of New York to be paid to him by my Exers hereafter named that is when he shall arrive to the full age of twenty one years & not Before but if in Case my said

Great Grant son John Van Buren should die before the age of twenty one years without Issue then in that Case it is my said Express will and order that the Before mentioned fifteen pounds Currant money aforesd shall Decend upon my own Children before named and be Equally Divided amongst them share & share alike otherwise the which sum is to be in full share & proportion of my Estate whatsoever

Lastly I hereby nominate Constitute & appoint my Loveing Sons John VanDyck Mattys Van Dyck Rutgers Van Brunt Symon DeHart to be my sole Exers of this my Last will and Testament & Do Deligent take care that everything and article to be Duely and Truely performed According to ye true Intent and Meaning hereof

And I do hereby utterly Disallow Revoke and Disannul all & every other former Testament wills and Legacies bequests and Executors by me in any ways before this time named & Bequeathed Ratifying and Confirming This & no other to be my Last will and Testament

In Witness whereof I have hereunto set my hand seal this sixteenth day of May in the year of our Lord Christ Anno Domini one thousand seven hundred and Thirty five

his
John Van (X) Dyck [L.S.]
mark

Signed sealed published pronounced & Declared by the said John Van Dyck as his Last Will and Testament in the presence of us the subscribers

Cornelius Van Brunt
Joost Van Brunt
Theo Elsworth
Christopher Codwise

APPENDIX E

ENTRIES IN AN OLD DUTCH FAMILY BIBLE OF JAN VAN DYCK (1682-1764) AND ANNA VERKERK, HIS WIFE

Entries

Anno 1706 den 5de Jun:
Ben ick Jan Van Dyck met Anna Ver Kerck Getrouwt.
1707, den 18th Apryl, is myn Doghter Juentye geboren.
1708, den 10de April, is myn Doghter Catrina geboren.
1709, den 5de November, is myn Soen Jan geboren.
1710, den 18de Mey, is myn Soen Roelof geboren.
1714, den 28de Augustus, is myn Soen Mattys geboren.
1716, den 3de October, is myn Soen Abraham geboren.
1718, den 12de October, is my Soen Simon geboren.
1721, den 28th June, is Isaac, my Soen, geboren.
1723, den 12 November, is myn Soen Jacob geboren.
1725, den 16 June, is myn Doghter Anna geboren.
1743, den 12 Mert, is myn soen ... [illegible] gestorven.
1752 den 24 Mert, is myn schoen Son Johanes Emans gestorven.
den 27 Mert, is Anna Emans gestorven.
den 1 April, is Tuentye Emans gestorven.
1754, den 27th June, is der boven geschreven Anna Verkerk overleden.
1764, der 18th Dec., is der boven geschreven Jan Van Dyck overleden.
January 13th, Anno 1684, Ben Ick Anna Verkerk.

Translation

In the year 1706 on June 5th:
I, Jan Van Dyck and Anna Ver Kerck were married.
1707, 18th April, my daughter Juentye was born.
1708, 10th April, my daughter Catrina was born.
1709, 5th November, my son Jan was born.
1710, 18th May, my son Roelof was born.
1714, 28th August, my son Mattys was born.
1716, 3rd October, my son Abraham was born.
1718, 12th October, my son Simon was born.
1721, 28th June, my son Isaac was born.
1723, 12th November, my son Jacob was born.
1725, 16th June, my daughter Anna was born.
1743, 12th March, my son ... [illegible] died.[1]
1752, 24th March, my son Johannes Emans died.
27th March, Anna Emans died.[2]
1 April, Tuentye Emans died.[2]
1754, 27th June, the above mentioned Anna Verkerk died.
1764, 18th December, the above mentioned Jan Van Dyck died.
January 13th, Anno 1684, I am Anna Verkerk.

Death of Anna Verkerk

Unfortunately the Old Dutch Family Bible of Jan the Fourth has not been found, from which we could compare for accuracy the transcribed record with the original entries.

The author is of the opinion, based upon the evidence available, that the date of death of Anna Verkerk given as June 27, 1754 is incorrect and should have been written June 27, 1764 (error in the tens digit). If this is correct, she was eighty years old on January 13, 1764 (born January 13, 1684) consistent with the tombstone inscription reading "Anna wife of Jan Van D--e when she died upwards of 80 years old".

Accepting 1754 as the year of death, the assumption runs counter to known facts: (1) In 1754 Anna would have been only 70 years old; (2) The will of Jan Van Dyck made April 12, 1757 creating a life estate for her attests that she was living in 1757.

Birth of Ruloff (Roelof) Van Dike

Because of a similar transcribing error, the birth of Ruloff was May 18, 1711 rather than May 18, 1710 as is noted in the text (Cook 18).

History

Some facts are clear. The words "January 13th Anno 1684, I am Anna Verkerk" may be interpreted "I, Anna Verkerk, was born January 13, 1684".

When Anna (Ann/Annetje) was seven days old, her parents, Roelof Ver Kerk and Catherine, took her to the Breuckelen Dutch Reformed Church to be baptized. The Baptismal Register records the baptism on January 20, 1684 (with four others that day) as follows:

> Annitje; parents: Roelof Verkerck, Catrijn Zijmens;
> witnesses: Jan Dircksen van der Vliet, Geertje Verkerck"
> (van der Linde 123)

One hypothesis suggests that the bible came into the hands of Anna Verkerk when she was a young lady or, perhaps, at the time of her marriage, and to signify ownership at that time she wrote in it her name and birthday. Upon the death of her husband, who made most of the entries, the bible was probably handed down to the first born son, John Van Dike of the Fifth Generation. This is indicated by the estate inventory of John Van Dike that lists "1 large Dutch Bible" (SA).

The Van Dyck family record together with a record of the Henry family were given by Mary Steen Henry Obdyke to the Genealogical Society of Pennsylvania and published March 1928 in Volume 10, No 2 (GSP 10:178-178). Miss Obdyke was a granddaughter of the Reverend J. Addison Henry of Philadelphia, who was said to be in possession of the bible in 1890 when the records were photographed by William H. Rue of that city (SCHQ 4:264).

Neither the bible nor the photographic reproduction of the records has been found. The author would welcome any relevant information.

A summary of the Henry family genealogy follows:

Rev. Symmes C. Henry, born June 7, 1797,
died March 22, 1857
M January 17, 1826
Catherine Rowley, born May 22, 1801

Six children including
James Addison Henry, born October 28, 1835
died August 8, 1906
M July 25, 1861
Mary Service Steen, born February 1, 1837

Two children including
Margaret Steen Henry, born April 23, 1862
M April 3, 1890
William Austin Obdyke

Mary Steen Henry Obdyke
born March 3, 1893, Wayne, Pa.
Unmarried

Josephine Austin Obdyke
born October 23, 1896, Wayne, Pa.
M May 6, 1919
John Kittera Garriques

Miss Obdyke's mother and father were married in the Princeton Presbyterian Church, Philadelphia, of which the Reverend J. Addison Henry was the pastor in 1890. Her sister Josephine was married in the Radnor Presbyterian Church, Wayne, Pennsylvania.

APPENDIX F

EAST AND WEST JERSEY: THE PROPRIETARY PERIOD

On old maps a line is seen running north and south dividing New Jersey into two parts called East Jersey and West Jersey. The division line has its origin in the original proprietors, Lord John Berkeley (_____-1678) and Sir George Carteret (ca1613-1679), to whom a vast tract of land was conveyed in 1664 by the Duke of York, James the brother of Charles II. England and Holland in this period were contending sea powers. The conveyance, in effect, constituted part of a plan to seize control of the New Netherland colony settled by the Dutch.

The Berkeley-Carteret partnership lasted about ten years. Lord Berkeley having become disenchanted with the colonization venture offered his halfshare for sale. It was purchased by John Fenwick and Edward Byllinge, members of the Society of Friends and close associates of William Penn (1644-1718). As a result, a survey became necessary to define a boundary. Carteret retained title to the land on the east side while Penn and his associates received title on the west side, the two parcels being described in a deed dated July 1, 1676 between George Carteret and the trustees of Byllinge. Said William Penn: "We have all that side on Delaware river from one end to the other; the line of partition is from the east side of Little Egg Harbor, straight north, through the country, to the utmost branch of Delaware river; with all powers, privileges, and immunities whatsoever. Ours is called New West Jersey; his is called New East Jersey". (Barber/Howe 20).

Carteret remained the sole proprietor of East Jersey until his death in 1679 when, as ordered by his will, the East Jersey province was placed on the market for sale by his widow and executors to pay his debts. Curiously the purchasers were William Penn and eleven of his friends who became known as the "twelve proprietors". Soon thereafter their numbers increased to twenty-four, each of the twelve taking on a partner.

The twenty-four proprietors, all principally interested in monetary gain in selling off their respective parcels, devised various methods and schemes for governing. The net result was a different government in each small domain inevitably creating confusion and dissention among the colonists. Finally, the proprietors, weary of administration, surrendered all governmental authority to the British Crown, formally accepted by Queen Ann on April 17, 1702.

It is interesting to note that although New Jersey was then united into a single province, the terms East and West Jersey remained for many years prior to the Revolution.

APPENDIX G

WILL OF JAN VAN DYCK (1682-1764)

In the name of God Amen, The Twelth Day of April Anno Domini One thousand Seven Hundred and fifty seven. I John Van Dike of the Corporation of New Brunswick in the County of Middlesex and Eastern Division of the province of New Jersey yeoman, being now (thanks to God) in good health and of Sound and perfect mind and memory Do make, and publish this my Last Will and Testament in manner following -

And first I nominate constitute and appoint Ann my now wife Executrix and all my sons named John, Ruloff, Mathias, Simon, Isaac, and Jacob Executors of this my said Last Will -

Item. I Give Devise and bequeath unto my Eldest Son John and to his heirs and assigns forever all that Farm & Tract of Land Situate in the County of Somerset whereon he now Lives which I purchased of Gershom Wiggins Containing about Two hundred and Thirty Acres to the same more or less as also my Silver Tankard which is marked with the first Letters of my name in a Cipher -

Item. I Give Devise and bequeath unto my Son Ruloff and to his heirs and assigns forever, all that Farm & Tract of Land whereon he now Lives Situate in the said County of Somerset containing about Two hundred and Thirty Acres, to the same more or less, which I purchased partly of the widdow [of] Thomson Hollinshead and Francis Hollinshead and partly of Thomas Leonard Esq -

Item. I Give Devise and bequeath unto my Son Mathias and to his heirs and assigns forever, all that Farm & Tract of Land whereon he now lives Situate at Maples Town in the County of Middlesex, which I purchased of Thomas South containing about Two hundred acres to the Same more or less, as also the Sum of fifty pounds Currency of East New Jersey at Eight Shillings per Ounce, to be paid unto him my Said Son Mathias his heirs or assigns by my Son Isaac or his heirs at or before the Expiration of One Year after my Decease -

Item. I Give Devise and bequeath unto my Son Simon and to his heirs and assigns forever, all that Farm & Tract of Land whereon he now Lives Situate near fresh pond in the County of Middlesex, containing about Three hundred acres more or less, which I purchased of Andrew Johnston Esq. as also the Sum of One hundred Pounds Current money of East New Jersey at Eight Shillings per Ounce, to be paid unto him my Said Son Simon his heirs or assigns, by my Said Son Isaac or his heirs at or before the Expiration of One Year after my Decease -

Item. I Give Devise and bequeath unto my Son Isaac and to his heirs and Assigns forever, all that Farm & Tract of Land whereon he now Lives, Situate at Maples Town in the County of Middlesex, containing about Two hundred and Sixty four Acres to the Same more or less which I purchased partly of Benjamin Pridmore and partly of Fredrick Dolhason, Provided he my Said Son Isaac his heirs Executors or administrators Shall and Do pay well and truly unto my Said Son Mathias his heirs or assigns the Sum of Fifty Pounds Current money of East New Jersey at Eight Shillings per Ounce, and the Sum of One hundred Pounds of like Current money unto my Said Son Simon his heirs or assigns at or before the Expiration of One Year after my Decease, according to the Legacys by me to them given

Item. I Give Devise amd bequeath unto my Son Jacob and to his heirs and assigns forever, all that Tract of Land Situate near Rockyhill in the County of Somerset which I purchased of John Harrisson containing about One hundred and fifty Acres to the Same more or less and also one other Tract of Land near the Same place containing about fifty acres more or less which I purchased of Thomas Yates Esq and also One Other Tract of Land adjoining the aforesaid Last Mentioned Tract Containing about Thirty five acres more or less which I purchased of Thomas Soden -

Item. I give and bequeath unto my three Daughters, Tuentje (wife of Johannes Emans) Catharine (wife of Gerradus Beekman) and Ann (wife of Albert Voorhees) to Each and Every of them my Said Daughters the Sum of Two hundred and fifty pounds Current Money of East New Jersey at Eight Shillings per Ounce, to be paid by my Executors as follows that is to Say the Sum of Two hundred Pounds in part thereof to be paid and Equally Divided amongst them my Said Daughters or their respective heirs at or before the Expiration of One Year after My Decease, Two hundred Pounds more and in further part thereof to be paid and Equally Divided as aforesaid at or before the Expiration of Two Years after My Decease, One hundred Pounds more thereof to be paid and Divided as aforesaid Three Years after My Decease, One hundred and fifty Pounds more thereof to be paid and Divided as aforesaid four years after my Decease, and the residue being One hundred Pounds more to be paid and Equally Divided as aforesaid at or before the Expiration of five Years after my Decease -

Item. I Give and bequeath unto Ann my now wife all my homestall Farm and Tract of Land whereon I now live containing about Six hundred Acres which I purchased partly of John Moss and partly of Benjamin Harrisson, Together with about Eighty Acres of Woodland which I purchased of Samuel Drake, as also all my real and personal Estate which is not herein before bequeathed, During her natural Life and it is further my Will and I Do order that after the Decease of my Said wife all my said homestall Farm and said Eighty Acres of Woodland with all other my real and personal Estate whatsoever and wheresoever (Except what is herein before particularly given and Devised by me to my Children as aforesaid) Shall be Sold by my Said Executors or the Survivors of them as Soon as conveniently may be after the Decease of my Said wife, and for the Doing Executing and performing thereof I Do by these presents give grant will and Transfer unto My Said Executors or the Survivors or Survivor of them, full power and authority to grant allien bargain Sell Convey and assure the Same and Every or any part thereof in Such proportions as they in their Discression Shall think fit, to any person or persons, and to their heirs and assigns forever in fee Simple, by all and Every Such Lawful ways and means as to my Said Executors or the Survivors or Survivor of them and his or their Council Learned in the Law Shall Seem fit or necessary, and all the money arising from the Sales thereof I Do hereby Give and bequeath unto all my aforesaid Children named John, Ruloff, Mathias, Simon, Isaac, Jacob, Tuentje, Catharine, and Ann and to their respective heirs, and assigns forever, to be by Amongst and Between all them my Said Children or their respective heirs Equally Divided in Even proportions and like Shares, being one ninth part thereof to Each of them or their respective heirs or assigns -

And it is likewise my Will and Desire and I Do order that in Case it Shall or may happen that any Dispute or controversy Doth arise respecting the right and Title of any of the said Lands herein before by me Given and or particularly Devised to all or any of my aforesaid Six Sons, that Each and Every of them my Said Six Sons Shall and Do pay an Equal part of the Cost and Charges which Shall or may accrue thereon, and in Case any part of the Said Lands So by me Devised Shall or may be recover'd from any of my Said Sons by Law for want of my not having a Sufficient Title to the Same, in Such Case Each of my aforesaid Six Sons or their respective heirs Shall bear any Equal proportionate part of the Loss as the Land Shall be valued by Indifferent men by them to be Chosen and agreed upon, and Each of my Said Sons or their respective heirs Shall pay their proportion in money to any one or more of them or their heirs so Looseing any of their Land according to Said Valuation. In Witness Whereof I the said John Van Dike have hereunto Set my hand and Seal the Day and Year first herein before Written -

Sign Sealed published pronounced and Declared by the Said John Van Dike as his Last Will and Testament the word (before) between the 5th and 6th lines from the Top of the 3rd page being first Interlined in the presence of us the Subscribers

/S/ Jacob Bergen — /S/ Jan Van dyck *[seal]*
/S/ Peter Berrien
/S/ John Berrien

Memorandum that on the twenty fifth day of January, in the year of our Lord One Thousand Seven hundred Sixty five, Jacob Bergen & Peter Berrien, two of the subscribing witnesses to the foregoing Will appeared before me John Smyth duly authorized etc. and they being Sworn on the Holy Evangelists of Almighty God on their Oath do declare that they were present and did see Jan Van dyke, the testator above named sign & seal the foregoing Instrument & heard him publish pronounce & declare it to be his Last Will and Testament: that at the doing thereof the said Testator was of sound mind & memory to the best of their knowledge and as they verily believe: and that John Berrien the other witness was also present & signed as an evidence thereto as each of the deponents did in the presence of the said Jan Van dyck - Also that at the same time John, Ruloff, Matthias, Simon, Isaac & Jacob Van dyck the executors in the foregoing Will named came before me and were duly qualifyed by takeing the oath of executors by Law appointed.

/S/ John Smyth

APPENDIX H

ROCKINGHAM FOR SALE

Margaret Berrien, widow of Judge John Berrien, resided at Rockingham after her husband's death in 1772 until 1783. On July 5, 1783 she placed an advertisement in the Royal Gazette, a New York City newspaper, reading as follows:

> FOR SALE- That very healthy and finely situated farm, 'Rockingham'. The property of Mrs. Margaret Berrien. This farm lies on the River Millstone, about five miles from Princeton, on the road leading from Princeton to Morristown. It contains about 320 acres, a good proportion of meadows and woodland. The soil is good for wheat and natural grass, so that a great quantity of the best English meadow may be made with little trouble or expense. The place is well watered. The house contains upwards of twenty rooms of different kinds, including a kitchen very conveniently contrived and genteely finished, and cellar almost under the whole. There is also a very good barn, and stables, coach-house, granary and fowl house, all painted; a curious smokehouse, and other outbuildings. There are several fine young apple orchards containing the best grafted fruit in our country, besides a variety of pears, plums, peaches and cherries, raspberries and currants. There is also a small tenement on the said farm of three rooms, with a cellar and milk-room, and the whole farm abounds in springs of the best water. There are several thousand very thrifty red cedar trees, a great number of which have been trimmed and properly cultivated. (SCHQ 1:86).

Although Cornwallis surrendered to Washington at Yorktown, Virginia, on October, 19, 1781, peace negotiations were still being conducted in Paris in July of 1783.[1] Meanwhile British troops occupied New York City while Washington and his Continental Army were in Newburgh, New York. A body of men who had served the patriot cause marched on Philadelphia demanding clothing, rations and money which the Continental Congress, financially destitute, was unable to provide. Elias Boudinot, the president, thought it wise to terminate sessions in Philadelphia and chose the small village of Princeton, where he once lived, as a safe meeting place where Congress could carry on its business.

Rockingham was selected as a residence and headquarters for Washington who was invited to attend the sessions of Congress. Mrs. Margaret Berrien agreed to take the property off the market and rent it to Washington.

APPENDIX I

HENDRICK CORTELYOU OF TEN MILE RUN AND HIS ANCESTRAL LINE

A scholarly treatise by John J. DeMott traces the origin of the Cortelyou family in seventeenth century Holland from the ancient Dutch city of Utrecht to the tiny Dutch settlement on Long Island called New Utrecht (SCHQ 1:103-106). In the final paragraph DeMott says: "The sons and grandsons of Jacques, the pioneer, came from Long Island to New Jersey in 1701, or soon thereafter. The numerous Cortelyous in Somerset and adjoining counties now are therefore all direct descendants, of eighth, ninth and tenth generations of Jacques Cortelyou, of Old and New Utrecht".

Complementing DeMott's analysis, The Cortelyou Genealogy by John Van Zandt Cortelyou recounts not only the genealogy but much of the history of the Cortelyou family in America. Published in 1942, it reflects intensive research and study. Said the author: "This book, as far as the writer himself is concerned was begun in the 1890's. But it was not earlier than twenty years ago that the work began to develop to any great extent. During the last eight years, however, practically all of my time has been devoted to it".

Jacques Cortelyou was born in Utrecht, Holland, about the year 1625, the son of Walloon parents who had fled religious persecution in provinces of present day Belgium and France. Matriculated at the University of Utrecht, the seat of learning in Western Europe, Jacques was a mathematician, philosopher, linguist, and by profession a surveyor. After coming to America in 1652, he married Neeltje Van Duyn about 1655/56. Six children survived infancy:

Jacques (ca1660-1731)
Cornelis (ca1662-ca1690)
Pieter (Peter) (ca1664/65-1757)
Helena (ca1666-1720)
Maria (ca1669-____)
Willem (ca1671-before1693)
(Cortelyou 65-67)

Jacques Cortelyou's son Peter and two of Peter's associates, in 1699, purchased from the proprietors 3,000 acres on the east side of the Millstone river extending from the Griggstown toward Franklin Park and Ten Mile Run (SCHQ 6:159). In 1712 Peter sold 300 acres between the old Indian Path and Middlebush road to Garret Stryker (SCHQ 5:185,186). In general the record discloses that in the capacity of surveyor, land investor, as well as in other pursuits, Peter enjoyed a long and productive life and survived all his siblings. Succumbing to the infirmities of old age, he died at his home on the Nyack bluff overlooking the Narrows in his ninety-third year (Cortelyou 77-81).

It was Peter's brother Jacques, however, who was the progenitor of the Somerset County Cortelyous. Among seven children of his marriage to Altie I. Boerman was a son Hendrick born April 18, 1711. Pursuant to the will of his father who died in 1731, Hendrick inherited 300 acres in Somerset County.

As a young man, Hendrick left New Utrecht on Long Island and established a home for his family at Ten Mile Run. In the colonizing era navigable roads were indispensable to human habitation, and in the year 1735 we find Hendrick in the company of three other men having laid out a road described in homely terms incorporating landmarks peculiarly known to the settlers but now lost in obscurity. For example, "A road laid out from Basking Ridge to ye west of the bridge on the north-west branch of Dead river, beginning at ye south side of Cornelius Breasin's said land which he now lives on ... then south-east of Robert Pain's house, and so along as the path now goes. Round the north-west corner of the Long Hill and so as the path goes to Dan Lewiston. Thence along the said path till it comes in the main road being a two-rod road". A full description of this primitive, meandering byway cut through trees and thickets was officially recorded on October 7, 1735 by the clerk of Somerset County in Road Book A (SCHQ 1:101).

Hendrick Cortelyou of the Third Generation of the Cortelyou family in America married a Dutch girl, Antie Albertse Van Voorhees, by whom he had five children, one of whom named Hendrick was born October 10, 1736. And there, in the Ten Mile Run cemetery, peacefully lie Hendrick Cortelyou and his Dutch wife, Johanna Stoothoff, amid fifty-three Cortelyous and twenty-seven Van Dycks (SCHQ 4:66,136,137,140,141). Accordingly, it should come as no surprise that three Cortelyous of the Fourth Generation intermarried with Van Dycks.

Summerized genealogically, the ancestral line of Hendrick Cortelyou of Ten Mile Run stemming from Jacques Cortelyou, the Dutch settler of Old and New Utrecht, is as follows:

First Generation

Jacques born ca1625, Utrecht, Holland, died 1693, New Utrecht, Long Island
Married Neeltje Van Duyn 1655/56
Seven children survived infancy including Jacques
(Cortelyou 65-67; SCHQ 1:103-106)

Second Generation

Jacques born ca1660, died May 3, 1731
Married first Marretje Hendricks Smack October 4, 1685
Eight children
Married second Altie I. Boerman January 10, 1706
Seven children including Hendrick
(Cortelyou 68-76)

Third Generation

Hendrick born April 18, 1711, died before March 5, 1777
Married first Antie Albertse Van Voorhees August 3, 1731
Five children including Hendrick
Married second Catrina Hooglandt August 19, 1742
Of eight children three married Van Dykes:
- Hermanus (Harman) (1747-1816) married Catherine Van Dyke
- Altie Cortelyou (1749-____) married Ferdinand Van Dyke
- Marya (Maria) Cortelyou (1752-____) married Jan Van Dyke

(Cortelyou 89-91,108-110)

Fourth Generation

Hendrick born October 10, 1736, died October 31, 1800
Married Johannah Stoothoff
Eleven children
Buried in the Ten Mile Run cemetery
(Cortelyou 89-91;SCHQ 4:136,137)

APPENDIX J

CORNELIA VAN DYCK

Was Cornelia, wife of Henry Berrien, the daughter of John Van Dike (1709-1777/78) of the Fifth Generation?

Cornelia and her husband Henry Berrien were born in the same year in Somerset County. They lived all their lives in Somerset County and are buried in the Ten Mile Run cemetery. Inscriptions on their respective monuments disclose:

Cornelia born December 8, 1743, died May 8, 1824
Henry born February 16, 1743, died May 16, 1806
(SCHQ 4:65)

Upon the marriage of Cornelia to Henry Berrien about the year 1765, Cornelia bore nine children baptized in the Dutch Reformed Church in keeping with Dutch tradition (Heiss 14,28,29). Neither a marriage certificate nor a marriage record has come to light and may not exist.

A Berrien Family Genealogy compiled by Margaret Kilpatrick Baumeister and Margaret Grant Plumb published in Transactions of the Huguenot Society of South Carolina (1968) states that Henry Berrien married "Cornelia Van Dyck 12/8/1743 - 5/8/1824, Somerset Co.,N.J." (THSSC 73:75). No authority, however, is cited. Based upon the totality of evidence, the author concludes that the statement is probably correct and that Cornelia was a member of the family of John Van Dike of the Fifth Generation.

By his marriage of seventeen years to Margaretta Barcalo on January 15, 1732, John Van Dike fathered at least three children (Cook 22). Other records may have been lost. The birth of a fourth child - assuming this child to be Cornelia born in the year 1743 - is possible and consistent with the family history.

Margaretta Barcalo died July 5, 1749. The following year John Van Dike married Garritie (Charity) Bergen by whom he had nine children. By this time a close affinity had developed between the Van Dike and Berrien families plainly exhibited by the Dutch settlement history, a relevant factor. Briefly, Henry Berrien's father, Peter Berrien (1714-1781) born at Newtown, Long Island, and his older brother John (1711-1772), a lawyer and later an eminent jurist, settled in the Millstone Valley in or about the year 1735. Judge Berrien's home, which he named Rockingham, nestled along the banks of the Millstone River at Rocky Hill while Peter's home lay on the Assunpink trail about a mile to the east. Earlier, in 1711, Jan Van Dyck (Jan the Fourth) bought 300 acres at Ten Mile Run where he settled with his family on the Middlesex side of the old Indian path. In short, these two Dutch families living in close propinquity in the Millstone Valley were intimately acquainted. Thus it is not surprising that intermarriages followed and that in the Ten Mile Run Cemetery lie twenty-seven Van Dikes and eight Berriens (SCHQ 4:65,140,141).

Cornelia was approaching her seventh birthday when John Van Dike married Charity Bergen, daughter of Frederick Bergen and Gerryte Veghte, on July 24, 1750. No evidence has been found that Charity married earlier or had born a child. On the other hand, if Charity had given birth to a child named Cornelia, this child would have become a foster daughter of John Van Dike; hence another possibility.

Therefore, a search of the archival documents for a possible clue of filial relationship was indicated.

The third child of the marriage of John Van Dike and Charity Bergen was a son Jacob, an ardent patriot of the American Revolution. A wealthy landholder residing near Griggstown, Somerset County, Jacob played a significant role in public affairs. Upon the death in 1806 of Henry Berrien, intestate and presumably quite suddenly, the intestate law mandated the appointment of an administrator to settle his estate. Cornelia chose two individuals, namely her son-in-law, William Duryea (Heiss 14), and Jacob Van Dike, evidenced by their respective signatures in the records of the Estate of Henry Berrien, Deceased filed in the Somerset County Court on June 3, 1806 (SA). Given the fact that Cornelia looked to representatives of both families to administer her deceased husband's estate viewed in the light of the interfamilial background strongly suggests that she was a member of the family of John Van Dike. They were persons she could trust for this assignment.

More compelling testimony springs from another archival document lodged in the Somerset County Court, namely the will of Charity Bergen dated August 9, 1787 and probated February 25, 1788 (SA). Assuming that Cornelia was the "daughter" of John Van Dike who at twenty-one years of age became the bride of Henry Berrien, it would be natural for Charity Van Dike to refer to Henry Berrien as her son-in-law.

In fact, she did!

Charity Van Dike's will recites:

> *Lastly I Do hereby Nominate an appoint my son Jacob and my Son in Law hendrick Berrien to be Executors of this my Last Will and Testament ...*

Concerning the will of John Van Dike, a question of course arises. Why did John bequeath to his daughters Ann, Margaret, Jane, Tuentje, Elsie, Catherine and Sarah the residue of his estate in equal shares to the exclusion of Cornelia? Was his love any less for Cornelia?

Only a speculative answer can be given. Nevertheless, it is worthy of note that upon perusing the estate inventory of Henry Berrien, it reflects a man owning substantial property and assets for the period in which he lived. His station in life may be termed of a high order. A picture is presented of a widow living comfortably on a Dutch plantation served by farmhands and servants. In these circumstances John, the testator, upon balancing the equities, may have considered that she was well provided for. Further he may have seen no need to incorporate a verbal explanation in his will.

APPENDIX K

WILL OF JOHN VAN DIKE (1709-1777/78)

IN THE NAME OF GOD AMEN the fourth Day of February Anno Domini One thousand Seven hundred and Seventy five I John Van Dike of the County of Sommerset and Eastern Division of the Province of New Jersey Farmer being much indisposed in Body through Gods Goodness of Sound and Disposing Mind and Memmory do Make and Ordain this to be my Last Will and Testament in manner and form following - to wit - Imprimis I hereby will order and direct that all my Just Debts and funeral Charges be Paid by My Executors herein after Named or the Survivors or Survivor of them as Soon as Conveniently May be after my Decease - Item I Give Devise and Bequeth Unto my Eldest Son John and to his heirs and Assigns for Ever all that farm and Trackt of Land Situate in the County of Sommerset Whereon he now Lives Which I Purchased of Jeames Murrey Esq Containing about two hundred Acres be the Same More or Less as also one Other three angel Lot of Land which I Purchased of Sammuel Nevil Esq Containing about three Acres be the Same More or Less Which Lot is Adjoining the Before Mentioned Trackt of Land and also the Wood Land of the Plantation Whereon Cornelus Tenbrook Now Lives and is Situate at the North West Corner of____ Pattent Provided he my Said Son John his heirs Executors or Administrators Shall well and truly pay unto my Executors here after Named the Sum of five hundred Pounds Money at Eight Shillings per ounce Within Six Month after my Decese of which five hundred Pounds he has already Paid the Sum of two Hundred and fifty three Pounds Nine Shillings and Seven Pence as by my Several Receipts therefore may appear Item I Give Devise and Bequeath unto my son Fredrick the one half Part of all that Trackt of Land Which I purchased of Hew Mac Can Situate at Elamantonk in the County of Hunterdon and the Other half part to my Son Abraham and to Each of their heirs and Assigns for Ever to be Equally Divided Between them the said Fredrick and Abraham their heirs and Assigns Provided they the said Fredrick and Abraham Shall Sepperately and Each for himself well and truly Pay the Sum of One hundred Pounds Money at Eight Shillings per ounce within Six Month after My Decese Item I Give Devise and Bequeath Unto my son Jacob all that Trackt of Land Situate in the County of Sommerset which I purchased of Garrit Williamson Containing about Sixty four Acres be the Same More or Less also One Other Trackt of Land near the Same Place which I Purchased of Samuel Nevil Esq the above mentioned three angel Lot of three Acres Excepted Containing about Ten Acres be the Same More or Less also one other Trackt of Land Situate in the County of Middlesex which I purchsed of Jacob Van Dike Containing about fifty Acres be the Same More or Less to his heirs and assigns for Ever Item I Give and Bequeath Unto Garritie My Now wife all My home stall Farm Whereon I now Live containing about three hundred and Sixty Acres be the Same More or Less which Was Partly Given and Bequeathed Unto Me by My Father John Van Dike by His Last Will and Testament and Partly I purchased of John Ver Kerk as also all My Real and Personal Estate Whatsoever and Wheresoever Except What is herein before Given Devised and Bequeathed During her Natural Life or During the time She Shall Remain my Widow but if She Should happen to Marry again it is my Will and I do Order She Shall have Only So Many household furniture as She brought with her at the time of her Marriage with Me and one Negroe Wench Which I Give her in full Consideration and lew of the Dower of my Said wife and it is further My Will and I Do order that after the Decese of my Said Wife or her Remarrige all my Said home stall farm with all my other Real and Personel Estate Whatsoever and Wheresoever Except what is herein before Given and Bequeathed in any Convenient time after the Decese of my Said Wife or Remarrige Shall be Sold by my Executors or the Survivors of them and the Moneys arising from the Sales thereof to be Divided among my Children hereafter Named and in Manner and form following to wit to my son Roelof the Sum of one hundred Pounds Money at Eight Shillings per ounce over and above his Equal Share and also the one Equal Eight Part of the Said Remainder of my Estate to my Daughter Ann the One Equal Eight Part - the One Equal Eight Part I order to be Left in the hands of My Executors the Anuel Intrest Whereof to be Paid to My Daughter Margrit by my Said Executors Yearly and Every Year During Her Natural Life and After her Decease to be Equally Divided among her Children - the one Equal Eight part to my Daughter Jane - To my daughter Tuntie the one Equal Eight part - To my daughter Elsie the One Equal Eight Part - To my daughter Cathrin the one Equal Eight Part - To my Daughter Sarah the one Equal Eight Part - and it is further My Will and I Do order that if any of my Said Children Should happen to Dye without Issue that Such Shares and Portions Shall be Equally Devided among all of my Surviving Children herein before Named.

Lastly I do hereby Nominate Constitute and appoint Garitie my Wife Executrix and my three Sons by Name Fredrick Abraham and Jacob and my Son in Law Sammuel Stout and my Brother in Law Henrey Bergen to be the Executors of this My Last Will and Testament and do Confirm unto my Said Executors by Name the Several Powers and Authorities herein before giving to my Executors and I do hereby Disannul and Make Void all former Wills and Testaments by Me in any wise made and do Ratifie and Confirm this and no other to be my Last Will and Testament

In Witness Whereof I the Said John Van Dike have hereunto Set my hand and Seal the Day and Year First herein before Written

Signed Sealed Published and
Declared by the Said John Van Dike
as and for his last will and
Testament in the Presence of us
who were present at the Signing
and Sealing thereof the Words
Sealing thereof the Words /S/ John Van Dike [*seal*]
the above mentioned three angel Lot
of three Acres Excepted) Between
the twentyth and twenty first line
from the Top being first Interlined

/S/ Roelof Van Dike
/S/ Jos. B. Cock
/S/ Jacob Van Dike

Roelof Vandike and Joseph L Bad Cock Two of the witnesses of the within Will being duly Sworn on the Holy Evangelists of Almighty God Did Severally dispose & Say that they Saw John Vandike the Testator therein Named Sign & Seal the Same and heard him publish pronounce and declare the within writing to be his Last Will & Testament, and that at the doing thereof the Said Testator was of Sound & disposing Mind and memory, as far as these Deponents know & as they Verily Believe, and that Jacob Vandike the other Subscribing Evidence was present at the Same Time and Signed his Name as a Witness to the said Will together with these Deponents, in Presence of the Said Testator.

Sworn at Somerset the
23rd Day of May 1778 /S/ Roelof Van Dike
Before me J_____Sexton Surrogate /S/ Jos. B. Cock

Frederick Vandike, Jacob Vandike, Samuel Stout, & Henry Bergen, Executors in the within Testament Named being duly Sworn on the Holy Evangelists of Almighty God did Severally depose & Say that the within Instrument contains the true Last Will & Testament of John Vandike the Testator therein Named, as far as they Know, & as they verily Believe, and that they will well and truly perform the Same, by paying first the Debts of the Said Deceased, and then the Legacies in the Said Testament Specified, so far as the Goods, Chattels, and Credits of the Said Deceased can thereunto extend, and that they will make and Exhibit unto the Prerogative Office of New Jersey, a true and Perfect Inventory of all & Singular the Goods, Chattels and Credits of the Said Deceased that have or Shall come to their knowledge or possession or to the Possession of any other Person or Persons for their use, and Render a first and true Account when thereunto lawfully Required ____

Sworn at Somerset the /S/ Frederick Van Dike
23rd day of May 1778 /S/ Jacob Van Dike
Before me J_____ Sexton Surrogate /S/ Samuel Stout
/S/ Henry Bergen

APPENDIX L

PROFILE OF MARGARET NEVIUS VAN DYKE

The delightful memoir of Margaret Nevius Van Dyke which she entitled As I Remember the Days of My Childhood reveals extraordinary sensitivity, keen insight, candor, vigor - all an integral part of her personality. She was a remarkable woman whose life spanned seventy-five years of the nineteenth century and seventeen years of the twentieth. Endowed with a fine intellect and a voracious reader since early childhood, she could discourse easily on the Bible, theology, geography, ancient history and the classics. Until a few days before her death, her mind was sharp and clear. Fluent with her pen, she contributed an article to the public press when nearing her ninetieth year. Small wonder, then, that she paints such a vivid picture of life on a Dutch plantation of the Van Dyke family in the days of slavery when the nation was young.

Margaret Nevius (1799-1862), her mother, was of French lineage. William J. Van Dyke (1795-1865), her father, was a descendant of Jan Thomasse Van Dyck who left Holland to settle in America in 1652 (Appendix R). This undoubtedly explains her strong character and personality composed of distinguishing traits inherited from her French and Dutch ancestors.

Margaret Van Dyke was born October 4, 1824 in the house of her maternal grandfather, David Nevius, the oldest of eight children, three girls and five boys. Shortly after her birth the house burned to the ground, the fire consuming a valuable clock and many family possessions that had come from Holland. She grew up in the old Van Dyke homestead in Mapleton (near Princeton) known as the Castle or, as Margaret preferred to call it, the Stone Cottage. Her great grandfather, Mathys Van Dike (1714-1784), son of Jan the Fourth, erected in 1756 a two story house of cut fieldstone along the banks of the Millstone on a 200 acre tract devised to him by his father's will probated in 1765 (Appendix G; Bailey 397,417).

For Margaret, in her eighties, the Stone Cottage was a treasure trove of precious childhood memories. There she heard Grandfather Matthew Van Dike say long morning prayers with the family and household slaves gathered around, and always grace before meals. There her Black Mammy, Peggy, whom she adored, taught her basic moral precepts instilled with loving, motherly care. And sometimes impressed with whippings judiciously applied - "all the whippings that I remember distinctly, and I now think I never had a stroke too much"[1]. There, too, she explored every nook and cranny and with equal zeal the wonders of nature outdoors; read books in quiet haunts; and happily romped and played with her brothers and sisters all of whom in their mature years, like Margaret, led markedly productive and dedicated lives. An In Memoriam appearing in The Presbyterian[2] shortly after her death on December 5, 1916 recounts briefly:

... One sister, Elizabeth Van Dyke, married the Rev. Dr. J. Kingsbury Wight, a distinguished Presbyterian divine. Her remaining sister, Anna Wilhelmina Van Dyke, married Dr. Beldon, a well known physician of New Jersey. Her brother, Dr. Edward B. Van Dyke, graduate of Princeton College, was a leading physician and surgeon in Philadelphia, and served in the Medical Department of the army during the War of the Rebellion. Her brother, Henry Van Dyke, was likewise a graduate of Princeton, and by profession a lawyer, being in his day one of the leaders of the New Jersey Bar in corporation practice. Her brother, William Van Dyke, was a hero of the Civil War, was captured in battle by the enemy and incarcerated a long while in Libbey Prison as a prisoner of war; her brother, James Van Dyke, lost his life in the Civil War, fighting on the side of the South, where he had many bloody relations and with whom he cast his fortunes in that great conflict. Her brother, Augustus Van Dyke, died in the great West, which he helped to develop.

A few days before her twentieth birthday, September 18, 1844, Margaret married Thomas Shields Malcolm, born in Philadelphia March 23, 1821. An honors graduate of Brown University and a recipient of the Doctor of Divinity from Princeton Theological Seminary at the age of twenty, Reverend Malcolm was recognized as an outstanding theologian, author and eloquent pulpit orator. His career in the ministery took him and Margaret to Kentucky and subsequently to Philadelphia. Six of their children lived to adulthood, all of whom Margaret survived except her only son, Frank[3].

An obituary in the Princeton Packet[4] epitomizes a long rewarding life:

Mrs. Margaret Nevius Van Dyke Malcolm, daughter of Margaret Nevius and William J. Van Dyke of Mapleton, passed away last week at Elm Hall, Marion, Philadelphia, the home of her son-in-law, General Bowman, at the honorable age of ninety-two years. She was born at Stone House, the home her Van Dyke ancestors had erected early in Seventeen Hundred, the first stone house built in New Jersey. And her early life was associated intimately with Rutgers and Princeton University, to whom her family furnished Presidents and Professors, besides liberally endowing them with financial benefits. Of old and noble French and Dutch lineage, in her life she preserved their traditions. She was a true aristocrat feeling the value and responsibility of birth and breeding. Of brilliant intellect with a mind cultivated by years of wide and varied reading, and intercourse with the great intellectual and social lights of several generations. She was a great scholar and in her books had traveled over and under the whole world; its formation, history, religion and politics she would discourse of interestingly for hours. Her love of home, flowers, nature, humanity, of all things beautiful, was a passion and they were reflected in her lovely face and figure. In her trailing white robes, a style of dress she adopted and never changed for seventy years, she was the very incarnation of grace and charm.

To the last she was in full possession of her wonderful mind, meeting death calmly and with great dignity.

Mrs. Malcolm was the widow of the late Rev. Thomas Shield Malcolm, D.D. of Philadelphia, a distinguished theologian and philanthropist. She is survived by several daughters, Mrs. Wendell Bowman, and Mrs. George M. Dallas Peitz of Philadelphia, and Mrs. Frank McLaughlin and Miss Ann Van Dyke Malcolm of New York.

APPENDIX M

MILITARY RECORDS RE: DEATH OF JOHN VAN DIKE (1709-1777/78)

When and where did John Van Dike of the Fifth Generation die?

Warren B. Stout, author of Ancestral Line of the Somerset Van Dykes published in the Somerset County Historical Quarterly in 1915 said without citing authority: "John Van Dyke died at Harlingen December 4, 1777, and is supposed to be buried in the grounds surrounding the church" (SCHQ 4:265), which was accepted by Cook (Cook 22). It is unfortunate that Stout did not disclose his source, which appears compatible with the factual picture. Meanwhile, accounts have been published claiming that Jan the Fifth met his death on the Monmouth County battlefield. In fact, the documentary evidence is to the contrary.

Born in New Utrecht, Long Island, on November 5, 1709, Jan the Fifth would have been in his sixty-ninth year when that historic battle was fought on June 28, 1778. The record clearly shows that three years earlier, on February 4, 1775, he made his will proclaiming "being much indisposed in Body" (Appendix K). The strong inference, therefore, is that by reason of age and senility he was unable to engage in military combat and would not have been accepted for service in the ranks in any event.

Only many years after the Revolution when lips were sealed were stories written asserting, among other things, that John Van Dyke was killed at the Battle of Monmouth. The storytellers were evidently unfamiliar with the historic facts. The probate records of the Somerset County Court establish that on May 23, 1778 - a month before the battle - five members of his family believing him deceased appeared before the Surrogate Judge. Thereupon John's two sons, his son-in-law and his brother-in-law were duly sworn as executors of his estate pursuant to the directive in his Last Will and Testament. Surely they knew all the facts and circumstances then existing and were not mistaken.

Turning now to the military records extant, a search conducted in the National Archives in Washington, D. C., fails to disclose any pension or military record relative to John Van Dyck/Dike/Dyke from New Jersey serving in the Revolution. It should be noted, however, that the archives are incomplete. Many governmental military records were destroyed by fire on November 8, 1800 and there was later destruction and theft in 1814 when the British occupied and burned down the National Capitol (Peterson 7).

The name John Van Dyck/Dike/Dyke does appear on military lists of Revolutionary War soldiers. William S. Stryker, recognized as New Jersey's foremost military historian, compiled a list in 1872 of New Jersey men who fought in the Revolution.[1] On Stryker's list is one "John Van Dyck" in "Captain Vroom's company, Second Battalion, Somerset" with the rank of private (Stryker 798). There is no doubt that this private is the same man appearing on a list of fifty-five soldiers in Captain Vroom's company, officially known as the Millstone Company, set forth in a history of Somerset County by James P. Snell[2] (Snell 31,32). Was he Jan the Fifth?

When one examines New Jersey's revolutionary history, it is manifest that this Private John Van Dyck was not John Van Dike of the Fifth Generation born in New Utrecht in 1709.

In the spring of 1775 military preparedness was the order of the day in the thirteen colonies in the wake of a skirmish with the British regiments stationed in Boston under General Gage, the royal governor of Massachusetts and commander of the King's troops in North America. Well known is the fact that a military encounter erupted on April 19, 1775 at Lexington and Concord - later immortalized by Emerson as the "shot heard round the World" - sounding an alarm throughout the colonies. The response was immediate and fervent. In New Jersey the Provincial Congress hastily met in Trenton to adopt rules and regulations for the purpose, as it said, "of defending the cause of American freedom". The Congress, in part, ordered that "one or more companies, as the case may require, be immediately formed in each Township or Corporation, and to this end, that several Committees in this Province do, as soon as may be, acquaint themselves with the number of male inhabitants in their respective districts from the age of sixteen to fifty, who are capable of bearing arms".

On May 3, 1775, a plan of action was agreed upon at a meeting of the principal freeholders and officers of the militia of the Township of Hillsborough in Somerset County held at the house of Garret Garretson for the purpose of raising a company of volunteers "to consist of 60 men, who are to be exercised twice per week, and to be ready at a minutes warning to march in defense of the liberty of our country"; and further providing that "the men so voluntarily enlisting in said Company shall receive one shilling and sixpense for every part of the day they are employed in being exercised by any of the officers, and the officers in proportion" (Snell 31).

Thus as a direct result of this urgent call to arms, the Millstone Company was formed in May of 1775. Its boundaries began at the mouth of the Raritan and encompassed a large area of Somerset County in the Millstone Valley. And in the ranks of the Millstone Company was a certain Private John Van Dyck who, we may reasonable assume, met the qualifications for enlistment.

The settled history, therefore, scarcely equates Jan the Fifth with the said private in the Millstone Company composed of able bodied men under fifty years of age capable of bearing arms. On the contrary, the facts point to Jan's nephew bearing the same name and residing in the Millstone Valley, the first born son of his brother Mathys (Matthias) and his wife Neeltje Laen (Eleanor Lane) married June 12, 1746. This John Van Dyck was born April 17, 1747, married Marla (Marya) Cortelyou, and fought in the Revolution (Cook 24; Cortelyou 110). In all probability, he was the able bodied recruit who at the age of twenty-eight in May of 1775 volunteered for military duty in the Millstone Company commanded by Captain Peter D. Vroom.

Clarence Stewart Peterson has most likely uncovered the same man. His compilation of all known military dead in the American Revolution representing an exhaustive search over many years lists a "John Van Dyke" from New Jersey with the rank of "Private" who "died" in 1778[3] (Peterson 170).

Samuel Stelle Smith is accredited as the leading authority on the Battle of Monmouth. Based on primary sources, Smith's work describes every phase of the battle hour by hour as it actually happened. Said Dr. Peter J. Guthorn in the Preface: "The work is outstanding because only primary sources have been employed. All quotations are from statements made by those who were actually on the field of battle and only if they were made within a short time of the battle, not in reminiscenses years later". Every soldier from New Jersey engaged in the struggle who was a casualty is specifically identified by name and rank whether in the Continental Army or the Militia Regiments. Of seventeen casualties broken down into five catagories, three were "killed", one was "missing", two "died of fatigue", ten were "wounded" and one was "sick in hospital". The name Van Dyck/Dike/Dyke does not appear[4] (Smith,S.S. 31,32).

Suffice to say, accepting credible authority including facts gleaned from the military records extant and the revolutionary history associated with the County of Somerset where Jan the Fifth resided, the evidence is convincing that this Dutch patriot did not march with the troops and play the role of a soldier in his sixty-ninth year.

Nor was he killed on the Monmouth County battlefield on June 28, 1778.

APPENDIX N

ENTRIES IN THE FAMILY BIBLE OF MARY SCHENCK SCOTT, SISTER-IN-LAW OF JACOB VAN DIKE (1754-1827)

MARRIAGES

Jacob Vandike was married to Sarah Schenck December 2nd 1786.

DEATHS

John R Schenck departed this life of dropsy May 13th, 1810, in the 63rd year of his age.

Eve Schenck, departed this life of pleurasy, Nov 21st 1810 in the 61st year of her age.

Sarah Vandike, departed this life, May 30th, 1811 of typhus fever in the 42nd year of her age.

Jacob Vandike, departed this life, Feb 4th, 1827 in the 72nd year of his age.

Sarah Vandike Oppi departed this life June 6th of Typhus fever in the 22nd year of her age.

Sarah Vandike Oppi departed this life, of dysentary at Bethlehem July 27th 1828 aged 17 years and 3 months.

Richard Scott departed this life February 29th 1815. In the 84th year of his age.

Mary Scott departed this life January 12th 1822 in the 80th year of her age.

John Scott, departed this life March 25th 1817. In the 51st year of his age.

Charles Van Dyke died Jan. 6th 1854

William Van Dyke died May 26th 1877.

BIRTHS

Jacob Vandike was born December 24th 1754.

Sarah Schenck daughter of John & Eve Schenck
was born Jan 24th, 1769.

Mary Schenck daughter of John & Eve Schenck
was born Jan 9th, 1776.

John Schenck Vandike was born Sept 25th, 1801.

Jacob Vandike was born July 15th 1806.

Sarah Vandike wife of Isaac Oppi
was born July 27, 1789.

William Van Dyke was born April 8th 1822

Elizabeth Ann Van Dyke was born Jan. 26th 1827

Alice Van Dyke was born Dec. 17th 1848.

Mary E. Van Dyke was born March 16th, 1850

Frank Van Dyke was born Dec. 11th 1851

Charles Van Dyke was born Dec. 27th 1853

John S. Van Dyke was born May 23rd 1857

The original donee of the bible was MARY SCHENCK SCOTT younger sister of Sarah Schenck, wife of Captain JACOB VAN DIKE born December 24, 1754.

The following handwritten inscription precedes the title page:

Mary Scott her Book
God give her grace therein to look
Bought at New Brunswick 1804

APPENDIX O

ENTRIES IN THE FAMILY BIBLE OF JACOB VAN DIKE (1754-1827)

Jacob Van Dike was born December 24th, 1754

Married to Sarah Skenck December 2nd, 1786

Sarah Skenck was born January 24th, 1769

Sarah Van Dike was born February 27th, 1784

John Skenck Van Dike was born September 25th, 1801

Jacob Van Dike was born July 15th, 1806

John R. Schenck departed this life May 13th, 1810
in the Sixty Third Year of his Age

Eve Schenck Departed this life Nov. 21, 1810
in the Sixty First Year of her Age

Sarah Van Dike Departed this life May 30th, 1811
in the Forty Second Year of her Age
Aged 42 years 4 months 6 days

Sarah Van Dike Oppie Departed this life June 6th, 1811
in the Twenty Second Year of her Age

Sarah Mary Van Dike Oppie was born March 26, 1811

Isaac Oppie Departed this life April 29th, 1811

Sara Van Dike Oppie Departed this life May 9th, 1811
in the 5th Year of her Age

John Van Dike and Frederick Van Dike Departed this life
June 23rd, 1811

Jacob Van Dike Departed this life February 4th, 1827
Aged 72 years, 1 month and 9 Days

Sarah V. D. Oppie Departed this life at Bethlehem July 21st, 1828
Aged 17 years 3 months and 25 Days

APPENDIX P

WILL OF JACOB VAN DIKE (1754-1827)

In the name of God, Amen.

I Jacob Van dike of the County of Somerset and State of New Jersey being of sound and disposing mind and memory do make this my last will and testament.

In the first place I order and direct all my just debts and funeral expences to be first paid out of my estate.

I give devise and bequeath to my son John S Van dike his heirs and assigns for ever, my two farms, situate in the township of West Windsor in the County of Middlesex. These two farms are on Penns Neck.

I give, devise and bequeath to my son Jacob Van dike, his heirs and assigns for ever the homestead where I now reside. Also the fifty acres of land which I purchased of Abraham Quick adjoining the said homestead. Also fifty acres of woodland near the Sand Hills in the County of Middlesex - to my said son Jacob his heirs and assigns forever.

I give and bequeath to my two sons John and Jacob all my horses, cows, cattle, hogs, sheep - all my farming utensils, my waggons, riding chair and waggon and harness - All the hay that may be cut and all the grain that may be gathered at the time of my decease, to be divided between them share and share alike.

I give and bequeath to my son Jacob Van dike all my household and kitchen furniture.

I give and bequeath to my son Jacob Van dike the sum of one thousand dollars to be paid to him at the time of my death out of such of my obligations as he may select.

I give and bequeath to my grand daughter Sarah Mary Van dike Oppie the sum of two thousand dollars to be paid to her at the age of one and twenty. And if she should die before the age of one and twenty, and without lawful issue, then I give and bequeath the said two thousand dollars to my two sons John and Jacob, to be divided equally.

I give, devise, and bequeath all the rest and residue of my estate, both real and personal to my two sons John and Jacob to them their heirs and assigns forever.

I do hereby nominate, constitute and appoint my two sons John and Jacob executors of this my last will and testament.

In witness whereof I have hereunto set my hand and seal this twenty second day of August, Eighteen hundred and twenty five.

Signed sealed Published and declared by the said Jacob Vandike as and for his last will and testament in our presence who at his request have hereunto subscribed our names as witnesses

/S/ Jacob Van Dike [SEAL]

/S/ S. Morford
/S/ Tho. White
/S/ Jas. S. Green

James S. Green, Esquire Being duly Sworn according to law did depose and say that he saw Jacob Van Dike the within Testator Sign and Seal this Instrument of writing and heard him publish pronounce and declare the Same to be his last will and Testament and that he was of sound and disposing mind memory and understanding at the time of the execution thereof: and that S Morford and Tho. White the other subscribing witnesses were present and Subscribed their names as witnesses together with this deponent in the presence and at the request of the Testator.

Sworn & Subscribed
at Somerville Feb. 15th 1827
Before me W Frelinghuysen Surrogate

/S/ Jas. S. Green

John Van Dike and Jacob Van Dike the Executors within named being duly sworn depose & say that the within writing contains the last will and Testament of Jacob Van Dike, dec. as far as they know and as the verily believe: and that they will well and truly perform and fulfill the Same by paying first the debts of dec. and then the Legacies therein Specified so far as goods Chattels & Credits can thereunto extend and Exhibit unto the Surrogates Office of Somerset a true and perfect Inventory of all & Singular the Goods Chattels Rights & Credits of said dec. that shall or may come to their knowledge or possession of any other person or persons for their use ____

Sworn & Subscribed at
Somerville Feby. 15th 1827.
Before me
/S/ W. Frelinghuysen, Surrogate

/S/ John S. Van Dyke
/S/ Jacob Van Dike

APPENDIX Q

JUDGE JOHN VAN DYKE (1807-1878) AND THE HONEYMAN STORY

Judge John Van Dyke was a great grandson of Jan the Fifth (1709-1777/78) and a cousin of John Schenck Van Dyke (1801-1852) as seen below:

V Jan the Fifth (1709-1777/78)

VI	Jacob (1754-1827) (Appendix N & O)	Abraham (1753-1804) M Ida Stryker (Cook 22)
VII	John Schenck (1801-1852) (Appendix N & O)	Abraham (1776-1854) M Sarah Honeyman (Daughter of John Honeyman) (SCHQ 4:265)
VIII	William (1822-1877) (Appendix N)	John (1807-1878) M Mary Dix Strong (See Diary of Mary Dix Strong Van Dyke, RUL/SCA)

Since his father, Abraham Van Dyke (1776-1854) married Sarah Honeyman, a daughter of John Honeyman, Judge John Van Dyke was a grandson of John Honeyman. Born in Ireland of Scotch parentage, John Honeyman came to America in 1758 as a soldier under General Wolfe, serving as one of his bodyguards. He married Mary Henry of a Scotch-Irish family, settled near Griggstown about 1772, and during the Revolution was said to be a spy of George Washington (SCHQ 5:275). Honeyman died on August 18, 1822 in the "93rd year of his age", inscribed on his tombstone in the burial ground of the Lamington Presbyterian Church, Bedminster Township, Somerset County (SCHQ 2:315).

In 1873 there appeared in a magazine, Our Home, an article entitled "An Unwritten Account of a Spy of Washington" by John Van Dyke (1807-1878) recounting events which, he claims, took place in 1776 (RUL/SCA). At the outset the author says that he "makes no claim to the power of invention" and "proposes to create neither persons nor circumstances," and asserts that he is "in possession of a number of facts, with which he has long been familiar, derived from the most unmistakable sources" (Emphasis by John Van Dyke).

One problem, however stands out which should concern an historian or anyone interested in serious research. The author fails to cite any authority for the alleged facts or the socalled "most unmistakable sources". What are the sources? Why was this important episode suppressed for nearly a century?

The spy story dramatically told in impressive detail recounts the capture of John Honeyman, a notorious British spy, by the colonial forces who brought him before Washington in December 1776. At a secret meeting Honeyman, said to be playing the role of a double spy, disclosed to Washington important military intelligence which led to the Continental Army's victorious engagement at a low point in the Revolution, the rout of the Hessian Troops quartered in Trenton on Christmas Day. Washington ordered Honeyman locked securely in a log-cabin prison well guarded. However, the same night Washington cleverly masterminded Honeyman's escape enabling him to return to the British lines and leaving the impression that he was serving the British. But that is not the end of the story which incorporates a dramatic climax after word of his escape reaches Honeyman's neighbors in Griggstown. Honeyman's house, says the author, was "surrounded at midnight by a crowd of his exasperated neighbors, who, by arrangement, had approached it from different directions supposing he might be there", and "demanded the surrender of the traitor". Mrs. Honeyman told them that she knew nothing of her husband's whereabouts which "only increased the demand and tumult." Finally she handed a paper to a young man serving as their "leader" who read aloud a message allegedly written by Washington himself ordering that the wife and children of John Honeyman be protected from all harm and annoyance. This effectively quelled the disturbance and the crowd gradually dispersed. The author, going one step further, quotes Washington's message verbatim as follows:

AMERICAN CAMP
NEW JERSEY, Nov. A.D., 1776.

To the good people of New Jersey and all others whom it may concern:

It is hereby ordered that the wife and children of John Honeyman, of Griggstown, the notorious Tory, now within the British lines, and probably acting the part of a spy, shall be and hereby are protected from all harm and annoyance from every quarter, until further orders. But this furnishes no protection to Honeyman himself.

GEO. WASHINGTON,
Com.-in-chief.

And, continues the author, "This paper was not only signed by Washington, but was all written by him, and remained in the family for many years afterwards. It was seen and read by the children as well as by many others."

When the story drew criticism shortly after its publication in 1873, Judge Van Dyke wrote A.V.D. Honeyman, In Memorium 1874), that "he did not hear the story directly from his grandfather but from Aunt Jane eldest of John Honeyman's seven children" who was about thirteen years old when the document was supposedly read to the threatening mob surrounding the Honeyman house in Griggstown. Aunt Jane, he says, "had a perfect recollection of everything that happened ... She had often seen, and read, and heard read, Washington's order for protection, and knew it by heart, and repeated it over to me ..."(Menzies 80).[1]

This explanation is seldom, if ever, mentioned when the story is resurrected by other writers and published years later. Nor is its authenticity inquired into.

Several versions published in this century are couched in a style making it appear authentic - genuine history, not legend. Some accounts even include the order purportly written and signed by Washington, although the author, John Van Dyke, never saw the document - its existence based solely on heresay - and all the characters in the exciting tale having long since died when it first appeared in the magazine article in 1873.

APPENDIX R

THREE VAN DYKE LINES

I	Thomas, of Amsterdam, Holland 3 sons, no daughters known (Cook 1)		
II	Jan Thomasse (ca1605-1673) Arrived in New Amsterdam (New York) in 1652 5 sons, 2 daughters (Cook 1-3)		
III	Jan Jansen (1648/49-ca1736) 2 sons, 6 daughters (Cook 7)		
IV	Jan (1682-1764) 7 sons, 3 daughters (Cook 18,19; Appendix E)		
V	John (Jan the Fifth) (1709-1777/78) 5 sons, 8 daughters (Cook 22,23; Appendix J)		Mathys (Matthew) (1714-1784) 2 sons, 6 daughters (Cook 18,24; Appendix E)
VI	Jacob (1754-1827 2 sons,1 daughter (Cook 22; Appendix N & O)	Frederick(1751-1811) 3 sons,3 daughters (Cook 22, SCHQ 6:189,190)	Matthew (1752-1832) 7 children survived childhood (Cook 24; PR)
VII	John Schenck (1801-1852) 1 son (Appendix N & O)	Rachel (1793- _____) (SCHQ 6:189,190)	William J. (1795-1865) 8 children (PR; Appendix L)
VIII	William (1822-1877) 3 sons,2 daughters (Appendix N & O)		Margaret Nevius (1824-1916) 1 son, 5 daughters survived (PR; Appendix L)
IX	John Schenck (1857-1906) 3 sons, 1 daughter (Appendix N & O)		

APPENDIX S

HENRY VAN DYKE (1852-1933)

Henry Van Dyke, famous as an author, poet, lecturer and pulpit orator, was professor of English at his alma mater, Princeton University, in his later years. As revealed by his writings, he loved fishing, nature and the great outdoors emulating his Dutch ancestors who earned their living from the land.

A member of the Ninth Generation of the family, the ancestral line of Henry Van Dyke stems from Jan the Fifth as follows:

V		John (Jan the Fifth)
	B	November 6, 1709
	D	1777/78
VI		Frederick
	Bp	November 3, 1751
	D	June 23, 1811
	M	December 11, 1778 Lydia Cole
VII		Frederick Augustus (a medical doctor in Philadelphia and one of the first to enter the profession)
	Bp	February 3, 1790
	D	1875
	M	Eliza Anderson
VIII		Henry Jackson
	B	March 2, 1822
	D	1891
	M	1845 Henriettta Ashmead
IX		Henry Jackson, Jr.
	B	November 10, 1852
	D	April 10, 1933
	M	December 13, 1881 Ellen Reid

TABLE of ABBREVIATIONS: AUTHORITIES AND SOURCES

A

Aitken	Aitken, William B. Distinguished Families in America Descended from Wilhelmus Beekman and Jan Thomasse Van Dyke: G. P. Putnam's Sons, 1912.
Anthony	Anthony, Katherine. Dolly Madison, Her Life and Times: Doubleday & Company, Inc., 1949.
APJ	Asbury Park Journal
APPL	Asbury Park Public Library

B

Bailey	Bailey, Rosalie Fellows. Pre-Revolutionary Dutch Houses and Families: Dover Publications, Inc., New York, 1968.
Barber/Howe	Barber, John W. and Howe, Henry. Historical Collections of the State of New Jersey: S. Tuttle, New York, 1845. Reprint 1990 Heritage Books, Inc., Bowie, Maryland.
Brecknell	Brecknell, Ursula C. Montgomery Township, An Historic Community 1702-1972. Montgomery Township, New Jersey, Bicentennial Committee, 1972 (RUL).

C

Carrick	Carrick, Elizabeth Bates. The Rockingham Story: The Rockingham Association, Princeton, New Jersey, 1978.
CMCL	Cape May County Library, New Jersey.
Cook	Cook, Richard Wilson (1903-1981). A scholarly compilation of the Van Dyck Family in America simply entitled Van Dycks, 1954 (RUL). See Appendix A.
Cortelyou	Cortelyou, John Van Zandt. The Cortelyou Genealogy: A Record of Jacques Cortelyou and Many of His Descendants: Copies in the hands of Cortelyou families in New Jersey, printed by Brown Printing Service, Lincoln, Nebraska, 1942.
Cranmer	Cranmer, H. Jerome. The New Jersey Canals, State Policy and Private Enterprise, 1820-1832. Dissertation in partial fulfillment of the requirements for degree of philosophy, Columbia University, June, 1955 (SCA).

D

DAB	Dictionary of American Biography, Vol IX: Charles Scribner's Sons, New York.
Danckaerts	Danckaerts, Jasper. Journal of Jasper Danckaerts 1679-1680, edited by Bartlett Burleigh James and J. Franklin Jameson, Barnes & Noble, Inc., New York, reprint 1952.
DC	Death Certificate.

E

Eid	Eid, Joseph. Trollies in the Coast Cities: March 1979 (NTPL).
Ellis	Ellis, Franklin. History of Monmouth County, New Jersey, 1885 (APPL).

F

FANT	Fiftieth Anniversary of Neptune Township, 1879-1929: Published by the Asbury Park Press, 1929 (APPL, NTPL).
FAW	Benjamin Franklin's Autobiographical Writings. Edited by Carl Van Doren: Viking Press, New York, 1945.
Fitzpatrick	Fitzpatrick, John C. Editor of The Writings of George Washington from the Original Manuscript Sources, 1745-1799, Volume 27: United States Government Printing Office, Washington, D.C.
Flexner	Flexner, James Thomas. George Washington, Anguish and Farewell, 1793-1799, Volume 4: Little, Brown and Company, Boston, Massachusetts.
Friedel/Israel	Robert Friedel & Paul Israel with Bernard S. Finn. Edison's Electric Light, based on Edison's papers. Rutgers University Press, New Brunswick, New Jersey, 1987.

G

GLIF	Genealogies of Long Island Families from the New York Genealogical and Biographical Record, Vol. 1, including an excellent work: The Rev. Johannes Theodorus Polhemus And Some of his Descendants by I. Heyward Peck exhibiting an exhaustive study of the Polhemius/Polhemus ancestry: Reprint Genealogical Publishing Company, Inc., Baltimore, Maryland, 1987.
GMNJ	Genealogical Magazine of New Jersey.

Goodrich	Goodrich, Peggy. Ike's Travels: Published by the Township of Neptune, Monmouth County, New Jersey, 1974 (NTPL).
Gordon	Gordon, Thomas F. Gazetteer of the State of New Jersey: Daniel Fenton, Trenton, New Jersey, 1834.
GSP	Genealogical Society of Pennsylvania (1895-1947).

H

Hageman	Hageman, John Frelinghuysen. History of Princeton and its Institutions: J. B. Lippincott & Co., Philadelphia, 1879.
HCR	Harlingen Church Records.
Heiss	Heiss, E. Renee. A Genealogical History of the Berrien Family: Gateway Press, Inc., 1982, Baltimore, Maryland. Available from the author, R. D. 7, Laurel Drive, Vincentown, New Jersey.
Hoagland	Hoagland, Christopher C. Gleanings from the History of the Protestant Reformed Dutch Church of Harlingen, Somerset County, New Jersey (RUL).
HSP	Historical Society of Princeton, Bainbridge House, 158 Nassau Street, Princeton, New Jersey.
HTN	History of the Township of Neptune. The Neptune Township Bicentennial Committee, 1976 (NTPL).

J

Jones	Jones, E. Alfred. The Loyalists of New Jersey in the Revolution: New Jersey Historical Society, Newark, New Jersey, 1927.

K

Kalm	Kalm, Peter. Peter Kalm's Travels in North America. Published in Stockholm, Sweden in 1753. English version of 1770 edited by Adolph B. Benson: Wilson-Emerson Inc., 1937.
Kammen	Kammen, Michael. Colonial New York. The author, currently professor of American History and Culture at Cornell University, has uniquely condensed in a single volume the diverse aspects of colonial New York. KTO Press, a U. S. Division of Kraus-Thomson Organization Limited, Millwood, New York, 1978.

Kull	Kull, Irving S. New Jersey A History, Vol.I: The American Historical Society, Inc., New York, 1930 (CMCL).

L

LC	Library of Congress
Lee	Lee, Francis Brazely. Genealogical and Personal Memorial of Mercer County, New Jersey, Vol.2: The Lewis Publishing Company, New York, Chicago (RUL).
Leiby	Leiby, Adrian C. The Early Dutch and Swedish Settlers of New Jersey: D. Van Nostrand Company, Inc., Princeton, New Jersey, 1964.

M

Malcom	Malcom, Elsa Barelift. Malcom-Cox with Allied Families, A Genealogical Record, 1982 (SL).
Malone	Malone, Dumas. The Sage of Monticello: Little Brown and Company, 1981.
MCHA	Monmouth County Historical Association, Freehold, New Jersey.
MCSC	Mercer County Surrogate's Court, Trenton, New Jersey.
Menzies	Menzies, Elizabeth G. C. Millstone Valley: Rutgers University Press, New Brunswick, New Jersey, 1969.
Morison	Morison, Samuel Eliot. The late Professor Morison taught at Harvard four decades. His prose is as scholarly as it is moving and entertaining, the product of comprehensive knowledge of the facts, his own seafaring experience, and journeys around the world to the bays, harbors, inlets and promontories first seen by those heroic European navigators of the fifteenth and sixteenth centuries. In The Great Explorers he captures the full drama: Oxford University Press, New York, 1978.
Myers	Myers, William Starr. The Story of New Jersey, Vol.III: Lewis Historical Publishing Co., Inc., New York (CMCL).

N

NBHC	The New Brunswick Historical Club. Charter and Ordinances of Ye Olde City of New Brunswick, forward by Austin Scott, February 12, 1913 (SCA).

NJRM — New Jersey Road Maps of the 18th Century published by the Friends of the Princeton University Library, Princeton, New Jersey, 1981

NTPL — Neptune Township Public Library.

O

OPN — Old Princeton's Neighbors. Federal Writer's Project, 1939.

P

Peterson — Peterson, Clarence Stewart. Known Military Dead During The American Revolutionary War 1775-1783: Genealogical Publishing Company, Baltimore, Maryland, 1967.

PFL — Philadelphia Free Library.

PHS — Presbyterian Historical Society. Philadelphia, Pennsylvania.

PNJHS — Proceedings of the New Jersey Historical Society.

Potts — Potts, Heston Nelson, Jr. The Dutch Schools in North America 1620-1750: Dissertation in partial fulfillment of the requirements for the degree of Doctor of Education, New Brunswick, New Jersey, June 1973.

PR — Princeton Recollector, a publication of the Princeton History Project, Elric J. Ellersby, Director (RUL).

PVDH — Pearl Van Dyke Harvey (1888-1967), the author's aunt. Four letters written at her home in Orlando, Florida, constitute an invaluable source of information supplementing the documentary findings.

R

Reickel/Bigler — Reickel, William C. and Bigler, W.M.H. The History of the Moravian Seminary For Young Ladies at Bethlehem, Pennsylvania, With A Catalogue of its pupils, 1785-1870: Fourth edition 1901, Moravian Seminary Library, Bethlehem, Pennsylvania.

Rogers/Sayer — Rogers, F.B. and Sayer, A.R. The Healing Art: A History of the Medical Society of New Jersey. Trenton,N.J., Medical Society of New Jersey, 1966.

RUL — Rutgers University Libraries.

S

SA	State Archives, Division of Archives and Records Management, Department of State, Trenton, New Jersey.
SCA	Special Collections and Archives, Rutgers University Libraries.
SCGQ	Somerset County Genealogical Quarterly
SCHQ	Somerset County Historical Quarterly
SCM	Somerset County Minutes, Meetings of the Justices and Chosen Freeholders, May 13, 1772 to September 2, 1822 (SL).
SL	State Library, Trenton, New Jersey.
SM	Somerset Messenger, an early newspaper published in Somerville, Somerset County, New Jersey (RUL)
Smith/SS	Smith, Samuel Stelle. The Battle of Monmouth: Philip Freneau Press, Monmouth Beach, New Jersey, 1964 (MCHA).
Snell	Snell, James P. History of Hunterdon and Somerset Counties, New Jersey: Everts & Peck, Philadelphia, 1881.
Steele	Steele, Richard H.,D.D. Historical Discourse Celebrating the One Hundred and Fiftieth Anniversary of the First Reformed Dutch Church in New Brunswick on October 1, 1867: Published by the Church Consistory, 1867 (SCA).
Stout	Stout, Warren B. Author of Ancestral Line of the Somerset Van Dykes (SCHQ 4:262).
Stryker	Stryker, William S. Official Register of the Officers and Men in the Revolutionary War: Printed by authority of the legislature 1972. Reprint Genealogical Publiching Co., Baltimore 1967.

T

Thompson	Thompson, J. Earle. An Elementary History of New Jersey: Hinds, Hayden & Eldredge, Inc., 1924.
THSSC	Transactions of the Huguenot Society of South Carolina. The Berrian Family Genealogy by Margaret Kilpatrick Baumeister and Margaret Grant Plumb: Huguenot Society of South Carolina, Charleston, South Carolina, 1918.

U

Updike — Updike, Frank M. The Princeton Baptist Church of Penns Neck Vol II, The Middle Years 1863 to 1912 (HSP).

V

Van Der Donck — Van Der Donck, Adriaen. A Description Of The New Netherlands edited by Thomas F. O'Donnell and translated from the original Dutch by Hon. Jeremiah Johnson: Syracuse University Press, Syracuse, New York, 1968.

van der Linde — van der Linde, A. P. G., translator and editor. Old First Dutch Reformed Church of Brooklyn, New York, First Book of Records 1660-1752. Sponsored by the Scholarship Committee of The Holland Society of New York: Genealogical Publishing Co. Inc., Baltimore, 1983.

Van Der Zee — Van Der Zee, Henri and Barbara. A Sweet and Alien Land: The Viking Press, New York, 1968.

VDFB/Author — Van Dyke Family Bible, a family heirloom in the author's possession.

VDFB/Princeton — Van Dyke Family Bible. Entrees from a bible found in a Princeton storehouse in 1944 (HSP).

Van Hoesen — Van Hoesen, Walter H. Early Taverns and Stagecoach Days in New Jersey. Fairleigh Dickinson University Press (CMCL).

Van Ness — Van Ness, Esther Oppie. William Oppie of Somerset County, New Jersey, and Some of His Ancestors (RUL).

Veit — Veit, Richard F. The Old Canals Of New Jersey: New Jersey Geographical Press, Little Falls, New Jersey (CMCL).

Voorhees — Voorhees, David William. Dr. Voorhees, a Research Fellow at New York University, has written and lectured extensively on Jacob Leisler, a colorful Dutch figure executed in 1691, which marked a turning point in New York colonial history. Currently Dr. Voorhees is director of a project devoted to collecting, translating and publishing the papers of Jacob Leisler numbering over 2000. See Appendix C.

VS/Del — Vital Statistics, Delaware.

VS/NJ — Vital Statistics, New Jersey.

VS/Pa — Vital Statistics, Pennsylvania

VS/Va — Vital Statistics, Virginia

W

Wacker	Wacker, Peter O. Land & People: Rutgers University Press, New Brunswick, New Jersey, 1975.
Wall	Wall, John P. The Chronicles of New Brunswick, New Jersey 1667-1931: Thatcher-Anderson Company, New Brunswick, New Jersey.
Wertenbaker	Wertenbaker, Thomas Jefferson. The Founding of American Civilization: Charles Scribner Sons, New York, 1938. Also Princeton 1746-1896, a history of Princeton University for 150 years from its founding by Jonathan Dickinson at Elizabeth in 1746, then known as the College of New Jersey: Princeton University Press, Princeton, New Jersey, 1946.
Weslager	Weslager, C.A. A Man And His Ship: Peter Minuit and the Kalmar Nyckel: Kalmar Nyckel Foundation, Wilmington, Delaware, 1989.
Wickes	Wickes, Stephen, AM,MD. History of Medicine in New Jersey and of its Medical Men: Martin R. Dennis & Co., Newark, New Jersey, 1879 (CMCL).
Woodward/Hageman	Woodward, Major E.M. and Hageman, John F. History of Burlington & Mercer Counties, New Jersey, Everts & Peck, Philadelphia, 1883.
WWTM	West Windsor Township Minutes.
WWTMR	West Windsor Township Marriage Records.

Addendum, July 1, 1996

Macy	Macy, Jr., Harry Amsterdam Records of the Jan Thomaszen Van Dyck Family, NYG&B Record, 126(4):239-242, October, 1995

NOTES

FIRST GENERATION

1. Holland is intended to be synonomous with The Netherlands, the official name of the Dutch government. The chief city is Amsterdam in North Holland, one of the eleven provinces.

2. John Cabot (ca1451-1498), originally Giovanni Cabotto (his name appears in various forms), probably born in Genoa, sailed twice in the service of King Henry VII of England searching for a shorter route to China (Cathay) and the East Indies. In May of 1497 he left Bristol in a small ship, Mathew, with a crew of eighteen and first sighted land on June 24 (St. John the Baptist Day) which the king named New Isle and later called newe founde lande. Cabot spent shortly less than a month exploring the rocky eastern coast line of Newfoundland, once going ashore to claim possession for King Henry VII. On August 7, after only eleven weeks at sea, Mathew returned safely to Bristol, a marvelous navigational feat for that time. In May of the following year Cabot departed Bristol with a flotilla of six ships. Shortly one ship returned, but Cabot and the other four ships were lost without a trace. There is no evidence that John Cabot ever set foot on the mainland of North America (Morison 39-73).

3. The general belief that Peter Minuit (ca1580-1638) purchased Manhattan Island from the Indians, as textbooks usually declare, has never been documented. It should be noted that Peter Schaghen's letter to the States General says, "they have bought the island Manhatten from the wild men" which unfortunately, is the only evidence of this historic event. For further explanation see the Purchase of Manhattan Island, Appendix B.

SECOND GENERATION

1. Cook corrects other accounts listing in error four additional children (Cook 2). Stout confirms Cook (SCHQ 4:263).

2. The Guilden Otter, the vessel that brought Catherine Polhemus and her children to America in 1656 to rejoin her husband, the Reverend Johannes Theodorus Polhemus, infra, set sail from Holland on June 4 and reached New Amsterdam on September 4 (GLIF 1:613). When Peter John Van Berckel, the Burgomaster from Rotterdam and the first Ambassador to the United States arrived in Philadelphia on October 11, 1783, it was after a "tedious and tempestuous voyage" of fifteen weeks (Carrick 17).

3. John J. DeMott, a noted genealogist, in The Origin of the Cortelyou Family says: "It was common practice for students to Latinize at least part of their names. Following this custom, Jacques called himself "Jacobus" (James). To this he added "Ultraiectinus" (or Ultrajectinus), meaning "of Utrecht" (SCHQ 1:104).

4. Colonial New York by Michael Kammen, page 68.

5. Henricus Selijns (1636-1701) served the Reformed Dutch Church in Brooklyn from 1660 to 1664 under a contract with the Dutch West India Company and conscientiously kept the church records during this period (van der Linde XX-

XXIX). Two very interesting letters written by him to the Classis of Amsterdam contain precious history not only relating to the church but the Dutch people themselves (ibid 226-233). Selijns was preceded by Johannes Theodorus Polhemus (1598-1676), a brilliant man and a refugee from an aborted Dutch colony in Brazil, who arrived in New Amsterdam by accident in September 1654 aboard the French frigate St. Charles. His wife Catherine and their children returned to Holland on another ship (GLIF 1: 612,613). Domine Polhemus remained in New Netherland, later joined by his wife, and ministered to the people of Midwout (Flatbush) on Sunday mornings and alternately in New Amersfoort (Flatlands) and Breuckelen (Brooklyn) on Sunday afternoons (GLIF 1:619). At that time Midwout, New Amersfoort and Breuckelen were the only Dutch settlements on Long Island and had neither a clergyman nor a church. Of necessity the inhabitants attended church in New Amsterdam (GLIF 1:614). When Domine Selijns arrived in 1660, a list of the Brooklyn congregation, twenty-five in all, were turned over to him. The list was prepared by Domine Polhemus whom the consistory highly praised as the "Rev., godly, and very learned Domine Johannes Polhemus with appropriate expressions of gratitude for his ministry" (van der Linde 12,13), recorded in this ancient volume currently lodged in the archives of the Gardner Sage Library in New Brunswick, N J.

6. All children survived him with the possible exception of his daughter Annetje (wife of Peter Jansen Staats) whose date of death has not been found.

THIRD GENERATION

1. Tryntje Thyssen was a descendant of the Lane family (Laenen, van der Laen, de la Lanon et al) of North Belgium, once part of The Netherlands. The family resided in the Walloon district in close proximity to the Dutch country and spoke Dutch. Tryntje was fifteen when her parents emigrated from Belgium. Her mother died on the passage. It was, therefore, her father Matthys Jansen Laenen, a widower, and four children (Tryntje, born ca 1648 was next to the oldest) who, in March 1663, arrived in New Amsterdam and settled in New Utrecht (SCHQ 2:110-114).

2. The author is indebted to Dr. David William Voorhees, a research fellow at New York University, for material on Jacob Leisler. For further detail, see Profile of Jacob Leisler, Appendix C.

3. A poll was a naturally hornless cow, ox, or similar farm animal; also referred to as a polled animal.

4. Husband of his daughter Jannetje (Cook 8) and referred to in his will as "Capt. Rutgers Van Brunt" (Appendix D).

5. Deed dated September 14, 1726 recorded July 31, 1729 (SCHQ 4:263).

6. Jan's will made May 16, 1735 and probated November 9, 1736 in the Surrogate's office, New York, refers to "Catleyntje Deceased", mother of "Three Sons & Three Daughters". Eva died February 16, 1723/4 (Cook 7). It may be presumed that Mayke (date of death unknown) was deceased in 1735 since she is not mentioned in the will. His great grandson to whom he left a legacy of fifteen pounds to be paid at the age of twenty-one years was John Van Buren,

son of his granddaughter "Tuentje Richon Deceased which was the wife of Doctor John Van Buren Junr". Jan identifies himself as "John Van Dyck of New Uytrecht in Kings County on the Island Nassau in y province of New York yeoman" and appoints his sons and sons-in-law "John Van Dyck Mattys Van Dyck Rutgers Van Brunt Symon DeHart" executors of his will. See Appendix D.

FOURTH GENERATION

1. "Ver" is the Dutch contraction of "ver der" and "kerk" means church; hence "of the church" (GMNJ 41:49).

2. The date of marriage is from the Dutch Family Bible of Jan Van Dyck (1682-1764) and his wife Annetje Verkerk. See the family record in Dutch with English translation in Appendix E.

3. Dates marked with an asterisk are from the old Dutch Family Bible. Other dates are from Cook's Van Dyck genealogy unless otherwise noted.

4. Richard W. Cook and Warren B. Stout cite the year 1711 which is probably correct (Cook 18;SCHQ 4:264) since the third child (Jan) was born November 5, 1709. The year 1710 was apparently an error in transcription from the old Dutch Family Bible. Appendix E.

5. Prior to the year 1743 only about a dozen baptismal records by the church organizer, Reverend Paulus Van Viecq, have survived. There is then a gap until July 13, 1743 (SCHQ 8:123,124).

6. The division of New Jersey into two parts stems from the original proprietors John Lord Berkeley (-1678) and Sir George Carteret (ca1613-1679) who received a deed in 1664 from the Duke of York (James the brother of Charles II, the English king). From the outset they experienced difficulty for a sound governmental structure eluded them. Soon Lord Berkeley became disenchanted with the colonization venture and sold his share to John Fenwick and Edward Byllinge, members of the Society of Friends and close associates of William Penn (1644-1718). A boundary line had to be drawn defining ownership and control, which brought into existence two Jerseys, East and West. See Appendix F.

7. The Pennsylvania Gazette published by Benjamin Franklin (1706-1790) became the most popular newspaper in the American colonies with a circulation between eight and ten thousand.

8. Copy made by Gerard Bancker March 8, 1762 from John Dalley's 1745 survey (NJRM).

9. It appears that Cook accepted the statement of Warren B. Stout that Jan Van Dyck "settled at Fresh Ponds, Middlesex County, N.J., about three miles from Spotswood" (Cook 18, SCHQ 4:264), clearly at variance with the documentary evidence.

10. Benjamin Harrison was a grandson of John Harrison, Senior, who soon after 1702 built the first gristmill on the east bank of the Millstone.

11. Will of Jan Van dyck (as he signed his name) dated April 12, 1757 probated January 25, 1765 (SA). See Appendix G.

12. Evidenced by a deed dated December 16, 1740 from Gerardus Beekman (son-in-law of John Van Dike) to John Van Dike conveying 300 acres in Middlesex County. The deed recites, "It being a part of a Larger Tract of Land Lying within the said County which He the Said Gerardus Beekman Bought & Purchased of Eupham Johnston Andrew Johnston William Shiner & Lawrence Smith Exors to the Last Will & Testament of Doctor John Johnston of Perth Amboy Deceased ... " by a former deed of conveyance dated March 14, 1739 (SA). It appears that Andrew Johnston, Esq., one of the executors and son of the decedent, was the party consummating the transaction and attorney of Doctor Johnston's estate.

13. Evidenced by a deed dated February 9, 1727 from Benjamin Pridmore of the Township of New Brunswick to Jan Van Dyke conveying a certain tract in the "Township of New Brunswick Beginning on the East Side of Millstone River at a tree Standing by the said River ... containing Two hundred acres of Land Together with ... Houses, Buildings, Edifices, Stables, fences, & Pastures Meadows, Brooks, Ponds, Woods ..." (SA). The deed of Frederick Dolhason has not been found.

14. The reference is to John Harrison, Junior, the eldest son of John Harrison, the Great Landholder. The 150 acre tract is confirmed by a deed from John Harrison of the City of Perth Amboy to John Van Dike dated May 1, 1723 described in terms of trees, neighboring landowners, chain lengths, brooks, etc. "Containing on[e] hundred and fifty Acres of Land Bee ye same more or Less" (SA). The deeds of Thomas Yates, Esq. and Thomas Soden have not been found.

15. John Berrien's niece, Elizabeth Berrien (ca1740-ca1780), married Colonel Henry Van Dyck (1743-1824), Jan's grandson (THSSC 73:47;Heiss 14;Cook 23). His nephew John Berrien (1751-1797) married Neeltje Van Dyck (1755-), Jan's granddaughter (THSSC 73:48;Heiss 6;Cook 24); and his nephew Henry Berrien (1743-1806), presumably married Cornelia Van Dyck (1743-1824), Jan's granddaughter, both of whom are buried at Ten Mile Run (SCHQ 4:65) (See Appendix J). During the years 1797-1800, Henry Berrien and Jan's grandson Jacob (1754-1827) (Sixth Generation), residents of Franklin Township, Somerset County, were chosen freeholders (Woodward/Hageman 814).

16. See Rockingham for Sale, Appendix H.

17. "... the word (before) between the 5th and 6th lines from the top of the 3rd page being first inserted in the presence of subscribers" (signature page). See Appendix G.

18. The early Dutch settlers crossed streams at fording places on the Indian path into the Millstone Valley. These areas were identified in terms of distance from Inian's Ferry on the Raritan in New Brunswick. Hence the names Ten Mile Run, Six Mile Run and Three Mile Run. The cemetery is in the area of Ten Mile Run.

19. A Cortelyou Genealogy by John Van Zandt Cortelyou, a scholarly work extensively researched, accounts for twelve marriages between the Cortelyou and Van Dyck families. See Appendix I.

-NOTES-

20. Stone cutter's error! See Illustration.

21. Formerly Ruth Hayes Cortelyou, born September 4, 1910 at Ten Mile Run, a descendant of Jacques Cortelyou, the pioneer settler. She died April 5, 1992.

22. Jeanette Gibson, born August 18, 1897, died January 29, 1990. She lies beside her husband.

23. A reading of the inscriptions in 1915 reveals seven Gibson interments (SCHQ 4:138).

24. Among the inscriptions is one reading "C.D.H., 1762" (oldest date) probably signifying "Cornelius DeHart" who died in that year (SCHQ 4:142). Marguerite Durick's source is evidently Franklin Township Historical Notes by Judge Ralph Voorhees (SCHQ 5:27,28,191). Simon DeHart, of French descent, sailed from Holland to New Amsterdam in 1664 and prior to 1673 bought a farm of about 300 acres at Gowanus, Long Island. His grandson Cornelius settled along the Old Indian Path at Six Mile Run in 1720, ibid.

25. The common ancestor, Jacques Cortelyou (ca1625-1693) of New Utrecht, was, as we have seen, the great grandfather of Hendrick Cortelyou (1736-1800) who lies in the Ten Mile Run Cemetery and the grandfather of Hendrick Cortelyou (1711-1777) who married Antie Albertse Van Voorhees to whom Marguerite Durick refers.

26. Died February 20, 1841, age 85 years, 4 months, 20 days, "A patriot of the Revolution" (SCHQ 4:138).

27. An error probably in transcribing her notes. "Dike" is spelled with an "e" as the name appears on the tombstone of Captain Jacob Van Dike who served in the Revolution (SCHQ 4:141). See the Sixth Generation.

28. After defining the boundaries covering an immense area, the document declares that it shall be "henceforth Called known and distinguished by the name of the City of New Brunswick", and concludes on the last page, "In America the thirtieth Day of December in the fourth year of our Reign In the year of our Lord Christ one thousand Seven Hundred and Thirty". It is interesting to note that Middlesex County in New Jersey was the only county in America containing two cities incorporated by a royal charter; the other was Perth Amboy, on August 4, 1718 (NBHC).

29. Cook names thirty-one children of Jan (John), Ruloff, Mathys and Simon, but unquestionably there were many more since Cook's work does not include children of Tuentje, Catrina, Isaac, Jacob and Anna, all of whom married (Cook 18,19).

30. Old Dutch Family Bible, Appendix E.

31. The author concludes that the date of death of Annetje Verkerk in the old Dutch Family Bible was transcribed erroneously with respect to the year; namely, June 27, 1754 should have been written June 27, 1764 (error in the tens digit). The year 1764 is consistent with the tombstone inscription to the effect that

Jan's wife Ann died when she was "upwards of 80 years old". For further analysis on this point, see Appendix E.

FIFTH GENERATION

1. From an Old Dutch Family Bible. See Appendix E. Cook and Stout differ by one day (Cook 18;Stout SCHQ 4:264).

2. A "yacht" at this time was a light sailing vessel used commercially for profit. The word came into English from the Dutch yaght derived from the earlier Low German jacht or jachtshift, literally a fast hunting ship used by the pirates or against them.

3. The church building constructed of wood seen by Peter Kalm was undoubtedly the First Reformed Dutch Church of New Brunswick erected by the Dutch prior to 1717, which existed upwards of fifty years until replaced by a second church edifice in 1767. It is said to have stood "on the corner of Burnet and Schureman, then called Dutch Church Street, and at that date it was called the church of the 'River and Lawrence Brook'. The building fronted the river, and occupied the corner lot, subsequently and for many years in the possession of Dr. William Van Deursen ... Its dimensions, according to a plan in the volume of records ... was fifty feet broad and forty feet deep. There were seven pews on each side of the pulpit, and eight along the middle aisle. The total number of pews in the building was fifty, and the church accommodations was three hundred" (Steele 24,25).

4. Cook did not include Cornelia in his Van Dyck genealogy, apparently because John Van Dike named seven daughters in his will who were the subjects of specific bequests. Cornelia was not among them. There is strong evidence, although not conclusive, that Cornelia, who is buried beside her husband, Henry Berrien (1743-1806), in the Ten Mile Run cemetery was the daughter of John Van Dike of the Fifth Generation and his wife, Margaretta Barcalo. See Cornelia Van Dyck, Appendix J.

5. Deed of conveyance dated November 21, 1928 from William I. Robinson and Anne E., his wife, to William A. Johnson, Sr. recorded in Vol K21, page 208, Recorder of Deeds Office, Somerset County. William A. Johnson, Jr. was born September 3, 1905.

6. Deed dated March 23, 1855 from Cornelia Voorhees, widow of Frederic V.D. Voorhees, deceased, et al, to John P. Oppie and Henry S. Drake, recorded in Book V2, page 483 et al, Recorder of Deeds Office, Somerset County. Cornelia was the daughter of the Rev. Henry Polhemus (SCHQ 5:115).

7. There have been several intermarriages between the Van Dyke and Voorhees families (Cook 18,19,22,26). Frederick Van Dyke Voorhees of Montgomery Township manumitted a slave named Hannah on March 12, 1827 (SCHQ 2:47).

8. The nearest newspapers were small weeklies in Philadelphia and New York. In Philadelphia William Bradford (1686-1742) published in 1719 The American Weekly Mercury. In 1729 Benjamin Franklin (1706-1790) purchased an interest in The Pennsylvania Gazette (December 1728) started by the eccentric Samuel Keimer (1688-1739), and with unusual writing skill and imagination turned it into a great

success. The first newspaper in New York was The New York Gazette established by William Bradford in 1725. In 1733 the New York Weekly Journal was published by John Peter Zenger (1697-1746) who was arrested the following year and charged with libel. He was acquitted by a jury.

9. Will of John Van Dike dated February 4, 1775 probated at Somerset May 23, 1778, lodged in the Division of Archives and Records Management, commonly called the State Archives (SA). See Appendix K.

10. His date of birth unknown. Customarily, following Dutch tradition, his parents would have arranged for his baptism soon after birth, a matter of weeks. A family bible recording his death in 1811 states his age as "74 years" (Bible and Family Records, GSNJ,#2162,RUL) thus indicating his birth in 1737, five years earlier. Would his parents have delayed baptism of their child until he was five years old? Was John the Tory the source of this information?

11. Of 1200 men, 456 were killed and 420 were wounded. Washington wrote home to his brother: "Dear Jack: As I heard since my arriv'l at this place, a circumstantial acct. of my death and dying speech, I take this early oppertunity of contradicting both, and of assuring you that I now exist and appear in the land of the living by the miraculous care of Providence, that protected me beyond all human expectation; for I had 4 Bullets through my Coat, and two Horses shot under me, and yet escaped unhurt . . . . Pray give my Compl'ts to all my F'ds. I am Dr.Jack,y'r most Affect.Broth'r" (John C. Fitzpatrick, Editor, The Writings of George Washington from the Original Manuscript Sources, Vol.I, p.152).

12. Legend has it that John the Tory was at Fort Duquesne (Pittsburg) and at Fort Ticonderoga: "When first he saw the French and the Indians in war paint coming, his knees knocked and he trembled in every limb - but the instant the first bullet whizzed by he rushed fearlessly at the enemy" (Aitken 208).

13. Franklin's Autobiographical Writings selected and edited by Carl Van Doren (FAW 780,781).

14. Col. Henry Van Dike born December 25, 1743, nephew of Jan the Fifth (Cook 23).

15. In 1771 Hillsborough was separated from the "Western Precinct" of the county and raised to township status.

16. Referring to the Synod of Dordrecht located in the province of South Holland, one of the first towns in the Netherlands to embrace the reformed Christian religion and throw off the yoke of Spain in 1572.

17. From an article entitled The Famous Frelinghuysen Controversy by the Rev. William Stockton Cranmer, D.D., Somerville, N.J., published April 1916 (SCHQ 5:81-89).

18. Title of an article by the Hon. James J. Bergen, Somerville, N.J., published July 1914, based on a scholarly work by Dr.E.T.Corwin in six large volumes (SCHQ 3:173,174).

19. The practice of <u>double-dating</u> began after the calendar was changed from the Julian to the Gregorian. It was the year 1582 that the calendar was reformed by Pope Gregory XIII who ordered that Thursday, October 4, 1582, was the last day of the Julian calendar and the next day was Friday, October 15, allowing the calendar to catch up with the solar year. However, the protestant countries were very slow to adopt the new calendar. The ecclesiastical calendar, essentially following the Julian calendar, had New Years Day fall on March 25, the Feast of the Annunciation (Luke 1:26-28), while under the new system the year began on January 1, as it does today. In Great Britain and her colonies the switch to the Gregorian calendar did not occur until 1752. Thus double-dating reflected both calendars <u>before</u> the year 1752 when the date fell between January 1 and March 24.

20. Deed dated "this Nineteenth day of February, in the Reign of our Sovereign Lord George the Second of Great Brittain, France & Ireland & King and in the year of our Lord, One Thousand and seven hundred forty nine and Fifty" (HCR)

21. Inventory of John Van Dike sworn by two appraisers at Somerset May 23, 1778 before J. Seaton, surrogate of the Somerset County Court (SA).

22. With his marriage to Martha Custis, Washington managed several hundred negroes, most of them legally attached to the Custis Estate. In 1786 he owned in his own right 216 blacks which by natural increase numbered 317 in 1799 (Flexner Vol IV 113, 437, 444). He seriously considered several plans to free them but could find no practical solution. By his will he gave them their freedom (Flexner Vol V 385-392). Jefferson, who deplored the evil was one of the first Americans to propose a specific plan of emancipation, which called for freeing all the slaves in Virginia (Malone 316,317). Similarly, Madison proposed a series of successive curbs by Congress leading to emancipation and colonization, and in his will bequeathed a considerable sum to the Virginia Colonization Society of which he was one of the founders (Anthony 319,320).

23. Margaret Nevius Van Dyke died at ninety-two years of age on December 5, 1916 at Elm Hall, Merion, Pennsylvania, the home of her son-in-law, Major General Wendall P. Bowman (Death Certificate VS/PA, <u>Princeton Packet</u>, December 15, 1916). She was the widow of Thomas Shields Malcom, D.D., of Philadelphia, a distinguished theologian, pulpit orator and philanthropist. See Appendix L.

24. Col. Henry Van Dike (1743-1824), nephew of John Van Dike (Cook 23)

25. A spinning wheel designed for wool fiber larger than the treadle type usually portrayed. The spinner maneuvered the soft carded wool with long deft strokes from a standing position.

26. From spinnestere (Middle English) meaning to spin.

27. The will of John the Tory dated May 31, 1811 and probated August 8, 1811 refers to his daughter "Margaret the wife of Abner Houton" and appoints "my son-in-law Abner Houton" one of his executors. On the probate record he signs his name "Abner Houghton" (SA).

28. Abraham Van Dike (1753-1804) named as executor in the will was not present with his brother , suggesting that he was in military service. Enlistments were often of short duration, a term of a few months. Frederick and Jacob also served in the Revolution (Cook 22). Arranging a convenient date in time of war doubtless presented problems.

29. His will made three years earlier on February 4, 1775 says "being much indisposed in body" (SA).

30. In a genealogy of the Somerset County Van Dyke families, Warren B. Stout says: "John Van Dyke died at Harlingen December 4, 1777, and is supposed to be buried in the grounds surrounding the church" (SCHQ 4:265), but cites no authority, indicating that this is based on rumor. For further analysis, see Military Records Re: Death of John Van Dyke (1709-1777/78) in Appendix M.

SIXTH GENERATION

1. Died September 12, 1809 in his eighty-sixth year and lies in the Ten Mile Run Cemetery (SCHQ 4:141;Cook 19).

2. New Jersey Patriot, Vol 1,No 27, Princeton, February 15, 1827 (LC).

3. Printed and published by S. Walter, Washington Square, Boston.

4. See entries in the Family Bible of Mary Schenck Scott, sister-in-law of Jacob Van Dike (1754-1827) in Appendix N.

5. See Entries in the Family Bible of Jacob Van Dike (1754-1827) in Appendix O.

6. Mary Schenck Scott was forty-one when her husband John died in 1817 (VDFB/Author). The record establishes that she died childless.

7. Born September 12, 1774. Jacob's daughter Sarah married Captain Isaac Oppie on November 8, 1806 (Van Ness 42,44). They had two children: Sarah above and a second daughter named Sarah Mary born March 26, 1811 (VDFB/Author;VDFB/Princeton;New Brunswick Gazette, October 1806).

8. It was not unusual for men to embrace both professions. Jonathan Dickinson, a Scottish clergyman and the first president of Princeton College, wrote a paper on "The Throat Distemper" (Kull 1270).

9. During the building of the Delaware and Raritan canal, Irish immigrant laborers succumbed to cholera and a number were buried in the Ten Mile Run Cemetery in unmarked graves (SCHQ 4:64). There stands today in this cemetery a monument in their memory, supra. Cases of cholera were reported in 1833 in Newark, along the Passaic River, in Belleville and Acquackanonk (Passaic), Paterson, Whippany, Jersey City and Elizabethtown (Rogers/Sayre 85,86).

10. Notice of the meeting published on June 27, 1766 in the New York Mercury reads as follows: "A considerable number of the Practitioners of Physic and Surgery, in East New Jersey, having agreed to form a Society for the mutual improvement, the advancement of the profession and the promotion of the public good, and desirous of extending as much as possible the usefulness of their

scheme, and of cultivating the utmost harmony and friendship with their brethern, hereby request and invite veery gentleman of the profession in the province, that may approve of their design, to attend their first meeting, which will be held at Mr. Duff's, in the city of New Brunswick, on Wednesday, the 23rd of July at which time and place the Constitution and Regulations of the Society are to be settled and subscribed" (Wickes 44). On May 21, 1816 eight physicians met at the house of Daniel Sargeant and organized the Somerset County Medical Society (SCHQ 5:235).

11. Notice in the Somerset Messenger April 26, 1827.

12. Confirming the date in Jacob's family bible (VDFB/Princeton) It is probable that neither family was present at her decease or burial.

13. The History of the Moravian Seminary for Young Ladies at Bethlehem, Pa., with a Catalogue of its Pupils 1785-1870 by William C. Reickel and W. M. H. Bigler (Reickel/Bigler 226,227).

14. Records of manumissions for the years August 27, 1805 and ending January 18, 1862 have been preserved in the Somerset County Clerk's Office (SCHQ 1:275-279;SCHQ 2:46-51).

15. Estate Inventory of Jacob Van Dyke, deceased, filed February 19, 1827 (SA)16. Appendix P. Also in the Somerset Messenger February 15, 1827.

SEVENTH GENERATION

1. Referring to her paternal grandfather, William Van Dyke (Eighth Generation). Anna Reed Van Dyke (1859-1947), her mother, lived in Hamilton Square in the vicinity of the Van Dyke family and was privy to the facts, as was her paternal grandmother, Elizabeth Ann Jewell Van Dyke (1827-1907).

2. A discrepancy in point of time. John Schenck returned before his father died as revealed by court documents, infra.

3. An example is found in the minutes of a Consistory Meeting of the Harlingen Reformed Dutch Church on October 25, 1769: "The reverend consistory, being gathered at the home of the minister, after calling upon the name of the Lord, [it] is resolved - That whenever persons present their child for baptism and [it] is found that they have lived with each other immorally and the child is thus not legitimate according to God's law, the immoral woman, as well as the man, shall make confession before the reverend consistory, who consider themselves obligated, so far as within them lies, to oppose such heaven-provoking sins, if it may yet please God upon their reform to spare a sinful, sinking land and people, even as the Lord spared Nineva in former times."(GMNJ 15:7).

4. Son of Col. Peter Dumont Vroom (1745-1831) of Dutch descent, a well known Revolutionary War Officer (SCHQ 2:129, SCHQ 5:254,256).

5. The common domestic bovine (Bos taurus).

6. Sixth Census on Enumeration of the Inhabitants of the United States as Corrected by the Department of State in 1840 published in 1841 (PFL).

7. Confirming 1801 as the year of his birth, supra.

8. The official title until the name was changed to Princeton University on October 22, 1896 (Wertenbaker 368).

9. Royal charter granted October 22, 1746 (ibid 22, 396).

10. Appraiser of the Estate of Voorhees Kovenhoven, deceased, August 31, 1843 (SA).

11. Daily True American December 3, 1852.

12. Book One covers the period June 3, 1793 to June 9, 1827, Book Two from April 14, 1828 to April 13, 1857.

13. Two constables were elected in 1827, 1832 and 1833; three in 1828-31.

14. One pound keeper was elected in 1827-29, 1832 and 1833; two in 1830; three in 1831.

15. Witness the peerless paintings of Jan Steen, Peter de Hooch, Gerardter Borch and other Dutch Masters.

16. Sixth Census of the Inhabitants of the United States as Corrected at the Department of State in 1840 (PFL).

17. The issue was Jackson's overzealous conduct in the Seminole Indian affair in Florida. Said Clay in the Senate Chamber on January 20, 1818: "Beware how you give a fatal sanction, in this infant period of our republic, scarcely yet two score years old, to military insubordination. Remember that Greece had her Alexander, Rome her Caesar, England her Cromwell, France her Bonaparte, and if we would escape the rock on which they split, we must avoid their errors".

18. Deed dated March 23, 1819 from William Kovenhoven of the County of Middlesex to Asher Temple recorded June 8, 1819 (SA).

19. The Trenton State Gazette in September 1835 advertised, "Penn's Neck Races" to "commence over this course on the first day of October and continue for two days. For particulars see handbills. Asher Temple".

20. Deed dated April 1, 1873 from Susan D. Rierson and Israel H. Rierson her husband, to Noah Reed, recorded in the Mercer County Clerk's Office on June 2, 1873 (Vol96,page149).

21. Deed dated February 1, 1879 from Isaac G. Waters aforesaid to the Trustees of the Princeton Baptist Church in consideration for the sum of $1600.00 recorded in the Mercer County Clerk's Office on February 6, 1879, (Vol 122,page 125).

22. From an article entitled "A Little Account of Nine Years at Princeton and Penn's Neck" by the Rev. L. O. Grenelle contained in the Ulyat papers in the Historical Society of Princeton (Updyke 26,27).

23. Letter dated October 12, 1783 to Washington's friend Chevalier DeChastellux while residing at Rockingham as a guest of the Congress (Fitzpatrick,Vol 27, pages 188-190).

24. Deed dated February 2, 1836 from John S. Van Dyke of the Township of West Windsor to the Delaware and Raritan Canal Company recorded in the Middlesex County Clerks Office on August 29, 1836.

25. James S. Green, Esquire, was a subscribing witness to the will of Jacob Van Dike (Sixth Generation) and doubtless was Jacob's attorney.

26. Jane (Jannitie) Van Dyke baptized November 20, 1757, daughter of Jan the Fifth and his wife, Garritie Bergen, married Gerardus Skillman (SCHQ 8:132). Their daughter Mary married John Joline who were parents of eight children including William Joline (SCHQ 6:190). The estate inventory of John Schenck Van Dyke lists four bonds payable by J V D Joline each in the principal sum of $250.00 (SA).

27. Rutgers University Library, Special Collections and Archives (SCA).

28. Author of "An Unwritten Account of the Spy of Washington" that has been widely published. See Judge John Van Dyke and the Honeyman Story, Appendix Q.

29. See Three Van Dyke Lines, Appendix R.

30. Frederick Augustus Van Dyke, born February 3, 1790, the son of Frederick and Lydia Cole Van Dyke (Cook 22;SCHQ 6:190), graduated from the College of New Jersey (Princeton) and practiced medicine in Abington and Philadelphia over sixty years. He was the grandfather of the renowned Henry Van Dyke (1852-1933), theologian, author, eminent lecturer and after-dinner speaker in demand everywhere; pastor of the Brick Church, New York, for seventeen years and beloved by his Presbyterian congregation; thereafter Professor of English Literature at Princeton University and ambassador to The Netherlands.

31. Bowling Green was originally a half acre park at the southern end of Broadway on the site of what was once Fort Amsterdam. In 1733, in order to provide recreational space, the city leased the ground to citizens as a green for lawn bowling; hence the name. By the twentieth century the mansions opposite the green were replaced by office buildings and known as Steamship Row because of the shipping firms that occupied them.

32. Inventory of the Estate of John Schenck Vandyke, deceased, dated December 16, 1852, filed in the Surrogate Court, Mercer County (SA).

33. Room names in quotation marks were assigned by the court appraisers.

-NOTES-

34. December 15, 1852 "Elizabeth Vandyke widow of John S. Vandyke deceased presented a written renunciation of her right to the administration of the estate of said decedent; which was filed" (SA).

35. December 16, 1852 "I William T. Sherman of the County of Mercer do certify that ... administration of the goods and chattels rights and credits which were of John S. Vandyke of the County of Mercer who died intestate was granted by me to Jacob Vandyke of the County of Mercer who is duly authorized to administer same agreeable to law" (SA).

EIGHTH GENERATION

1. Princeton Press, June 2, 1877.

2. William Van Dyke was thirty-nine on April 21, 1861 when South Carolina troops fired on Fort Sumter in the Charleston Harbor.

3. The Princeton Whig, Friday May 26, 1848.

4. "I do not know the date of Grandfather's marriage but presume it was on the Jewell farm which adjoins the Van Dyke acres" (PVDH).

5. Princeton Press, June 2, 1877

6. Inventory of the Estate of William Van Dyke dated June 6, 1877 filed in the Surrogates Court of Mercer County (SA).

7. Frank Van Dyke married Emma Cox, daughter of Charles Cox of Princeton, on July 4, 1875. The ceremony took place in New York (WWTMR).

8. John Schenck Van Dyke (1857-1906), Ninth Generation.

9. From the papers of John Schenck Van Dyke (1857-1906).

10. Estate of Elisha Jewell, deceased, in the Surrogate's Court, Mercer County (SA).

11. Frank Van Dyke died July 30, 1895 in Princeton (VS/NJ).

12. See Ninth Generation.

13. Will dated September 24, 1906 and probated April 16, 1907 in the Mercer County Surrogate's Office, Trenton.

14. Deed from Hetty G. Lane and Charles S. Lane, her husband, to Elizabeth A. Van Dyke, dated February 1, 1896, recorded in the Mercer County Clerk's Office, Book 206, page 266 et seq.

15. Following is the chain of title: (1) Deed dated February 1, 1896 from Hetty G. Lane et al to Elizabeth A. Van Dyke for a consideration of $2500 recorded in Volume 206, page 266 (Mercer County Clerk's Office); (2) Deed dated July 15, 1908 from Henry E. Hale, Executor of the Estate of Elizabeth A. Van Dyke to Anne Sill Douglas for a consideration of $4,000 recorded

in Volume 307, page 439; (3) Deed dated August 19, 1919 from Alice Sill Douglas to C. Carroll Mardon for a dollar consideration (stamps $8.00) recorded in Volume 430, page 289; (4)(Deed dated July 24, 1935 from Mary Clark Mardon, Widow, to Elsa Einstein (wife of Albert Einstein) for a consideration of $1,000, recorded in Volume 737, page 314.

16. Affidavit and Account of Henry E. Hall, Executor, filed in the Mercer County Surrogates Court on October 1, 1908 (MCSC).

NINTH GENERATION

1. A marriage record has not been found. Said Aunt Pearl: "I do not know the date although I have a hazy recollection of Mother saying they were married in New York City". As of June 9, 1900 when the Federal Census was taken for Neptune Township, Monmouth County, they had been married nineteen years (Federal Census 1900).

2. Born December 25, 1859 in Baltimore, Maryland (PVDH). Died June 21, 1947 in Arlington, Virginia (DC/VS/Va).

3. Died at Princeton, March 24, 1886, aged fifty-four years. (Princeton Press, March 27, 1886).

4. Originally settled by the Wyandotte Indians from Ohio in 1843, then by white settlers in 1853. It was incorporated as a city in 1858 with a population of 1,259.

5. Located on a terrace nearly two miles above sea level about 170 miles southwest of Denver, Leadville was another celebrated mining camp following the discovery of gold late in 1859. Prospectors returned the following spring and established a mining camp. In a few years the placer gold deposits were exhausted.

6. This was the shortest and most convenient route to Asbury Park. A timetable in his personal effects entitled, Pennsylvania Railroad, Amboy Division, schedule in effect May 2, 1886, shows a connection at "Jamesburg for Monmouth Junction" and "Jamesburg for Sea Girt and Long Branch". This was the route taking James A. Garfield (1831-1881), fatally shot on July 2, 1881, to Elberon (Long Branch) by a special Pennsylvania Railroad train in the early morning hours of September 6, 1881 in the hope that the invigorating sea air would speed his recovery. The president died at Elberon on September 9, 1881.

7. The earliest document that has come to light evidencing a proprietorship. The record implies that there were other business ventures.

8. John S. Van Dyke is ordered to vacate the premises under a lease to "expire on the first day of April A. D. 1891". The document was apparently drawn by a lawyer.

9. The homely reminiscence of US Navy Commander Isaac Schlossbach, Retired, is drawn from Ike's Travels by Peggy Goodrich, former historian and curator of the Neptune Historical Museum, Neptune, N.J., and to whom the author is indebted. It can be fairly said of Commander Schlossbach's humble background

intermixed with hard work and play prepared him for a brilliant naval career embracing twelve scientific expeditions to the Arctic and Antarctic and one to the jungles of Central America. Ike attended the first submarine school in New London, Connecticut, in 1916, piloted primitive planes of the United States Navy in 1921, and served as an engineer and aviation instructor at the US Naval Academy. Small wonder, then, that he was honored with three Congressional Medals, one for the critical part he played in Admiral Richard E. Byrd's Antarctic expedition in 1933-35. Said Admiral Byrd, "Ike was the best damn navigator I ever had!" He died at the age of ninety-three on August 23, 1984 not far from his boyhood home (Goodrich 3-8,NTPL).

10. Deed dated April 18, 1890 from Emil Brown and Sarah, his wife in the Township of Neptune, County of Monmouth, West Asbury Park, recorded in Freehold in Deed Book 463, page 97 et seq. West Asbury Park, then part of Neptune Township, was annexed to Asbury Park on May 15, 1906 by a referendum of the voters.

11. Mortgage marked satisfied on August 17, 1893 recorded in Freehold, Monmouth County, in Mortgage Book 142, page 605 et seq.

12. Deed dated October 4, 1890 from Joseph Van Brunt and Mary E., his wife, of the Township of Neptune, to Anna Van Dyke, wife of John S. Van Dyke, for Lot 246, twenty-five feet wide and one hundred feet deep on Cookman Avenue recorded in Freehold in Deed Book 470, page 133 et seq.

13. The Asbury Park Journal & Asbury Park Evening Press, June 23, 1906.

14. Estate of Ellwood P. Wright deceased, No.27922, Surrogates Court, Freehold. The Asbury Park Journal, October 13, 1899.

15. Laboratory records at Menlo Park between October 22-27, 1879, establish that a carbonized thread lamp burned for thirteen and a half hours (Friedel/Israel 101-103,244).

16. The estate inventory of John S. Van Dyke, lists a "150 ampere dynamo" appraised at $60.00 and a "boiler and engine" at $100.00.

17. Asbury Park Daily Press, July 9, 1902

18. Lease dated February 20, 1902 for one year from John S. Van Dyke to Harlan P. Sanford of the Township of Neptune reciting an annual rental of $120.00.

19. Bill of Sale dated October 13, 1901 from Wallace N. Burr to John S. Van Dyke reciting a consideration of $93.00.

20. Letter dated May 26, 1888 by Wm. L. Clarke, Manager, Atlantic Coast Electric Light Co., serving Asbury Park, Deal, Allenhurst, Loch Arbor, Bradley Beach, Avon, Belmar, Spring Lake and Sea Girt.

-NOTES-

APPENDIX A

1. With Mr. Cook's kind permission. See a memorial by Kenn Stryker-Rodda (GMNJ 56:97,98).

APPENDIX E

1. Probably his son Abraham born October 3, 1716, who is said to have died "young" (Cook 18).

2. Anna and Tuentye Emans were children of Tuentje (Juentye) Van Dyck and her husband John (Johannes) Emans (Cook 18). Tuentye, the mother, was a beneficiary named in the will of her father dated April 12, 1757. See Appendix G.

APPENDIX H

1. The Treaty of Paris was signed September 3, 1783.

APPENDIX L

1. Princeton Recollector, January 1979 (RUL).

2. Publication of the Presbyterian Church, January 11, 1917, Presbyterian Historical Society, Philadelphia.

3. Elsa Barelift Malcom, compiler of the Malcom-Cox families, accounts for ten children.

4. Issue of December 15, 1916, Public Library, Princeton, N.J.

APPENDIX M

1. Official Register of the Officers and Men of New Jersey in the Revolutionary War by Adjutant General William S. Stryker authorized to be published by a joint resolution of the Senate and General Assembly of the State of New Jersey approved March 21, 1871 (SL).

2. History of Hunterdon and Somerset Counties, New Jersey, by James P. Snell, published 1881 (SL).

3. Known Military Dead During The American Revolutionary War 1775-1782, by Ex-Lieut. Clarence Stewart Peterson, M.A. originally published in Baltimore, 1959. Peterson makes a distinction between "died" and "killed".

4. The Battle of Monmouth by Samuel Stelle Smith published 1964, Philip Freneau Press, Monmouth Beach, N.J. (MCHA).

APPENDIX Q

1. The author is indebted to Elizabeth G.C.Menzies, author of Millstone Valley, published by Rutgers University Press.

INDEX OF SUBJECTS

INDEX OF SUBJECTS

INDEX of SURNAMES

INDEX of SURNAMES

Heritage Books
Bowie, Maryland
$22.50